ALEXANDER OF YUGOSLAVIA

KING ALEXANDER OF YUGOSLAVIA

ALEXANDER
OF YUGOSLAVIA

The Story of the King Who Was
Murdered at Marseilles

BY

STEPHEN GRAHAM

ARCHON BOOKS

1972

Library of Congress Cataloging in Publication Data

Graham, Stephen, 1884–
    Alexander of Yugoslavia.

    Bibliography: p. 317-318.
    1. Alexander I, King of Yugoslavia, 1888-1934. I. Title.
DR368.G7 1972   949.7'02'0924 [B]   73-122414
ISBN 0-208-01082-3

9 2
A 3 766 g

Mr

Printed in the United States of America

CONTENTS

ILLUSTRATIONS

ALEXANDER OF YUGOSLAVIA

CHAPTER I

VLADA THE CHAUFFEUR

IN the summer of 1934 there was living in Italy an uncouth ruffian who was frequently seen in the company of the elegant lawyer Pavelich, at Trieste, at Turin, at Brescia, at a villa on Lake Garda, at Borgotaro, at "Bulgarian Village" where there was an army of terrorists, mostly Croats but told to call themselves Bulgarians. Vlada the Chauffeur was, in fact, a Bulgarian *: he did not have to lie. The most redoubtable political murderer in Bulgaria, he had been lent for service abroad. Alleged to have committed some thirty murders, he was in some danger from the relatives of the deceased because blood calls for revenge. But with all provided, clothes, food, and plenty of money, he found himself in more comfortable circumstances and wrote to Bulgaria: "I prefer it up here. The people are more cultured."

He was a man of many false names—Georgiev, Stoyanov, Dimitrov, Chernozemsky, Suk, Kerin, Kelemen, Velichko; but he was most commonly known as Vlada the Chauffeur. To the most flourishing of his mistresses, Katia, who kept a restaurant in Sofia, he was known as Vlada. But his face was so unforgettable that no change of name mattered. When the photographs of the dead man appeared in the Sofia newspapers it was at once realized that the murderer of King Alexander was Vlada the Chauffeur.

* A Bulgarian citizen, although Macedonian by birth.

His head, emerging from a starched collar and crowned by a businessman's hat, arrested the attention. The big olive-shaped eyes had a stony impertinent glare of a man who cared for no one. It was a broad Tartar face. The slightly hooked nose brooded over a long, flexible, brutal mouth. His round ears stood out from his head as if always on the alert. He was not very young. His thirty-seven years were crowded with violent experience. There was something about him which would cause a man to beware of picking a quarrel with him in the street. Apart from that, he was powerfully built. But in a quarrel he would never have recourse to his fists. He was quick and certain with his revolver, a man who when ordered to kill never made a mistake.

The lawyer Pavelich was the chief, the *poglavnik*, the man whose command was law. More than that, he had the money and could pay for what he wanted. Vlada the Chauffeur, with village-school education and no language beyond his own, could not follow the intricacies of the lawyer's plots. All he understood was that Pavelich had enemies and wanted them removed. The chief was conducting a political feud with the aid of foreigners. That much Vlada the Chauffeur understood. He had been making clockwork bombs and teaching green revolutionaries how to jump cars and kill the occupants. He had taken squads in revolver practice but it had bored him. The pay was good but the adventure was slight. The leaders liked to have him as company because they appreciated having a bodyguard who was quick on the trigger. They did not send him on dangerous exploits: they kept him in reserve.

In the previous December they had picked a man in "Bulgarian Village," near Borgotaro, to go and kill King Alexander at Zagreb, given him bombs and revolvers, and promised him a king's ransom—simple-minded Peter Oreb. Vlada had not picked him to do the job. They had picked him. He was no good. He lost his head, got arrested, and then confessed all in the hope of getting a light sentence. The Oreb attempt had been badly conceived. They had sent a man who was merely an ex-smuggler. He had known enough to smuggle arms across a frontier but he had never killed a man. He had not even been sent on a dangerous raid to test his nerves. They did not do things that way in Bulgaria. But Ante Pavelich quite understood that the Bulgarian was a more sure assassin. The money which had been offered Oreb was waiting and could still be earned.

Alexander, who was unafraid of assassins, decided to make a state visit to King Boris of Bulgaria in Sofia. There was a great chance to kill him. But Vlada the Chauffeur would not go to Sofia. There was a warrant out for his arrest and he had but to set foot on Bulgarian soil to be arrested, on his face alone. Pavelich was enraged. He had publicly condemned Alexander to death. The King's death was required. Petty outrages such as blowing up passenger trains did not satisfy Pavelich's employers. They threatened withdrawal of financial support if something more disruptive of Yugoslavia were not achieved. Hungary had been forced, after complaint to the League, to disband a terrorist camp on her frontier. Italy might be forced to do the same at Borgotaro. Pavelich had publicly condemned Alexander to death and began to look ridiculous. It became urgent to make good his international boast that Alexander would be removed within the year.

Vlada the Chauffeur was ready. Alexander had announced that his next state visit would be to France.

After that he would go to England. He would never
go to England. The deed must be done in France. Vlada
the Chauffeur's light conscience is known. "Killing a
man," he once said, "is nothing more to me than removing a tree." *

Pavelich made his plans and organized a complicated
conspiracy to kill the King. He had the man who was
capable of doing it but this time he would leave nothing to chance. He would send a gang into France. If
the attempt failed at Marseilles it would succeed at
Versailles. If it failed at both places there was still
Lausanne where, on his return journey, the King intended to pay a visit to his oculist. Vlada the Chauffeur
was the silent man in many groups where the plans
were discussed in languages which he did not understand. When he was free he amused himself with
women. Despite his ugly face and big cavernous mouth
filled with gold teeth, he had a fascination for the sex.
He had married and divorced, married again, and had
had several other women in Bulgaria. It was said he
could not live without killing. It was equally true that
he could not live without women. Women and political
violence were his chief interests in life.

And the fearsome record of this man, even if only
partially disclosed, was not a handicap with a certain
sort of woman. It was possible to admire Vlada the
Chauffeur. That may explain the part played in the
murder of Alexander by the mysterious blonde girl,
Maria Vudrasek, who carried the bombs and revolvers
to Marseilles and handed them to the assassins on the
fatal morning. A young woman, she could hardly have
realized what she was doing. The share in the false

* Kraishumovich, Sofia correspondent of *Politika*.

glory of the exploit outweighed the censure of conscience.

It was, of course, dangerous to take this girl along. One of the leaders had been betrayed during the previous year by his mistress, Yelka, who, after gleaning all the information she could about the terrorists, had decamped and published her memoirs. But on the other hand a lady's suitcase was seldom submitted to more than a cursory inspection by the courteous customs officials of France. The presence of a lady was also useful in diverting suspicion. Then history held a parallel: Sophie Perovsky killed Alexander II of Russia. Why should not Maria Vudrasek have a hand in killing this other Alexander?

At length the plans were matured. The weapons were procured and they were absolutely first class. The helpers were chosen. One of the leaders gave his chauffeur, who was also his personal bodyguard, Pospishil, a man second only to Vlada. He was to have charge of the attempt at Versailles in case that at Marseilles failed. He and the others had some practice with the new Mausers and Walther pistols. It was explained to Vlada that the Mauser could be used with the rapidity of a machine gun but he was not interested in that. He intended to take aim. One shot would be enough.

Kvaternik made a journey into Switzerland to negotiate the exchange of a large sum of liras. It was a precaution. The Italians were their hosts and patrons. It would be invidious if any of the gang were arrested with Italian money on them. He returned to Turin and met Pavelich and Maria Vudrasek and Vlada the Chauffeur for the final arrangements. Some of the men were in Hungary. Pospishil was taking charge of them and bringing them along. Toward the end of September Maria Vudrasek set off for Paris with the guns and bombs wrapped in frocks and lingerie. She went alone but Pavelich journeyed in the same train so as to be able to report any mischance and give directions for the dispatch of a second consignment of weapons if the first lot happened to be seized at the Swiss or French frontiers. "Peter" was seen later in Paris, Avignon, Aix, and Marseilles. He escaped the vigilance of the police. Only one witness identified him subsequently with the help of a portrait of Ante Pavelich. But it was admitted by the other prisoners that "Peter" was their chief and that they obeyed him implicitly. For these and other reasons we assume that the man accompanying Maria Vudrasek was Pavelich himself, the *poglavnik*.

They departed on September 26. On the following day Kvaternik set off with the Bulgarian for Switzerland. He gave Vlada a Hungarian passport in the name of Rudolf Suk. He himself traveled as Eugene Kramer. He took two suitcases which gave them the appearance of ordinary tourists. Vlada the Chauffeur packed nothing. Kvaternik took a revolver, which he had to leave in a checkroom in Lausanne. The arm belonged to "Peter" and represented the last hope of the conspiracy. If Marseilles and Versailles failed, perhaps the chief himself would fire the final shot. But who was to act at Lausanne had not been settled.

They traveled second class. The other passengers did not look at them with interest. No spy passing by the corridor considered them. Kvaternik with a sheaf of newspapers, mostly Austrian and French, read all he could find about King Alexander's visit to France.

He did not try to conduct a conversation with the semi-illiterate Vlada. One would hardly have thought they were traveling together. He was a handsome, elegant young fellow. The son of Colonel Kvaternik of the old Austrian Army looked as if he had bought his attire in the best shops of Vienna; an Austrian dandy, he used perfume. He showed a colored silk handkerchief in the upper pocket of his coat and had fancy socks to match and patent-leather shoes. Vlada the Chauffeur, in a cheap ready-made suit he had bought in Budapest, heavy boots, soiled shirt, his face sunk in sleepy melancholy, looked an uncouth figure. One might have put him down as a commercial traveler, but it would have been hard to say what he was traveling in. A traveler in assassinations!

Kvaternik was young in the revolutionary movement. He had attempted to blow up police headquarters in Zagreb, the one crime held against him. He had no authority except that delegated by Pavelich. Before reaching Zurich, Kvaternik opened one of his suitcases and took out an old newspaper on which Pavelich had written his code sign in copying-ink pencil. Two big purple words were scrawled across two columns. Vlada noticed but made no comment. He had seen the *poglavnik* do it. He knew that Kvaternik was in command and that whatever that young fellow ordered was law, but he was indifferent. He knew he was the man on whom the plot depended, the killer. He was superior to Kvaternik. Had Maria Vudrasek traveled with them the chauffeur might have felt less indifference.

At Zurich, Kvaternik left his suitcases in the checkroom but kept the newspaper with the purple scrawl. He had to meet a Vienna express; which express it would be depended on whether Pospishil had kept to the timetable he had furnished him. With his rough companion he went to the general post office and collected a poste-restante telegram from Budapest and a letter from Paris. These were satisfactory. All was going according to plan. At one o'clock the three helpers would arrive from Hungary. There was time to go to a restaurant for a snack.

"This city far from Marseilles?" asked Vlada the Chauffeur.

"Got to get to Paris first."

"Plenty of time. We've got to collect the others," added Kvaternik, seeing by the Bulgarian's face that he was impatient.

At the lower end of the long platform at the station Kvaternik took his stand with Vlada the Chauffeur and unfolded his newspaper. He began to read as the train came in, holding the paper upside down but close to his eyes as if he were shortsighted. On the reverse side, visible to the passengers emerging from the Vienna express, was the purple handwriting of Pavelich.

Vlada the Chauffeur had given Kral lessons with the revolver. Kral had been sent to Budapest to learn to drive a car but he had also been given practice in jumping on the running board of a moving car, drawing a pistol from an inside pocket, and firing. Vlada also knew Pospishil by sight. He had driven Perchets, another chauffeur, to Borgotaro. The tall Raich, who had been recruited from South America, he had not seen before. Kvaternik must also have known Pospishil. Pospishil came right up to him and greeted him familiarly. Kvaternik handed him the newspaper. Pospishil handed it in turn to the others, who read Pavelich's message and made no comment.

"So we're all going to kill the King," said Raich

cheerfully, as they walked out of the station, but Kvaternik at once hushed him. "The walls have ears. Now please get our names right. I am Kramer. This is Rudolf Suk. Remember your own names. That is in case anyone questions you."

He led them to a restaurant and ordered a substantial lunch for the three newcomers and a double brandy for Vlada the Chauffeur. Then he went out to make sure that they had not been followed. At the corner of the street he picked up a Hungarian spy who had followed Pospishil and the others all the way from Budapest. He gave the disconcerting information that Pospishil and Raich had been eavesdropped on their way to Vienna by a Serbian agent circulating in the train. This agent had certainly telegraphed Belgrade that three terrorists were leaving Hungary at the same time the King was leaving Yugoslavia. If Belgrade acted promptly the French police would be waiting to arrest the party at the Gare de Lyon and the Gare de l'Est.

Even Zurich was not safe. Kvaternik returned and hurried the four men out of the restaurant and back to the station. He recovered his suitcases and took five second-class tickets for Lausanne. Lausanne was not on the direct route Vienna-Paris. There might already be detectives on the Zurich-Paris trains but they were less likely on the express from Trieste. Kvaternik put the men on the train and stood watching on the platform till the last moment, when he also got on. There were only Swiss passengers on that train. But Kvaternik took precautions. He ordered his companions to remain silent all the way to Lausanne. Let them smoke and admire the scenery but say nothing. Kvaternik was frightened by the chance of spies. He was a clever youth but not very brave. He did not intend to risk his own head in this adventure. He must post these dangerous men and then flee to safety in Italy. He had written a letter to himself to a poste-restante address in Switzerland and he intended to return and claim that letter on the day of the assassination, so insuring a complete alibi. He had foreseen most possibilities, including that of danger on the trains from Zurich to Paris, and it was part of the plan agreed on with Pavelich that they should switch from Zurich to Lausanne. But he had not expected that Pospishil, Kral, and Raich would be observed by a Serb agent. He decided that their appearance must be changed at the first possible moment lest a description of them had been wired to Paris and Marseilles.

At Lausanne they all got into the omnibus of the Hôtel des Palmiers, registered under their false names, and took rooms. Kvaternik paid for a night's lodging for them in advance and then led them out into the city. It was already dark, which was a favorable circumstance as he did not wish them to be observed. He took them to a large store where, first of all, he bought a capacious suitcase. Then they went to the clothing department and the three men from Hungary bought new suits. Kvaternik paid. Then they bought new boots and having packed these and the clothes in the suitcase they returned to the hotel. They changed their clothes. Raich had had a gray Palm Beach suit with a belt; now he had a dark wine-colored Swiss suit and braces. The original clothes of Pospishil and Kral could have been identified by any experienced detective as having been bought in Budapest. In Swiss attire they looked more restrained, rather of a better class. The three could well pass as tourists and were in glaring contrast to Vlada the Chauffeur who, in their company, looked more than ever like a gangster. He would have impressed Hollywood. They went to a barber's to get shaved, but he let the black stubble grow on his face. He did not understand this dressing up. One could shoot just as well in old clothes as in new.

Kvaternik packed the discarded suits in the new portmanteau and carefully hid the revolver which Pavelich had asked him to consign in the railway checkroom. Pospishil also had a pistol. He put that in too, because, if by chance arrested, it would look better if they had no arms upon them. Next morning he took the suitcase to the station and deposited it at the *consigne*, putting the receipt in his letter case.

Kvaternik decided that in any event he would not entrain his party from Lausanne. There might be complications at the French frontier. He preferred to enter France at an obscure customs barrier on the shore of the Lake of Geneva. It was a bright, sunny morning and they hired two boats and were rowed across the lake to Thonon. There they were regarded as a party of tourists amusing themselves in Switzerland, and had not the slightest difficulty in entering France. After taking a few drinks in the cafés, they went to the railway station and Kvaternik took tickets for Paris. In the train he handed out new passports in different names. Vlada the Chauffeur was still Rudolf Suk, a Hungarian, but Pospishil became Novak, Raich became Beneš—they were now Czechs; Kral became Hossek. Their new passports not only were forged documents but had forged visas and they were stamped "Vallorbes," as if the holders had entered France by the main frontier station. Their other passports stamped "Thonon" were taken by Kvaternik, who put them in his pocket.

The night train rushed across the dark country of France. There were but few passengers. Kvaternik had a compartment to himself. In the next two compartments were the four terrorists stretched out on the cushions. Vlada the Chauffeur snored; the others were too excited to sleep and lay smoking cigarettes far into the night. Kvaternik was up at dawn and at the first stop bought French newspapers. He stirred up the others to wash and make themselves presentable. "We are not going to Paris," he whispered. "We shall have to get out of this train soon." He handed them each a wad of French paper money. It was Pavelich's instructions that they all be treated well. "See they want for nothing, give them everything of the best. If you are stingy they may think they won't get a premium when it's all over."

At eight in the morning they all got out at Fontaine-bleau and had coffee near the principal bus stop. No one paid them the least attention. In truth there was nothing particularly remarkable about their appearance, except that Vlada the Chauffeur had not washed the sleep out of his eyes. He looked even more of a brigand and Kvaternik made a mental note to tidy him up in Paris. There was no time in Fontainebleau. The omni-bus for Paris was leaving in ten minutes.

Even the most vigilant police would not be inspect-ing the passengers by the motor coach. The bus was full. Vlada was wedged between two stout women with baskets. Kral, being a slow peasant, failed to get a seat and had to stand. Kvaternik was alarmed to see two Russians among the passengers but upon consideration concluded they were merely harmless *émigrés*. The omnibus blundered cheerily along through the morning mist to Paris without incident.

"Now," said Kvaternik, "you have several days in

Paris. Enjoy yourselves, see the town, eat at the best restaurants, visit the music halls. When I want you I'll tell you. I'll see you at your hotels every day. Don't pay for anything there. I'll settle the bills."

He then separated his party, took Vlada the Chauffeur and Raich to the Hôtel Regina on the Rue Mazagran. He promised to call for them in an hour. Then he took a taxi to the Gare d'Orsay and placed Pospishil and Kral in a big hotel near the station—a resort of visitors from Toulouse and tourists from Spain. Kvaternik then put his own bags in the Hôtel Belle Vue for a night before proceeding to the Commodore. Maria Vudrasek and her escort were in the Hôtel St. Anne. Thus the conspirators were distributed in four expensive hotels, places where there was but little curiosity concerning the business of guests if they were in a position to pay for costly accommodation.

Vlada the Chauffeur, still rather sleepy, was unimpressed by his sumptuous room at the Regina and he lay down on the bed as he was. He was awakened by Kvaternik knocking. Kvaternik was shocked by Vlada's appearance, a hotel bandit, nothing less. He took him out at once to a barber and had him shaved and shampooed. Then he got him a clean collar and tie. He still looked too rough. He took him to an outfitter's and bought him a good suit. It was dark brown, almost a chestnut color. Vlada satisfied himself that the left inside pocket of the coat was roomy, deep enough to take the whole of the long Mauser pistol. The shopkeeper watched him repeatedly put his right hand in that pocket and then draw it out in the action of raising a revolver but he did not understand the gesture.

As this brown suit might also be observed and remembered Kvaternik bought him a raincoat. Raich thought he would also like a raincoat. Kvaternik with a sheaf of bank notes was ready to pay for all they required. Vlada the Chauffeur was unusually pleased with the transaction. He despised the precaution of changing his attire in order to commit a murder but he was childish enough to like getting a new rig-out for nothing. He gave Kvaternik a mock salute. There remained but to buy him a new hat and he looked entirely respectable, a prosperous farmer, or a provincial inn-keeper come to town.

Raich was sent back to his hotel. Vlada the Chauffeur was taken to be paraded before Maria Vudrasek in the foyer of the Hôtel St. Anne. Kvaternik the dandy talked rapidly in German. He must have explained that he had bought the new clothes, as if he, Vlada, was not able to buy clothes for himself.

They had lunch at a restaurant near the Opera House. Pavelich was there. "You will never call me by any other name than Peter," said he in a low voice. But they had a table in a far corner and could not be overheard. The luncheon was a complete success because the blonde made eyes at the Bulgarian and breathed compliments across the hors d'œuvres.

Pavelich watched approvingly. Maria was playing her part. She was switching her electricity into the Bulgarian. Georgiev—Peter always thought of him as Georgiev—did not need it. He was a man without sympathy or nerves.

"I don't like the man I'm quartered with at the hotel," said Vlada, looking vindictively at Kvaternik. "He doesn't understand me."

"That's all right," said Pavelich. "You will be with Kral at Marseilles, so you had better not be seen with him much in Paris. Just a small precaution. Raich stays here to help Pospishil. He's our number four. Doesn't count for much, but he is willing to take the first place if we'd let him. He'd make a hash of it like Oreb. We keep him in reserve. You have Kral. You taught him. He's a stout fellow. You will do the big job. I know you won't make a mistake. Kral has to stand at a distance and make a disturbance so that you'll be able to get away in the confusion."

Pavelich glanced round the restaurant. There was no one near enough to overhear. "The bombs burst forward," he whispered. "They cannot injure the man who throws them. I think Kral has had sufficient practice. You'll have to be smart making the getaway, but the French police always lose their heads and arrest the wrong persons. And there will be swarms of people."

"I'll sell my life dearly," growled Vlada. "I don't want to go to prison again."

"You'll get another fifteen years if they catch you," whispered Kvaternik. "And you would not be amnestied until Italy makes war on France. That might not be for another five years."

The guillotine was never mentioned to Vlada the Chauffeur. He did not know that such a thing existed. And he imagined that a political crime would be as lightly punished as in his own country. He had already been in prison several times for murder but never for long. Now he had no measure of the crime he was about to commit. Killing the King of Serbia would be a mere incident in his career. He would survive to kill others. Kvaternik contrived to combine the holiday spirit with the grave reality of the plot. Vlada the Chauffeur was to have a whole week in which to enjoy himself in Paris. It was only September 30, and the King would not arrive in Marseilles until October 9.

They walked from the restaurant to the Place de l'Opéra and Pavelich pointed out a table in the Café de la Paix. That table or the nearest table to it would be their general rendezvous. Pospishil and Kral and Raich would be shown it also. It was easy to find; they could not make a mistake. It was convenient for Pavelich because the Hôtel St. Anne was just round the corner. Kvaternik would move to the Commodore on the Boulevard Haussmann and that was near. Later Pospishil and Kral would be moved from the Orsay Palace to the Terminus Gare St. Lazare and that would be nearer for them. Kvaternik took Vlada to his hotel and then went to see Pospishil. He had much to say to Pospishil because he would have charge of the attempt to murder Alexander at Versailles should Vlada fail at Marseilles.

Vlada the Chauffeur did not make the most of Paris because he slept a great deal of the time. He was never out when Kvaternik called for him. He was sprawling on his bed. The shops had no interest for him; he did not want to buy anything, was not looking for souvenirs. When Kvaternik made him a present he was not inclined to take it. Kvaternik gave each of the men a pocket compass. "What's the use of it?" asked the Chauffeur. "It will show you the way when you make your escape," explained Kvaternik. "If you want to get to Italy you keep going east. If you want to get to the Spanish frontier from Marseilles you will keep going southwest."

Vlada pocketed the compass with a derisive smile. It was not his intention to tramp across the mountains to Italy. Hé had his own plan of escape, perhaps in the company of the blonde. He would fix that but he naturally did not reveal his plans to Kvaternik. His only

Bulgarian refused to part with them. Vlada gave his old clothes to Pavelich, telling him he would require them later. The bombs were put in some old boots which Pospishil bought at a second-hand store and the pistols were wrapped in an old traveling blanket. The chargers and the spare ammunition were thrown loose into the suitcase. The case was strapped as well as locked and Kvaternik gave instructions to Pospishil to take it to the checkroom at the Gare St. Lazare and leave it there until it would be required. Pospishil and Raich would be left behind when the others went to Marseilles. They had better stay at Fontainebleau. That would be safer. A room would be taken for them at the Golden Lion Hotel. They would call each day at the post office for letters. In the meantime they must visit Versailles and study the best place for making an attempt on the King's life there. But they would receive instructions at Fontainebleau as to how to proceed. Vlada the Chauffeur and Kral had their passports changed again. They now became Czechs. The Bulgarian got the name of Petrus Kelemen and Kral became Silvestre Malny.

On October 6 Pavelich and Maria, Kvaternik, Vlada the Chauffeur, and Kral set off for Marseilles. But they did not go direct. There was still the chance that police agents might be watching for suspicious-looking characters among the passengers arriving at the Marseilles station. They went to Avignon and stayed a night at hotels there. The next day Pavelich, Vlada, and Kral went by omnibus to Marseilles. But they did not remain there, did not take rooms in hotels. The police might be interested in strangers in hotels. One could not be sure that the French would not take that precaution. Kvaternik had been sent to Aix-en-Provence, which is about an hour's journey from Marseilles, and had booked rooms for the party there. Pavelich introduced Marseilles to Vlada the Chauffeur. He was unimpressed. All he wanted to know was when the King was coming. Kral followed cloddishly along the Cannebière to the Bourse, to the Vieux Port. Peasant and tramp and then terrorist, he still remained peasant —dogged, unimaginative, waiting always to be told what he would have to do.

They had lunch facing the Vieux Port but it was dull without Maria. Pavelich, a man of culture and affairs, was bored by his inarticulate companions. Queer company for a man of his accomplishments! After lunch they at once took the omnibus to Aix. There, in a café on the main street, they found Kvaternik entertaining the blonde. Vlada the Chauffeur frowned. But Pavelich was relieved. Kvaternik was a highly educated young fellow and had a wealth of conversation. He was in any case better company.

Kvaternik had news. A message had come through before he left Avignon. The Queen of Yugoslavia had at the last moment decided not to accompany her husband on the destroyer. She was making the journey by rail and would endeavor to get to Marseilles in time to meet her husband there. A small calculation sufficed to show that that would be difficult unless she made part of the journey by air. Would the disembarkation of the King be delayed to enable her to meet him at the quay? It seemed more likely that the Queen would wait in Paris. They ought both to be killed because then there would be a historic parallel. Pavelich considered that the world would regard a dual assassination as poetic justice, the natural answer, somewhat delayed, to the murder of the Archduke Ferdinand and his consort at Sarajevo.

It was also important that Vlada the Chauffeur should know just who was going to be in the carriage with the King. If it should be some young vigorous minister he might have the presence of mind to strike the assassin's wrist at the moment of firing. Laval was capable of that as an act of mere self-preservation. In the case of the Queen's not being able to get there, would the French Premier go to Marseilles? Courtesy almost demanded it. But if it were old Barthou it would not be very dangerous, except for Barthou. Pavelich's organization had condemned Barthou to death as well as the King of Yugoslavia. He pretended to desire an understanding with Italy but he might oppose the forthcoming conquest of Abyssinia. He was also opposed to Hungary's policy of revisionism and had that year visited the capitals of the Little Entente. He was stubbornly tenacious of the terms of the iniquitous peace treaties. On the other hand, if Barthou were killed the French police would be forced to become more active. Pavelich and Kvaternik might be arrested before they could get out of the country.

"Well, Eugene, you can leave tomorrow evening," said Pavelich. He had promised Colonel Kvaternik that his son should come to no harm. Eugene had done his part and done it excellently. He had got the men through to Paris and Marseilles without a hitch.

Maria Vudrasek may have been annoyed. But Kvaternik had long since made up his mind to show a clean pair of heels. No fair lady could cause him to risk his head. His own program was worked out with the same meticulous care as that of bringing the assassins across Europe. He had never intended to stay for the shooting. "Kramer is leaving us," said Maria to Vlada the

Chauffeur. Vlada grimaced. "It makes no difference," said he.

Maria Vudrasek had already taken a room with twin beds for herself and her "husband." She had been busy while Pavelich and the others were in Marseilles. She had ripped the material from the top of one of the box-springs and carefully hidden the bombs and revolvers among the springs and straps. Then she had refixed the material again. She had security from inquisitive maids who might open her trunks to see what was the baggage the porter had been told to handle so carefully. This was at the Hôtel Nègre Coste.

Kral and Vlada the Chauffeur shared a room in the Hôtel Moderne. Kvaternik had a room to himself in the same hotel. He cynically registered himself and Vlada as brothers. The sleepy little town of Aix did not dream what guests it harbored on the nights of October 7 and 8, 1934. But the presence of the strangers was noticeable. Everybody who had seen them remembered them after the tragic event. Still, the police in Aix did not feel any responsibility for what might happen in Marseilles and they did not report the arrival of mysterious foreigners.

The omnibus connection with the port was a convenience and it is overlooked to what extent bus service has supplanted train service. Police agents watch the arrivals at the railway stations: they seldom pay any attention to those who come by bus. On the day before the crime the conspirators went by bus to Marseilles to study the best point for the outrage. They bought a plan of the city and the "official program and guide." The enormity of the plot which was nearing execution did not weigh upon the mind of Maria Vudrasek. She bought herself a frock at Chiffonette on the actual route of the King's procession and not very far from the place chosen for the assassination.

The real business which had taken them that day to Marseilles was quickly accomplished. The deed would be done as the King passed the Bourse, on the way to place a wreath on the monument to the soldiers who fell at Salonika. Vlada the Chauffeur would attack from the near side. Probably the King's car would observe French traffic regulations and keep to the right on the Cannebière. On the right-hand side he would be much nearer the crowds of sightseers. Kral, who was shorter than Vlada, would be able to watch from the steps of the Bourse. That would give him an advantage in throwing his bombs. It was very near the harbor and Pavelich and Maria Vudrasek could watch from the Vieux Port side and be in a position to get rapidly to a ship when the King had been killed. Actually, Pavelich had to get a message through to the men waiting at Fontainebleau if the attempt failed. But he refused to believe there would be failure. If Vlada the Chauffeur were successful he intended to leave Pospishil and Raich to shift for themselves. The man called "Peter" must get to the shelter of Italy at once.

The party was almost lightheaded and they lunched in a spirit of unusual gaiety. Vlada the Chauffeur was less gloomy than he had been during the whole of the trip. That action was on the morrow cheered him. He was tired of waiting and despised the many precautions. He knew he was going to succeed and he had his own plan of escape. Kral was also more lively and insisted on drinking to free Croatia. He believed he was doing something for Croatia. International politics meant nothing to him. He was a narrow-minded peasant who had been made into a fanatic by reiterated stories of the wrongs of the Croats. Kvaternik was in high spirits because his work was done and he was leaving that night for Switzerland and Italy. The only person who was at all somber was Peter. He still had much on his mind.

They returned to Aix in the gloom of the October afternoon. Their mood changed somewhat. Aix in the evening seemed sinister, as if the attempt were going to be committed there and not at Marseilles. The event of the coming day threw a shadow on the town of Aix. The conspirators hardly knew what to do with themselves. Kvaternik coached Vlada and Kral in what they had to do. Vlada must jump on the running board of the car and shoot the King. When he was sure he had done that he must step back and throw his bombs, then bolt. Kral must watch carefully and throw his bombs so as to help Vlada. If Vlada were knocked down or arrested he must throw his bombs directly at the King's car. He would use his pistols only in self-defense. Vlada was warned not to kill Barthou instead of the King. He must not fire at the French Foreign Minister unless the latter was so foolish as to put his body in front of the monarch to save him. How Barthou was to be saved from the bombs Kvaternik did not explain. Kral swore he would stand by Vlada, and Vlada told him he had better, because if he showed the white feather at the last moment he would shoot him dead like a fly. "I never miss, remember that."

"Not so rough," objected Kvaternik. "Mio is just as ready to die for the Cause as you are. You could not have a better helper."

Kvaternik went out for a few minutes and came back with a small suitcase. "Tomorrow morning at seven you take this to the Hôtel Nègre Coste and ask to see Peter. You will receive your weapons and Peter will give you final instructions."

"No more instructions, I hope," sneered Vlada.

Kvaternik smiled. He had no ill feeling. "I'm going now," said he. "You go to Marseilles and kill the King. It's au revoir. We'll meet again in Italy soon."

Kvaternik went to the Hôtel Nègre Coste to exchange a few words with Pavelich. Then he took a taxi to Avignon and caught the night train for Switzerland. Next day he went to Montreux and collected a letter addressed by himself to himself. He did so at the hour when the shooting would be taking place. Then he went to Italy to wait for Pavelich.

Early next morning Vlada the Chauffeur and Mio Kral were admitted to the double room occupied by Maria Vudrasek and her supposed husband. Pavelich was dressed. She was in pyjamas and dressing gown. She smiled radiantly on the two men, but Pavelich's expression was severe. He locked the door and took Maria's chemise from her bed rail and carefully draped it over the keyhole. He listened attentively to make sure there were no steps in the corridor outside. That meant he was only nervous. There was not the least likelihood of any last-minute suspicion on the part of the hotel management or the Aix police. Maria unfastened the material of the spring mattress and with her dainty hands and carmined nails scooped out the first of the bombs and handed it to Vlada. Kral stood there with the suitcase wide open and Vlada placed the bombs in as he received them. Then came the chargers for the Mauser and the Walther. They were tied up in a handkerchief. Maria drew forth one of the Mausers. Vlada rapidly opened the breach, looked down the sight, placed a charger in the slot, shut it up again, released the safety catch, and placed the revolver in his inside coat pocket. His lips set in a look of self-confidence. The other three weapons he allowed to be wrapped up and packed in the suitcase.

"Now I've very little more advice to give you," said Pavelich. "You will catch the one o'clock omnibus to Marseilles. You will not go earlier on any account. The King will almost certainly arrive about four and set off at once to place a wreath on the Salonika monument. A few minutes after four he will be passing the big building we pointed out to you. You will have taken up your stand there and you will kill him. I shall be there watching you to see that you do not fail, and I will pick you up and make good your escape. If I'm prevented, I'll meet you in the restaurant of your hotel here at Aix, you understand. But if I should be arrested or stopped you will not wait for me at Aix, but take a taxi to Avignon, get on the Paris train, and join Pospishil and Raich at Fontainebleau."

Vlada the Chauffeur was too much in awe of the *poglavnik* to make any objection to this program, but he suspected that Peter was planning to go away on a ship. He, Vlada, was not going to run to Aix with all the French police in hue and cry.

Pavelich unlocked the door of the room and looked along the corridor. There was no one stirring. Kral picked up the suitcase and the two men walked out. The door shut quietly behind them. They went back to the Hôtel Moderne and put the bombs and pistols and ammunition in their pockets and looked at themselves in the cheval glass. Their clothes looked bulgy, but they could not leave this arsenal in the suitcase. Some servant might open the case or throw it about and explode the bombs. They had breakfast, and later lunch, wearing their weapons.

Their room at the hotel had been paid for up to October 9. Kvaternik had settled the bill before he left. A maid came to them and asked whether they were keeping the room, but Vlada the Chauffeur waved his hand. When they went out to catch the bus they left the suitcase behind. It was empty, but that seemed to imply that they were returning.

At one o'clock they got seats in a packed omnibus of sightseers going to Marseilles to shout *Vive le Roi!* when King Alexander arrived. A stout passenger sat on one of Kral's bomb pockets and he had to stand up and rearrange his coat. A little after two they were in Marseilles. The shops were all open. Business was proceeding as usual, but there were already a lot of people standing about, waiting for the show, two hours before the King arrived. There were many flags flying. Kral began to feel nervous.

But Vlada the Chauffeur was not affected by the French street excitement and he did not sense that Kral was beginning to show the white feather. He was gruff with Kral as if the Croat were under his command. He got him along to the corner of the Bourse and, having found the place which had been chosen, he remained there, though there was long to wait. He had been warned not to start any conversation there lest they be overheard by police agents. But he did not wish to talk. The time of action was approaching.

Vlada the Chauffeur ignored the gathering crowds. He saw the street would not be lined with troops. There was no cordon of police. It was not going to be difficult. He watched the private cars still circulating on the Cannebière and in imagination tackled each one as it came along, rehearsing mentally his short run and leap onto the running board, then the flash of his revolver from his left inside pocket.

Kral gave a start as he heard the first boom of cannon announcing that the King's boat was in the harbor.

CHAPTER II

THE KING GOES TO MARSEILLES

1

HIDE yourself, you gipsy! But it does not matter where you go, we will find you and kill you."

So wrote Pavelich in April, 1934, in one of the propaganda sheets printed abroad at his expense. He called the King a gipsy because the dynasty of Karageorgevich is descended from an obscure family which had migrated to Shumadia from the Montenegrin border and directly from a cattle drover and trader known as Black George, *Kara Jorj*. This original Black George took the surname of Petrovich because his father's name was Peter. He drove pigs to market. He was fully armed and prepared to defend the swine with his life. He became a *haiduk*. There were episodes in his early life which show him as a raider and the sworn foe of Turks, several of whom he killed before he became a leader of men and led the Serbs in victorious revolt against their masters. The people of the Dinaric Alps where his ancestors lived are a blend. There is Turkish blood, there is Albanian, Montenegrin, Greek. But the type of the Karageorgevich family is predominantly Slav. Alexander, a proud man who never begged of anyone, a brave soldier, and a man who despised mere wealth, a man with no taste for a vagabond life—he could hardly be thought to be descended from a gipsy.

But Pavelich was angry. In December, 1933, he had

sent three men from Italy to kill the King at Zagreb.
Not only had the attempt failed but the men had been
caught, and one of them, Peter Oreb, had made a full
confession, incriminating Pavelich and compromising
Italy. The trial had taken place in March, in Yugoslavia, in a blaze of publicity. The position of Pavelich,
suborned by Italy, was made clear to the Yugoslavs,
perhaps to the world. On April 1 the three men had
been condemned to death.

Pavelich put a brave face on it, declaring in one of
his subsidized papers: "We condemn *Alexander the
Last*, and honor Oreb and his companions." He could
not afford to admit that Oreb had betrayed him. On the
other hand, the Italians were losing patience. If he
failed so disastrously in his plots they might have to
dispense with his services and expel him from the country. In order to safeguard his position Pavelich must
make another attempt and this time must succeed. He
organized the assassination at Marseilles so thoroughly
because his future career and personal safety depended
on his making good his boast that he would find "The
Gipsy" and kill him.

King Alexander, though with a price on his head,
was devoted to international peace. He was a soldier
by training but had become a pacifist. He knew the
dreadful reality of war. As a youth he had fought
through the Turkish and Bulgarian campaigns. In his
prime of manhood he had gone through the ordeal of
the Great War. He had seen enough of lands laid waste
and carnage. He was no firebrand. During all the
stormy period from 1918 to 1934 he threatened no one.
He was repeatedly threatened by Italy but he made no
martial response beyond perfecting the organization of
defense. To pacify tribal passions within his enlarged

territory he sacrificed the proud name of Serbia to call his kingdom Yugoslavia. That somber word is a collective description: it merely means South Slavia. It was, moreover, his fond hope that the embittered Bulgarians, who are also Slavs, might at some future date cast in their lot with Serbs, Croats, and Slovenes and make of Yugoslavia a still larger and securer collective unity. Unhappily, some Croats felt the sacrifice of their national name as deeply as did the Serbs, and the word Yugoslavia became for them a symbol of Alexander's centralist policy. Alexander did much to assuage the murderous blood lust which divided Serbia and Bulgaria after the war. It may even be said that he effected a reconciliation. He forgave the outrages on the Macedonian frontier. He made friends. His preoccupation in the summer of 1934 was peace.

King Alexander was well aware that he was threatened with death. He said, "Well, if I die in my bed I shall have a less bloody end than most of my ancestors." In the Great War he was frequently to be seen in the most dangerous places, calmly inspecting trenches and dugouts with bullets spitting past his ears. He always laughed when remonstrated with. He was familiar with death. So he took no measures for his personal safety. The activity of the police around his person annoyed him. Orders were given that detectives guarding him should keep out of his sight. When he visited Zagreb in December, 1933, ten months before the catastrophe of Marseilles, not even elementary precautions were taken for his safety. The would-be assassins with bombs in their pockets stood but a few yards from the royal car, unmolested, and only the fact that they lost their nerve saved the King and Queen from death. That evening Alexander went out on foot with Atsa Dimitrievich and mixed with the Croat populace. The crowd about the King was so dense that the Court Marshal perspired under his heavy overcoat. Any malcontent or hired assassin could have killed the King. Next day, although the plot to murder him had been discovered, the King said, "Come on, Atsa; let's go to the place where they wanted to blow me up"; and despite the marshal's protests they visited the crowded market place and watched the peasants and the townspeople shopping.

In the fatal year 1934 he took no precautions. He was not an Abdul Hamid who would have a double to make public appearances and take the risk of assassination. He went about his ordinary business and did not alter his plans. His first interest was to continue the good work with King Boris and try to bring Bulgaria into the Balkan Pact. That pact was one of mutual nonaggression. He hated the phrase so commonly applied to the Balkans, "the powder factory." "There will be no war in the Balkans," said he in 1933. "The one danger has always been in the interference of the great powers in Balkan affairs. But for the meddling of the great powers there would not be even a shadow of danger from this part of Europe." That was Alexander's view, although racial animosity, especially that of Serbs and Bulgars which grew out of the second Balkan War and the Macedonian question, was always dangerous even without foreign influence. The King meant, however, that the Balkan nations could settle their differences amicably if left to themselves. Alexander's object in deciding to visit King Boris in Sofia, in the summer of 1934, was to disentangle the Italian intrigue in Bulgarian politics. Boris had married an Italian princess and promise had been given that the children of the union would be baptized into the Roman

Church. Boris had taken the first step away from Rome in having his child baptized into the Orthodox Church. A small matter, perhaps, but Boris was a decent fellow and had given sign that he did not intend to be made the cat's-paw of Rome.

It was a dangerous visit. For Pavelich's threat must be taken seriously. He had the backing of the enemy, Italy. And Bulgaria had plenty of men who still hated Serbia and would count it virtue to hurl a bomb at the King. The Serbian Minister of the Interior, in coöperation with the Bulgarians, packed Sofia with police agents. A number of Bulgarians were placed under precautionary arrest, that is, confined to their homes for the period of the visit.

Alexander was indifferent to the danger he incurred. His Court Marshal, Atsa Dimitrievich, who was to some extent responsible for the monarch's safety, was apprehensive, the more so as he developed a poisoned foot and had great difficulty in keeping close to his King. He tells how Boris and Alexander talked far into the night. He was in an antechamber, resting one bandaged foot on a chair. A Bulgarian aide-de-camp said to him at midnight, "Why don't you turn in and go to bed?" He replied, "The King might want me. I cannot go to bed before my King." At three o'clock in the morning King Boris came in to him and engaged him in conversation. He was struck by the doglike fidelity of the Serbian general. That type was difficult to find in Bulgaria. He returned to Alexander and said to him, "That Dimitrievich is a pearl. That's a man worth having. Take care of him!"

General Dimitrievich, who had served with Alexander in the Turkish War and in the Great War and under him in the victorious advance from Salonika in

1918, was the King's most intimate friend and servant. As marshal his official duties related merely to ceremonial and receptions. But he had become unofficial bodyguard and confidential secretary. He kept the King's checkbook and wrote his checks. He was with him in the unconventional hours of the night when Alexander, in pyjamas, lighted cigarette after cigarette and turned the pages of the French classics of which he was so fond. A rubicund hearty fellow, with a broad open face and an endless flow of childish prattle, Dimitrievich was a man who was honest as the day. His favorite saying now is, "I loved my King alive. I love him dead." But one of the first acts of the government, after the King's death, was to remove the general from his position and to place him under "house arrest." No official reason was given for this disgrace, but the assumption was that the marshal had not done all that was humanly possible to safeguard the sovereign. It was not his business, but he had become the King's watchdog and he had not barked.

In truth, the poisoned foot was a drag upon the activities of the general. When in the autumn King Alexander discussed his plans for visiting France, he was willing that Dimitrievich should remain behind in Belgrade and nurse his foot. The King had decided to proceed to Marseilles by sea. In the past, when he had visited Paris, he had commonly made the journey via Italy and Switzerland. But relations with Italy were so bad that he was averse to traveling over Italian soil. In any case, he had a special reason for going to Marseilles. Even had he decided to go to Paris by rail he would have continued the journey to Marseilles. He wished to honor Marseilles, the port from which the first French contingents had sailed to Salonika and the support of the reconstituted Serbian Army in the war. He would place a wreath upon the monument in Marseilles dedicated to the *Poilus d'Orient*. There was another sentimental reason. By going on a destroyer from the Gulf of Kotor he would be on Yugoslav territory till he reached the coast of France. No third power would come between him and *la belle France*.

He compromised with Dimitrievich. He allowed him to go by rail. His marshal was highly necessary in Paris to supervise the King's part in the various ceremonies there. Atsa must see that all was in order there and then hurry to Marseilles to study the French arrangements for the visit, and to be on hand when Alexander disembarked.

No one advised the King not to go to France. The Queen herself had no misgiving. It is, however, conceivable that had the King had a responsible government, had Yugoslavia been at the time a limited monarchy, the ministers of the crown might have opposed the visit. But the King, having dissolved the constitution in January, 1929, had become virtual dictator of his country and was a law unto himself. He was a man who asked no advice, made his own decisions, and could not be shaken from his purpose. For some time he had developed a very great activity in the conduct of foreign affairs. His Foreign Minister, Bogoljub Yevtich, was capable but he was not allowed initiative. The initiative was the King's. Yevtich merely helped to conduct the King's policy. But the policy had the merit of being successful and permanent, not subject to the chance and change of party politics. In the Balkans and elsewhere some politicians can be bribed; but the King could not be bribed. Some states, such as Italy, are at much expense to give financial assistance to politicians in other states. The King of Yugoslavia could not be bought.

Nevertheless, the state visit to France was superfluous. It would have been sufficient to send Yevtich to Paris. The King's visit to Bulgaria was very risky, but it had some justification. It was a spectacular and dramatic act. It fired the imagination, and the extension of the royal hand of friendship to a bitter enemy was worth more than any pact signed by diplomats. Had the King's car been blown up in the streets of Sofia he would have been blamed for his foolhardiness. The old hatred of Serbs and Bulgars would have flared up once more and the last state of the Balkans would have been worse than the first. But nothing succeeds like success, and the King's achievement resounded in the press of the world. Alexander was becoming as famous as a diplomatist as he had been redoubted as a soldier.

But the visit to France was not worth the candle. There was no such glorious reward as peace in the Balkans. The most that could be expected was that France would pat Alexander on the back and say, "Good boy!" The visit was intended to be of an informative character. The King intended to stay only three days in Paris, certainly not long enough to go into the details of some new pact with France. It was said, during the trial of the assassins, that he had come to put his signature to a new pact of friendship. But that was not accurate. According to Yevtich he wished to communicate the results of his conversations with King Boris of Bulgaria and report to France the prospects of the new Balkan Pact which did not yet include Bulgaria. In the previous year he had discussed the future frankly with President Kemal in Stambul. He had also obtained a confirmation of his policy in the Court of Bucharest.

He wished to make it clear in the West that there was no longer any likelihood of an outbreak of war on the initiative of any of the Balkan States. That was important. He must clear the whole Balkans from the stigma of being possible warmakers.

After France it was the King's intention to visit England. He would, in any case, have attended the wedding of the Duke of Kent and the Princess Marina. And it was Barthou's intention to visit Italy. It was expected that while in Paris the King would discuss a proposed pact of mutual guarantee to embrace the coasts of the Adriatic and the eastern Mediterranean, such a pact to be signed by Yugoslavia, Greece, Turkey, Albania, and Italy. Barthou was anxious that a step should be taken to modify the dangerous hostility of Yugoslavia and Italy. The French were about to come to an understanding with Italy and did not wish it to be jeopardized by a conflict between Italy and Yugoslavia. Alexander was a thorn in the side of Mussolini.

It has become a fashion in France to declare that King Alexander desired peace with Italy. But the King was not a man who cried "Peace, peace!" when there was no peace. It was shown conclusively in March, 1934, in the Oreb trial, that the Italians were ready to pay for the murder of the King. Italy supported Pavelich and his gang, and even after the trial and its revelations Pavelich had publicly announced that the attempt at murder would be repeated. Had Italy been desirous for a peaceful understanding the first step must have been the expulsion of Pavelich from her territory.

In September, a month before the tragedy, Italy perpetrated a public insult of the Serbs. From the radio station of Bari she broadcast a description ridiculing the behavior of the Serbs at the battle of Kosovo. The broadcast was in the Serbian language and its offensiveness was calculated. At that time propaganda in the Serbian language was radiated from Bari, much as at a later date anti-British propaganda was broadcast to the Arabs. The Serbs retaliated by ridiculing the Italian Army and the defeat at Caporetto. It cannot be said that at the time of Alexander's departure for France there were conditions suggesting the possibility of an entente with Italy. On the contrary, Mussolini was a mortal enemy who had assassins in his employ. That was something which ought to have been taken into serious consideration before the King ventured into the slackly policed territory of France.

The King was warned but he replied that he would die when his time came and not before. And he would not change his plans. The Queen says she had become accustomed to the danger of being attacked. "How we escaped being blown to pieces at Zagreb I have never been able to understand." Her Majesty says that at this period the King had developed a nervous habit of looking behind him to see whether he was being followed. Alexander was not in the best of health in October, 1934—rather run down. In his pictures he looks as if he had really reached the end. There was a strange blankness in his face, as if in truth it had no future. But he expressed no misgivings. On October 4 he made up the royal party: his cousin, Prince Paul; Paul's wife, the Princess Olga; the Queen; Bogoljub Yevtich.

His departure was unannounced. He stole away from Belgrade in the night and was never seen in the capital again. The Prime Minister, Uzunovich, and General Zhivkovich, commander of the royal guard, were summoned and bade Their Majesties farewell at the little

suburban station of Topchider. A royal coach had been
added to the midnight express for Nish. It would be
disconnected at Lapovo and the royal party would proceed by another line to Mitrovitsa. The King was not
going direct to the port of embarkation, Zelenika. He
wished to show Prince Paul some beauty spots in Montenegro and take Princess Olga to the place where he
was born. So they went first to Mitrovitsa, which is near
the field of Kosovo, tragic battle of the Middle Ages,
when the Serbs went under the yoke of the Turk. But
Mitrovitsa had another association, if not for Prince
Paul, who was no soldier. From there the right wing of
the Serbian Army retreated over the mountains to the
sea in the most calamitous period of the Great War.
The left wing, which included Alexander, passed by
Prizren across Albania to meet what was left of the
other army near Scutari. What was then a series of cart
tracks and goat paths had become a modern highway
and motor road, the King's work. And Alexander's
party from the railway station at Mitrovitsa went over
the ground of that retreat in two smooth-going auto-
mobiles.

It was rainy weather and chill. The empty and soli-
tary region had a preternatural grandeur, the mountains' heights shrouded in leaden-colored vapor, fring-
ing downward in gray mist. The visible slopes of the
hills were covered with gray boulders, each commonly
about the size of a man, looking like fields of the dead
that had been turned to stones—ancient, passive, cruel.

The peasants, with bread and salt, came out of their
little stone cottages and shouted for the King. The affection of these hill folk for the King was boundless.
Was he not one of them by extraction? The ancestors
of Kara George had dwelt among those hills. No need

to guard him on that journey. The King had insisted on making the journey in an open car so that the peasants might see him as he passed by. He and Prince Paul and Yevtich were in the first car. The Queen and Princess Olga followed in a closed car. The rain came down in torrents and the men were drenched to the skin. So soaked were they that at Rijeka they stopped and changed into dry clothes. But the rain did not abate: it whipped them with the lash of the southwest wind. They proceeded to Cetinje, the capital of old Montenegro. The mountain city lay listless, draped in rain-washed bunting. Clouds and mist drove over the roofs of the houses. The flags drooped as at half-mast. But Alexander wanted to visit the house where he was born, the unpretentious stone cottage where Princess Zorka, daughter of King Nicholas, had given birth to him and then, a year later, had died. Alexander was orphaned as an infant. He never knew what it was to have a mother.

The party descended from the cars and the King pointed out to Princess Olga the room where he was born. Olga had never been in Montenegro before and this was new to her. The house is an officers' mess now. It is impressive in that it is unimpressive. It must remind Alexander and others that whatever his achieved greatness his beginnings were very humble, the son of a poor exile. The Karageorgeviches had been put to flight and a king of the Obrenovich line ruled then in Belgrade.

But there is something which haunts the imagination in this last visit of King Alexander to his birthplace, in the rain, four days before his death. What instinct prompted him to go there?

In the late afternoon the journey was resumed to

Budva, where a royal villa was being constructed, to Zelenika and the sea. Everyone was tired. They went on board the *Dubrovnik*. It was arranged that they spend the night on the destroyer. At dinner they discussed the weather. A great storm was raging on the sea and the outlook for the voyage was unpleasant. The King, even if he did wear an admiral's uniform, was a bad sailor. The Queen suffered from bile. Prince Paul tried hard to persuade them to cancel the voyage and go by train.

"We sent for timetables," says Prince Paul. "The King, having looked up the Innsbruck-Basle route, became delighted at the prospect of going by train and agreed to abandon the voyage. That was on the evening of October 5. I thought it was settled. We spent a night on that wretched ship. But in the morning, when the King saw the long faces of the commander and his officers, he said he could not disappoint them. They would all get medals if they conveyed him safely to Marseilles. Let the Queen go by rail. He would keep to the *Dubrovnik*."

Yevtich says, "The King asked the commander whether he could guarantee that in case of rough weather the *Dubrovnik* would not be forced to take shelter in some Italian port. The commander gave the necessary assurance and the King agreed to go by sea. The Queen, as you know, suffers from an internal complaint. It was thought she might be affected adversely by a rough voyage so she went by train."

The final decision was only arrived at on the morning of October 6, at early breakfast. There was then some sadness at the thought of the King going alone. But Alexander rallied the drooping spirits of the party. "One more little expedition before I go to France," said he. "Let us go to the Savina monastery before I sail!"

Yevtich tactfully remained on the ship, declaring that he had certain dispatches to get off. The rest went ashore and proceeded in the royal car to Savina, a little way along the shore from Zelenika, approached by a long quiet avenue of pines; a mile through the pines and not a soul to be seen. Alexander wanted to hold in his hands again the ancient cross, the treasure of the monastery. It had been a gift from Stephen Dushan, Tsar of the Serbs, in 1354.

The car drew up under cypresses before the white walls of the monastery church. There was an eerie silence; no sound of prayers; the monastery church was locked up. The Queen told me about this visit to the monastery: "The monastery was locked. We could not find anyone, either priest or monk, to open for us. We had not announced our visit and so were not expected. My husband said to Paul, 'I must show you the cross; come on, let's wake them up!' Then the boys did something they shouldn't have done. Of course it was very wrong. They found two ropes and rang the monastery bells. The bell my husband rang was very rarely sounded. It had a peculiar tone and must have greatly surprised those who heard it. A priest appeared as from nowhere, running over the flagstone paving toward us, and he was greatly surprised to see who it was that had arrived. The priest opened the church and the royal party bought candles, lighted them, and placed them before the altar. But we were greatly disappointed to hear that the old cross of Stephen Dushan was not at the monastery. It had been sent away. We inscribed our names in a book and went away. But afterwards we heard a curious story about this visit. I am not super-

stitious. I consider it rather a legend. We heard that
the bells the boys had rung each had a name. The bell
my husband had rung was called 'Death' and the bell
Paul had rung was called 'Life.' "

Three days before his death King Alexander had
tolled a bell for himself at the ancient monastery of
Savina.

They returned to the *Dubrovnik* and the King went
to his cabin and donned the admiral's uniform which
he hated. Admiral of a one-ship fleet! He would have
much preferred to have remained a soldier. All his life
he had worn military uniform but he was to die dressed
as a sailor! Queen Marie said good-by to her husband.
She confesses she had a strange feeling as if this were
not an ordinary farewell. She was troubled. She said to
Paul and Olga as they drove away that she had had
an unpleasant sense of something not being right.

There were officers and men seeing the King off.
Zelenika is a military station. There was the singing of
the national anthem. The *Dubrovnik* moved off from
the mole. Smoke surged into the dull atmosphere; the
keel of the destroyer cleft the green waters of the gulf.
The King in his admiral's uniform stood gazing at the
coast he had lived for and fought for. He said not a
word. Like a phantom he was removed from Yugoslavia.

2

THE story that a telephone message was received at
Zelenika asking the King to delay embarkation as the
police were desirous to follow up the movements of a
group of terrorists across Europe appears to be untrue.
Prince Paul, the Queen, Yevtich, all deny knowledge of
any such message. They must have known. The de-

parture of Pospishil, Kral, and Raich out of Hungary had been signaled to the police, but further trace of them had been lost. The King left Zelenika on the same day that a group of conspirators left Paris for Marseilles, but that coincidence was unknown to the authorities.

Atsa Dimitrievich, before he left Yugoslavia, had been a little apprehensive about the monarch's safety. No detectives had been deputed to accompany the King. No agents had been sent in advance to Marseilles and Paris to watch for suspect persons. Everyone in the gang except Vlada the Chauffeur and the blonde lady was known to the police. Their photographs were ranged in albums at the Ministry of the Interior. And Vlada the Chauffeur was "wanted" in Bulgaria. A posse of capable Balkan police would have had a fair chance of spotting some of the men. When the King had gone to Sofia the police had done their work well. "I do not understand why we are not taking the same precautions at Paris and Marseilles as we took in Sofia," said Dimitrievich over the telephone to the Belgrade chief of police.

"I have had no orders," was the reply.

"You had better take it up with Lazich," said Dimitrievich. Lazich was Minister of the Interior, a favorite of the King, who had promoted him to the Cabinet because of the way he had settled the Macedonian disorders, a man of fine character, though too obedient to the King's wishes. The King did not wish to be guarded in France and that was enough for Lazich. He said that the French had guaranteed in advance the security of the King and that they would not countenance the presence of Yugoslav police upon their national territory. Scotland Yard had also proffered its services and had been refused. That the exit of certain of Pavelich's men from Hungary had been reported did not impress Lazich. Hungary had, during the preceding summer, agreed to disband the terrorists encamped on her territory and it was natural that some bad characters should be leaving. Dimitrievich had no say. He was only the Court Marshal and it was not part of his duties to organize police protection.

The general was not in a condition to be very active in Belgrade. The King had sanctioned his journey to France by rail on condition that he took a sleeper and nursed his foot all the way. He set off for Paris alone and rather disgruntled. Perhaps he was jealous of Bogoljub Yevtich, who occupied his position with the King and voyaged in the *Dubrovnik* to Marseilles. He was used to having more say in the arrangements for a royal state visit. But he had been commissioned to do certain things. He must take a suite for the King and Queen at the Hôtel Crillon, in the Place de la Concorde. Alexander's bedroom must face the gardens at the back; he did not wish to be subject to the din of traffic at night. The general had also been told to get the plans of the reception from the French Minister of ceremonies and cut the ceremony to the indispensable minimum. The King loathed pageantry and show.

But in Paris the Serbian Court Marshal found himself regarded as a person of minor importance. Lacking the personal backing of the sovereign he was regarded as a supernumerary, a fussy old general with a game foot, trying to change the cut-and-dried plans of the French Republic. But he got the desired rooms at the Hôtel Crillon without difficulty and had decided to quit Paris for Marseilles when the message came through that the Queen had changed her plans and was going to Marseilles by train. Then, that she was too late to get there. It was imperative that the King and Queen should arrive in Paris together, unthinkable that the Queen should be waiting for her husband at the station. Dimitrievich wanted the Queen's car uncoupled at Lyons and then connected with the train bringing the King from Marseilles. Then the sovereigns would arrive together in Paris on the morning of October 10.

The French said this was unheard of. Such a thing was never done in France. The railway was privately owned and the officials would never agree to such a novelty. Dimitrievich was delayed. He sought telephonic communication with the Queen traveling on the Paris express. He was put through to her eventually at Liubliana. Queen Marie was indignant and would not hear of meeting her husband at the Gare de Lyon in Paris. Dimitrievich told the Yugoslav Minister, Spalaikovich, and he had more success. But it had taken the French a long time to agree to uncouple the Queen's coach. "The trouble is," Atsa explained, "that Yugoslavia is a small country. It does not count for much in France. Had it been the English King and Queen they would have done all that was required of them at once."

On October 8 the lame Serbian general went by night train to Marseilles, arriving at the port at half-past nine on the morning of the fateful day. He had but little time to look about him and see what arrangements had been made for the reception of the King. It may be urged that the Serb master of ceremonies had no standing in France, but no Serb official with authority got to Marseilles a day before the event. In the afternoon Dimitrievich was allowed to escort M. Jacques Piétri, the French Minister of Marine, on board the *Dubrovnik* and introduce him to the King.

3

THE King and his Foreign Minister, Yevtich, voyaged
to Marseilles. The only other company on the destroyer was the commander Pavich. Alexander spent
much of the time in his cabin, but he was not ill. For
once a rough sea seemed to have no power to upset him.
It did not interfere with the program of work on board.
He composed the speeches he would have to make in
France, and with the help of Yevtich compiled lists of
the distinguished Frenchmen he was likely to meet,
adding notes on their careers.

Yevtich alone knows how the King spent those days
on the sea. He is a short dark man, with glittering face
and ears on the alert, not a long-headed man nor having the appearance of a typical diplomat. But Alexander trusted him. Most of the King's chosen men were
trustworthy. There were no crooked characters, for the
King appreciated character even more than talent. Yevtich had one of those short, broad heads not uncommon
in the Balkans, rather like an earthenware jar with a
wide brim, not shaped to fine ends, but useful. He was
quick, intelligent, faithful, perhaps too impulsive. Af-
fectionately known as Boshko Yevtich, he returned
from Paris after the tragedy on a wave of passionate
popular feeling as the one leader in Yugoslavia, the
mouthpiece of the clamor for revenge. Had he had
effective backing from France or obtained complete international satisfaction for the crime, he would have
remained the leading figure in Yugoslav politics for
many years.

Most of what is here set down about the voyage is
derived from Boshko Yevtich. The King was not wist-
ful, neither reviewing his past nor thinking he had come

to a dead end in his reign. On the contrary, he was full of plans for the development of his policy both at home and abroad. He was cheerful and businesslike all the way:

"No, we did not play cards. That would have been a relaxation, but there was not time for that. But we listened to the radio. On the first day out the wireless did bring us something sensational, causing us a great deal of reflection. We heard Mussolini make a remarkable speech. In the square in front of the cathedral at Milan the Duce addressed the world."

It is possible that Mussolini knew that at that moment Alexander was voyaging toward probable death. That gives his speech, when one reads it after his death, a peculiarly dramatic quality. High functionaries of the Fascist Council must have known what was in the air.

"I know that Kerin [Vlada the Chauffeur] started from Turin. Pavelich was in Turin. It is impossible for the doings and movements of the terrorist groups in Italy to have escaped the vigilance of the Fascist authorities," said Yevtich.

One may take it that Mussolini knew something. The speech does not seem to have been addressed to King Alexander. The King, in a sense, was already dead. The words were spoken over the King's head to those who might come to power in Yugoslavia after Alexander had ceased to matter.

"What did Italy envisage as a result of the murder?" I asked Yevtich.

"Separatism and chaos. Italy considered she would then be free from the embarrassment of a hostile neighbor. The event has to be taken in conjunction with Italy's imperial policy. She intended going into Abyssinia."

Mussolini, in his speech, reviewed his relationship with each of the important powers in Europe and addressed himself first to Yugoslavia. "We do not see much prospect of improving our relationship with our neighbors beyond the mountains," said he. "At least, not so long as they continue to wound us in our most sensitive part. The first condition for a policy of friendship, a friendship which would be crystallized in diplomatic protocols, would be the discontinuance of those reflections on the valor of those Italian soldiers who shed their blood in the wildernesses of Krass and Macedonia. . . . Nevertheless, we who are confident and strong now demand, for the last time, the possibility of an understanding."

Mussolini was referring to the article in *Vreme* about the disastrous battle of Caporetto, when an army containing many Bosnian and Dalmatian units in the Austrian service routed the Italians, causing casualties amounting to several hundred thousands, a greater defeat than that inflicted on the Russians at Tannenberg. The article had greatly wounded Italy's martial pride. Nevertheless, Italy asked for an understanding with Yugoslavia.

"What did the King think of Mussolini's words?" I asked.

"He thought them hypocritical."

Curiously enough, the understanding which Mussolini demanded he did obtain after the King's death.

The radio continued to bleat his words through the southwest wind over the murky Adriatic. The Duce went on to speak of Austria. Murder was in the air. Chancellor Dollfuss had been shot the previous July.

"As regards Austria, we will defend with all our power the independence of the Austrian Republic, an independence now consecrated by the blood of a chancellor, a little man but with great spirit," declared the voice of Mussolini.

It was a less resolute and arrogant voice speaking in 1934, the voice of Italy before the Abyssinian conquest, before the Spanish adventure, before the inauguration of the Rome-Berlin axis. Mussolini warned those in Germany who vainly attempted to frustrate the historical destiny of Italy. No words of friendship for Germany in that speech! He was at that time more interested to have an understanding with France than with Germany; because if influential politicians in France could be won over he would have a force capable of hamstringing the efforts of England and the League of Nations when he attacked Abyssinia. He was feeling out Laval. He was able to report that "the relationship with France has greatly improved during the last year. If we get the understanding with France we require it will be most profitable and fruitful for European interests generally."

He then made a passing reference to England and the failure of the policy of disarmament. Now that the compromise of disarmament had failed, an improvement in the relationship of the various European powers was generally advantageous. Finally the Duce declared his faith that Fascism was the type par excellence of European civilization in our age.

"I at once sent a telegram to Belgrade instructing the press how it should comment on this speech," said Yevtich. "I asked them to refrain from provocative commentary, merely to report it objectively."

The *Dubrovnik* plowed its way across the Adriatic waves. Spray and rain came with the southwest wind; a short twilight, a night without stars. Yevtich and the

King sat below and worked on the speech which would have to be made at the great banquet in Paris in response to the President of the French Republic, words to be spoken the day after his death:

Je ne saurais mieux répondre aux éloquentes et cordiales paroles qui m'ont été adressées qu'en saisissant cette occasion, qui est une des plus solennelles dans ma vie, depuis la grande guerre, pour vous exprimer les sentiments qui animent toute la nation Yougoslave. . . .

Alexander was an admirable French scholar. From his earliest years of childhood in Geneva he was familiar with the French language. His father, Peter I, educated in Paris, a volunteer fighting for France in the Franco-Prussian War, spoke French well and was more allied in sentiment to France than to any other country. Yevtich's French could not compare with that of his sovereign. But he was able to judge the scope of the speech, how much could be said, what might better be omitted. Alexander's tendency was to praise France more than she deserved. For a long time France had been but passive in her friendship with Yugoslavia. France did not support Yugoslavia to the extent she expected Yugoslavia to support her in the eventuality of war.

Having composed this first important speech, the King jotted down a few words to say at the military school of St. Cyr, where his father had been educated. That was one of his engagements for October 11.

It is probable that during the night Alexander pondered Mussolini's speech. Italy "for the last time" demanded an understanding with Yugoslavia. Was that a threat? When had she previously demanded an understanding? Two years earlier Yugoslavia had gone to the limit in approaching the Fascists. The effort for reconciliation had culminated in a personal affront. Alexander was to have had an interview with the Duce, but at the last moment Mussolini rudely refused to meet the King, telling him to "put his house in order first." And since 1932 Italy had all the while aided and abetted terrorism in Yugoslavia. Mussolini had not even wished that the Yugoslav house should be in order.

It is possible that in 1932 Mussolini had meant to say to Alexander, "You have taken a step toward Fascism, but you have not gone the whole hog. When you adopt Fascist institutions I will meet you." Alexander had abrogated the constitution in 1929. Democracy had been tried, but the Yugoslavs had failed. Alexander, against his better judgment, had put himself in almost the same position with regard to his people as a Fascist dictator. He had slipped into the error of paternal government which might have worked in old Montenegro but was unsuitable for a large state and a complex of jealous races. It had proved difficult for the soldier to cope with the turbulent politicians and he had taken refuge in paternalism. But he had not quite abjured democracy. He consciously linked the destiny of his subjects to that of the democracies of the West, especially France and England, with the safeguards of the League of Nations. The King felt he must give the lie to Mussolini's prophecy that Fascism was going to be the type of European civilization in our era.

On the following day Alexander discussed with Yevtich his plans for the restoration of responsible democratic government in Yugoslavia. The dictatorship and the one-party regime had been a failure since their inception and the King was aware of it. The plans were not entirely new. He had had before him for some time

the draft of an amended constitution. He had at last
decided to yield to the advice of most of the dissidents
and have a decentralized kingdom. For democracy to
have a chance the jealous races must be placed in federal compartments. He would grant local state government on the American plan. Each of the existing provinces would become a self-governing unity with resident
governor, state elections, domestic budget, control of
education and police, but federated in the unity of
Yugoslavia with the King above party and above state.
He said he had decided to give effect to this after his
return from France. Then he would announce a general
election and appoint a premier responsible to Parliament. In his mind he had moved toward freedom. He
wanted to release the numerous leftist propagandists
and political prisoners languishing in jail. He would
recognize Soviet Russia.

M. Yevtich, in these long conversations on board
the *Dubrovnik*, was privileged to learn more of the
mind of the King than any other man. That future in
which, ironically, he could have no part exercised Alexander's mind unusually. He gave to his Foreign Minister his vision of the Europe to be. The forces making
for peace would become united: those making for war
would be isolated. The destinies of France and England were indivisible: if one fell the other fell. The
Balkan Powers were already consolidated. Free from
interference on the part of Italy, Austria, Hungary, and,
as he hoped, Russia, they would enter upon a golden
age of peaceful development. Nazi Germany might
ultimately absorb Austria, but that would not alter the
distribution of forces, because in a war Austria and
Germany would in any case act as one. Germany on the
Brenner Pass would be a curb upon the ambitions of

Italy. Czechoslovakia might be alarmed but she would have a counterbalance in the support of Soviet Russia. *Anschluss* would be less dangerous than the restoration of the Hapsburg dynasty, with its claims to the recovery of all the lost territory of the Austrian Empire.

The King discussed the terms of a note which he would have required Yevtich to send to Soviet Russia. He must obtain assurance from Stalin that Russia had no claim to territory in the Balkans, and that there would be no more subsidized propaganda for Communism, a mere formality because the Soviet eagerly desired a general understanding with the Balkan Powers and Czechoslovakia. Both the Litte Entente and the Balkan Pact would obtain the support of Russia.

King Alexander was obviously not a dominant factor in European politics, but more depended on him at that time than the world knew. "Had he survived for but one year," said Yevtich to me afterwards, "the face of European politics would have been altogether different." With him perished most of his plans. His vision of the future faded like an insubstantial dream.

The little destroyer went roaring into a new storm. The spray of the sea lashed the decks and in the sinister commotion of the elements the two men talked of peace far into the night. When they retired they could not sleep for the uproar of the sea. The *Dubrovnik*, seeking calmer waters, passed through the Straits of Messina rather than keep to the open Mediterranean. But Italian waters were rough, as if partaking of the character of Italian politics.

The turbines thundered through the Tyrrhenian Sea. At length, at a distance of 150 miles from the French coast, the French fleet coming from home waters signaled the *Dubrovnik*. A squadron of cruisers and torpedo boats, accompanied by submarines, crossed the dim horizon, grew near, maneuvered into position, and then accompanied her to Marseilles. The King, sitting between two guns, field glasses in hand, descried the *Colbert* and the *Duquesne*, the *Forbin*, the *Mistral*, and the *Fronde*, and the flagship of Admiral Dubois. The forenoon of the ninth was fair. The sea grew more calm, as if only the Italian part was stormy. The grand south coast of France broke through low mist, the picturesque littoral of Toulon, the cliffs of Cassis and Marseilles. The King watched the vague picture of Marseilles become clearer and clearer, the forts, the breakwaters, the shipping. Then the *Dubrovnik* made a slow approach to the dead water of the Vieux Port. Guns thundered a salute to the sky. The King of Yugoslavia had arrived.

CHAPTER III

O GOD! O MARSEILLES!

THE official preparations in Marseilles had an impromptu air, as if the monarch were arriving at very short notice. Paris was not coöperating. No extra police were drafted from other cities. No specials were sent from the capital. The Sûreté Générale was not in control. Even the Ministry of War failed to give orders that troops should line the route. It allowed a cavalry escort, trumpeters, and some detachments of white and black infantry, these for purposes of parade, not for security.

The crowds began to form in the early afternoon, but they were never dense. There was free movement and everyone had a view of the street. *Per contra*, anyone in the street could look over and examine the whole crowd. A capable detective must have noticed Vlada the Chauffeur with Mio Kral, and decided to keep them under observation. The Bulgarian was out of his setting and could be remarked. He had a revolver a foot long in one pocket, a revolver with three-inch-square cumbrous magazine, not easy to hide from sharp eyes. His lower pockets bulged with bombs and ammunition. He and his nervous companion were hanging about for a couple of hours before the parade started. Certainly, had there been six Serbian police agents watching the crowd during the afternoon these two must have been rounded up before the King's car came groaning up the Cannebière.

The swarms of journalists, press photographers, and newsreel men invading the city on the morning of October 9 must have shown that the press and the cinema scented a world event. But Marseilles persistently regarded the King's visit as a small affair. Incidentally, nothing was done to regulate the movements of the cameramen. Newsreel operators, especially of America, are among the most daring and intrepid men of our day. They caused delay and confusion. They filmed the murder marvelously and helped to make it possible.

There was, of course, pardonable excitement at the Vieux Port, where Barthou and the mayor of Marseilles and General Georges with other notables were ranged in a semicircle to greet the King when he stepped ashore. The cannon blazing from the forts and ships put men's nerves on edge. The low-flying seaplanes caused so much noise that the nervous men waiting could not hear themselves speak.

Foissac, who had to drive the King, came up in an old police car from the prefecture. He was himself a policeman doing duty as chauffeur, a peasant speaking with a strong Provençal accent. Foissac was also nervous. It was the first time in his life that he had been called upon to drive a king. He had driven better cars, but he had never driven a better man. "This car is more like a hearse than an automobile," said he to a police officer. "It won't go more than twenty miles an hour and it is very ancient. Wouldn't it be better to borrow the car of Monsieur the Mayor? After all—the King—it's not every day we have a king here."

"You think you are entered for a race, Foissac," rejoined the officer with a thin smile. "You must not

exceed a speed of five miles an hour. Keep her in first!
These are your orders."

This car, with the bloodstains on the upholstery and
the scratches on the paint work made by the assassin,
is now in a museum in Belgrade. It was and is a museum
piece. Much inferior to a Belgrade taxi, its date of
construction is 1927, but it does not possess its original
coach work which appears to have been renewed after a
smash. It has a broad, clumsy running board and a step
that looks like a converted tool box. It has been re-
painted a drab official black and has the flat, well-worn
cushions of an old taxi.

"Bring out the rubber-tired buggy!" The use of this
car was in itself a disgrace to Marseilles. In the service
of the police force it was commonly used for the arrest
of some high-placed courtesan or the wife of some great
crook like Stavisky. One can imagine such a dame in
the seat given to Alexander. She is being taken in this
car to the prefecture, accompanied by two gendarmes
with waxed moustaches. Very fitting!

King Alexander, wearing his admiral's uniform, little
white collar and tie, two-cornered admiral's hat with
gold braid inches deep, his breast slashed scarlet with
the Legion of Honor, stepped out of a little boat with
Piétri and Yevtich and Dimitrievich, on to the Quai
des Belges, where a squad of French marines shouted a
sevenfold hurrah. A group of veterans of the old
Salonika front stood to attention. Barthou greeted the
King a little patronizingly. The old Frenchman was
a friend, but at the Vieux Port he represented France.
He must not be servile. The King of Yugoslavia's importance must not be exaggerated officially. The King
had a grave, almost imperceptible smile. Perhaps he

did not like the roaring sound of the engines of the planes overhead, the thunder of the guns. He hated all fuss. It was an awkward official moment. But the bands played the national anthems of Yugoslavia and France. The cameramen clicked and snapped, the newsreelers wound their reels. The populace surging forward shrieked dementedly "Long live the King!"

A little girl in Provençal dress came forward, pushed by her mother up to the King. She curtsied and held up a bouquet of wild autumn flowers. That was unrehearsed and unofficial, a smile from *la belle France*. The King was touched. The constraint dropped from his features like a mask, and those who looked on could see that he had become happy in Marseilles.

Warm afternoon sunshine flooded across the scene and helped the camera men, who were still very busy. The hood of the old car was pulled down so that the King and Barthou could sit in the sun. The hood disclosed only half of the interior of the car. It gave air to those who sat in the back seats. General Georges would have a collapsible side seat, what the French call a *strapontin*, and he would be in the shade of the narrow wooden roof, an honor to be in the same coupé with the King and Barthou, but a most uncomfortable sitting posture for a famous general. The mayor led the King and the French Foreign Minister to the car, where they sat on the shallow gray cushions at the back. General Georges arranged his legs under the *strapontin* so as not to interfere too much with the gouty feet of the old French Minister. General Georges was attached to the person of the King for the period of his visit to France. He was guard of honor but he carried no weapons.

The three men were in the car for quite a while before

Foissac put in the clutch. They heard the clash of horses' feet, the cavalry maneuvering into position. The two mounted escorts, Colonel Piolet on the right, Captain Vigoreux on the left, stood waiting at the back. Yevtich, Piétri, and the mayor of Marseilles got into a second car, Dimitrievich and the local chief of police into a third. The procession formed up and was ready to start. It was ten minutes past four. But it was impossible to get going because eight cameramen barred the way. They were in a line in front of the King's car at a distance of a few feet. One of them acted as spokesman and addressed Foissac the chauffeur. "We should like one or two more shots," said he. "Perhaps you would not mind waiting a few minutes."

There seemed to be no one with authority to say "No." The cameramen had their way and it was a quarter-past four when they signaled Foissac that they were satisfied. Trumpeters and *gardes mobiles* rode up the Cannebière and the cars, in first gear, followed at a walking pace, greeted by salvos of *Vive le Roi!* The seaplanes descended, roaring toward the roofs, causing a noise as of great wings striking the walls on each side of the Cannebière. The engine of the King's car made a terrible din. But above the noise was the human hubbub of the people shouting for His Majesty. The King had to speak loudly. He turned to Barthou and said, "I am very happy to be in France." But these were the last words he ever uttered.

On Alexander's face there was a wan smile. He may have been happy, but his face was not radiant with happiness. It was a blank face with a faint smile. That smile, caught by the photographers while he was alive, remained long after he was dead and stands fixed forever in the death mask of the King.

King Alexander incessantly acknowledged the cheers of the populace, raising his hand to the gold braid of his hat. The noise was deafening. Overhead roared the low aeroplanes and from each side of the Cannebière blared the plaudits of the people. Only two minutes had elapsed. The car approached the Bourse. General Georges put his head out at the window on his left to look ahead and see where the cavalry escort was. Actually it was not at all near the King whom it was supposed to be escorting, but was gallivanting away in front as if it belonged to a circus procession.

At the same moment that General Georges put his head out of the window on the left something happened on the right. A man in brown, a bunched figure like a wild cat, had bounded onto the running board of the car. Such was the noise overhead and all around that General Georges thought that the shots which he heard were far away.

Colonel Piolet, with his horse indolently grazing the hood of the car, saw the man in brown jump on the running board of the car, but he thought it was a photographer.

The police agent, Celestin Galy, on duty at the Bourse on the right-hand side of the procession, saw the man leap onto the car and supposed it was some fellow who wanted to touch the King for luck.

Capt. Vigoreux, on the other side of the car, deafened by the roaring of the seaplanes overhead, thought he discerned the rattle of machine-gun fire, but he continued undisturbed on horseback following the car.

Foissac the chauffeur, driving the car, saw the man in brown disengage himself from the crowd on the pavement, plunge through the cinematographers who

VLADA THE CHAUFFEUR BEING STRUCK DOWN BY COLONEL
PIOLET JUST AFTER FIRING THE FATAL SHOTS

were filming the show, and approach the car. When he heard the shots he turned about, saw the assassin, and with one hand tried to push him off while he still continued to drive at a walking pace, but on second thoughts he stopped the car. The *vivas* for the King continued after the King was shot. No one seemed to have at once understood. The *vivas* continued and then suddenly changed to a hoarse roar of guttural conversation, like the sound of a gale entering a forest. There was a stamping and chafing, then a lurching, hoarse questions and exclamations, uneasy surging, surprise, screams.

General Georges had heard nothing from inside the car. He drew his head in at the window and looked round. Never can any man have had a greater surprise than he had then. Blotting out the opposite window was the monstrous visage of Vlada the Chauffeur, with protruding jaw and set blazing eyes, the blood lust incarnate. Alexander the King lay sunk in the right-hand corner of the car with a bullet near his heart. Barthou, moaning in agony, had slipped onto his knees on the mat. A hand with a long slim-barreled Mauser was covering Alexander, ready to fire again. All this General Georges realized in the twinkling of an eye. He did not hesitate. He flung open the left-hand door of the car and sprang into the street.

The agent, Celestin Galy, on duty in the street opposite the Bourse, was armed with a revolver, but he did not draw it. He heard the shouting of the crowd change to angry murmurs. He strode forward, but he did not hear the shots. He put his right hand on the shoulder of the assassin, who was crouching in at the window of the car, and he ordered him to get off. Vlada the Chauffeur at once turned upon him and shot him through the stomach. The police agent fell, rolling in agony in the street.

The mob then knew for certain that it was assassination. Pandemonium was let loose in the Cannebière. The policeman driver, Foissac, had got down from his seat and invited death by pulling the Bulgarian by the tail of his coat. But by that time General Georges had got round and he rushed up to the assassin to seize him by the collar. But Vlada the Chauffeur turned about with rapidity, covered General Georges with his Mauser, firing at once and wounding him in the side, then taking precise aim and shooting him in the region of the heart. The general tumbled backwards, but with two more shots the murderer put bullets through his right arm and his left arm.

Meanwhile Barthou, who had been shot in the right arm above the elbow, staggered out of the car into the street by the door which General Georges had left open. An artery had been severed. His blood flowed in a stream, gushed from him, splattering the pavement and the coats of the howling mob.

Yevtich got out of the second car, a diminutive, perturbed figure in frock coat and top hat, hurrying anxiously between policemen and sightseers. He got into the King's car by the open door by which Barthou had got out and at once he placed a hand on the breast of Alexander to feel his pulse. Dimitrievich got out of the third vehicle in bewilderment and fright.*

* According to General Dimitrievich, he reached the royal car before Yevtich and bending over the monarch he caught his last dying whisper, which was *"Chuvajte Jugoslaviju!"* (Save Yugoslavia!) In converse with the general I felt rather incredulous about this. If he had got there in time to hear anything I suggested that it might have been *"Chuvajte Kralitsu!"*

The murderer was not looking into the car any longer. He was at bay. For the moment unassailed, he held his revolver ready to repel attack. With his left hand he extracted another charger which he was prepared to insert in the Mauser the moment the first was exhausted. But he had become angry because it appeared that his helper, Kral, was leaving him in the lurch. If he, Vlada, was to make a run for it and escape, now was the moment for Kral to throw his bombs into the crowd. His eyes sought Kral. He fired two shots at the people on the steps of the Bourse. Perhaps that would startle Kral and make him do his duty. But Kral had a nervous brain storm. He was frightened by what he had seen. He slunk backward out of the lynching crowd and then ran to get into the provincial omnibus just starting for Aix-en-Provence. The newsreel men were still busy. For them it was the scoop of the universe, but they did not get the escaping Kral.

The drama was still going on. Colonel Piolet, who had clumsily backed his horse—he was an infantry officer—drew his saber and began a tardy attack upon Vlada the Chauffeur, beating him on the head. He was

---

(Take care of the Queen!) But Atsa Dimitrievich was very firm about it and imitated expressively with his lips how he had heard the words. Certainly it sounded more like an expiring sigh than an articulate sentence.

But upon reference to Bogoljub Yevtich I was informed that Dimitrievich never entered the King's car and that he did not see him until they reached the prefecture. That left me in rather a quandary, but as between the two men I felt that the Foreign Minister was the more likely to have the truth. Nevertheless, for state reasons it has generally been allowed that the King's last words were "Save Yugoslavia!" That was about the best thing he could have said under the circumstances and is most likely to be perpetuated in Serbian history.

egged on by women screaming. Two women had already been killed by spent bullets. The populace wanted to lynch the assassin, but it was not brave. It was stampeding. People were underfoot in the roadway and on the pavement. One can imagine the result if Kral had indeed thrown his bombs as he had been instructed.

Colonel Piolet had taken the murderer by surprise. Having received several blows on the head, the Bulgarian fell onto the running board of the car and rolled to the ground. He fired upward from the roadway. Then a plucky but overexcited policeman jumped on him and snatched what he thought was the revolver. It was the charger. Another policeman came up and shot Vlada in the head, quieting him but not killing him outright. The mob gained courage and surged forward, stamping on the prostrate terrorist, kicking him, shrieking and shouting. Police then came in swarms, elbowing the crowd roughly, fighting the mob. They made a cordon about the car.

Yevtich was still bent over the King. He had been joined by Colonel Pavlovich, the Chamberlain. They were still hoping that the King was not dead. They stretched his short body on the length of the two cushioned seats. Yevtich, with a small penknife used for opening letters, cut open the King's starched collar to give him air. But he could not unbutton the King's waistcoat. The admiral's uniform was too tight. It seemed to prevent his breathing. Yevtich began hacking through the broad red band of the Legion of Honor with his little knife. The French decoration seemed to tie death and the King together. Yevtich frenziedly cut it through. Then he sliced down the King's vest and opened the uniform; blood suddenly spurted from the released body onto his hands and face.

But he felt and found the wounds. He even noticed that the top of the King's right thumb had been notched by the fatal bullet that went to his heart. Alexander had been shot through his saluting hand, through the hand which acknowledged the shouts of *Vive le Roi!* There was blood now everywhere except on the face of the King, which was as white as marble. On his lips was the fading smile which had not quite faded. There was no sign of pain of any kind. Some last thought was on his face, but it was not fear of death, no, nor spasm of mortal agony. And nothing more could be done. There was a strange hush of death in the midst of a hurly-burly as of hell let loose. Yevtich was helpless and desperate and unspeakably moved. Alexander had been very fond of him. They were bound, not so much subject and sovereign as friend and friend, by deep affection.

When the murderer was down on the ground and the crowd had taken courage, surging forward once more, some men dashed to the car to stare at the dead King. There were wild, frightened faces looking down from the back of the car and hands outstretched along the upholstery, as if wishing to touch the dead King. Photographers demanded unimpeded view of the body. There was a confused jabbering as of angry apes. Anger was the note of the rapid French, anger against the assassin.

Foissac got back to the driver's seat and on orders from the chief of police started up again. He now went into top gear and, sounding lustily on his horn, clove a way through the people. That was strange. The dead King continued upon the line of route. Prostrate on the cushions, he looked up to the dim bunting with eyes that did not see. Only the crowd in the immediate vicinity of the Bourse had realized what had happened. The car got quickly through the excited mob and reached masses of sightseers who were still waiting for the King. From the Cannebière into the Rue St. Ferréol, where the public were all cheering and still crying *Vive le Roi!*

But the car drew up at the prefecture. Tea was set out there because it had been intended that after the ceremony of placing a wreath on the monument to the fallen soldiers King Alexander, M. Barthou, and other notables should return to the prefecture for tea before His Majesty went to the railway station to take the train to Dijon to meet the Queen. The King's body was carried into the chief magistrate's room and laid upon a sofa. Blood now trickled from the lips which still preserved their vague smile, making it possible to believe that the King yet lived. Several doctors had offered their services, but were not allowed to examine the wounds. A gendarme had been sent posthaste to a hospital to fetch the most highly qualified doctor in Marseilles. He reached the hospital at 4.30 P.M. and Dr. Assali, chief medical officer of colonial troops, came at once. Dr. Assali took one glance at the body, took up a wrist, felt for the pulse, and then gave an almost indignant glance at the people gathered round, as much as to say, "Why did you bring me here?" "Life has ceased," said he.

He entrusted the examination of the dead body to another doctor and hurried to the military hospital to see what he could do for General Georges, who lay unconscious there. It was found that King Alexander had been shot twice, first through the chest and then through the abdomen. It was the first bullet that had

Exclusive News Agency, London

THE MURDERED KING BEING
LIFTED FROM THE CAR

Wide World Photos, Inc.

THE DEAD KING BEING BORNE TO THE HOUSE OF THE
PREFECT OF POLICE

killed him, not actually passing through the heart, but near enough for death to have been almost instantaneous. In his subsequent evidence to the court, the second doctor, Raoul Olmer, declared: "Nous n'avons pu que constater le décès qui avait dû être très rapide."

General Georges was the next to receive attention. His condition was parlous in the extreme. He had been shot through the left breast, through the abdominal wall, and through both arms. The metal in a Serbian decoration had deflected one bullet from his heart. He lay between life and death for five months, but Dr. Assali saved him.

The plight of Barthou in the Hôtel Dieu was not so desperate, had he received prompt attention. But Marseilles had completely lost its nerve that afternoon. Barthou was allowed to bleed to death. He was lying on a tilted operating table, the idea being that on an incline he would lose less blood. His arm had been tied with a girl's handkerchief, at the wrist, while the wound was above the elbow! Dr. Bonnal, when he arrived and saw this, was indignant. He administered ethyl chloride and worked on the wound, finding at once the two extremities of the severed artery and joining them again. Had this been done at once when Barthou arrived in hospital there is little doubt but that he would have been saved. But it was too late. The old man had lost too much blood. Other doctors arrived and commenced a transfusion, but during that transfusion Barthou died.

In another ward Celestin Galy was speechless in agony. In the women's ward were Yolande Paris and Mme. Durbec, one shot through the right hip, the other through the right thigh. Both died.

In another room lay the murderer with bleeding

CHAPTER IV

MIO KRAL

MIO KRAL admitted afterwards that his courage failed him, or, as he put it, he did not throw his bombs because so many women and children might be killed. That failure to support the principal assassin at the critical moment in the Cannebière saved him from the guillotine. But Kral's obligation as helper was not merely to facilitate escape. He had his Mauser and his Walther, loaded and ready, and abundance of reserve ammunition. In case the Bulgarian had been arrested or shot, or for some other reason failed in his attempt, the principal role fell to Kral. He understudied the principal actor. But considering his mental state there was no strong supposition that he could have himself committed the murder unaided.

Kral was only twenty-seven, a poor, narrow-brained degenerate from a family ruled by the Austrians before the war, one of those pious peasant Catholics who seldom have enough converse with intelligent priests to get fanaticism smoothed out of their frustrate souls. He had become a tramp. He had left his village and wandered into foreign lands, been put in prison for vagabondage. But a serious talk with a simple father might have lured Kral away from murder. Priests had no influence in Pavelich's camps. The assumption of the approval of the Church was used by him without the permission of the Church. In all the evidence given afterwards there never was one word about a priest. Pavelich knew well enough that "Thou shalt do no murder!" holds good for Catholics as for others.

Mio Kral kissed the Cross and went to kill the King. He had been told that what the *poglavnik* decreed was blessed by Holy Church. He agreed that his own life was forfeit if he failed to obey instructions and also that his soul was damned. He desired a glorious role, a martyr's crown. But he did not know himself. The cannon firing in Marseilles, the expectant crowd, the tension, the shots, the minute of great noise and drama, were too much for his emotions. He slunk back out of the mob and fled precipitately.

He got onto an omnibus plying between Marseilles and Aix-en-Provence. In a sense he was fortunate. Not one of the other passengers was agitated. Those Frenchmen who had witnessed the drama were still discussing it in the streets. Not for them to take a bus to Aix! Not even the driver of the omnibus knew what had happened. Mio Kral drove to Aix ahead of the news. That was well for him because a nervous foreigner might well have come under the observation of the police. The police of Aix knew nothing. No telephone message had conveyed the dire news. Kral returned to the hotel from which he had departed at midday and there was nothing peculiar in that.

He expected to be met at the hotel. He would have to confess that he had left his comrade in the lurch, that he had not thrown his bombs. But he was ready to admit that his nerve had failed him. He believed the King to be dead. The main object was achieved and it was likely that Pavelich would be lenient to him. He could face Pavelich, though he had not been able to face mass murder. He sat in the restaurant of the hotel and smoked cigarette after cigarette. He ordered nothing, said he was waiting for someone.

Those who organized the murder were callous in the extreme. Beyond giving them pocket compasses they made no provision for the escape of the assassins. At the moment of the crime Kvaternik was already in Montreux, in Switzerland, receiving the letter written by himself to himself. He had done his allotted part and left the rest of the responsibility to Pavelich. He would not have been on hand to organize an attempt at Versailles had the Marseilles plot failed. It was not he who was going to forward instructions to Pospishil and Raich waiting at Fontainebleau.

But there is no doubt that the murder in Marseilles was watched by someone who had authority, probably "Peter," who did not have to have a message from Pavelich ordering the men to obey him because he was himself Pavelich. Unidentified by anyone in the frenzied crowd, he looked on critically while Vlada the Chauffeur carried out his orders. With him no doubt was Maria Vudrasek, the blonde lady. Had there been a failure, it was he who would have given immediate instructions to Pospishil and Raich. Equally upon him devolved the duty of facilitating the escape of Kral and Vlada the Chauffeur, supposing them not to have been arrested. Was he to have picked up the two assassins at the hotel at Aix? Of that we cannot be sure. Perhaps Kral was merely waiting for the Bulgarian on the chance that he might have made a dash for it and escaped.

In truth, had Kral thrown his bombs there is a fair chance that in the confusion and panic the two men might have escaped the flustered police and both got on to the Aix omnibus. A provincial omnibus was the last place likely to be searched for the assassins. It was shrewdly calculated. There was at least a chance.

But the observer, having realized that the King was dead, insured his own safety by making an immediate escape. He did not notify Pospishil and he left Kral to shift for himself. Kral had not carried out instructions. He had not thrown the bombs. His blood was on his own head.

Kral was more and more nervous. The news had not come to Aix, but it might come at any moment. When it was dark he went up to his room and ripped the covering from the spring mattress on his bed, hid the bombs, the pistols, and the ammunition and then tacked the covering in place again. He had no particular originality. He did what he had seen the blonde lady do. He had not freed himself from incriminating evidence, supposing he had been arrested that evening. Mattresses are liable to be shaken. The whole hotel might have been blown up. Better for him to have dumped them in the Rhone.

Better not to have waited two hours at the hotel. Time was precious if he wished to escape before the hue and cry. But he was expecting someone. The man who was to have warned Pospishil must pick him up. How otherwise was he to get away from France, how get to the safety of Italy? There was only one thing he knew, go north to Switzerland by the way he had come, like a dog, by Avignon to Paris, to Fontainebleau, to Thonon, across the Lake of Geneva. Then would come the adventure, going east by compass over the mountains of Switzerland to Italy.

At length the news came to the hotel. There was a lot of animated talk. Kral did not understand French but he guessed what it was about. Someone off the seven o'clock bus came into the hotel and was a center of interest. He had seen everything. One might have thought from his gestures that he had been in the middle of it, that bullets had flown by his head. His story provoked murmurs and exclamations of indignation from the men, sighs of horror from the women. Perhaps he was not entirely believed, but another man came rushing in with next day's edition of the Marseilles *Matin* with staring headlines, sensational pictures of the crime, photos of Alexander and Barthou.

Kral, in indescribable agitation, rushed out of the hotel and sat in the first taxi he could find. "Avignon!" said he in a hoarse voice and he had to repeat it several times before the taxi driver understood that the passenger wanted to be driven all the way to Avignon, a big fare. The taxi driver was engrossed, reading the evening paper but he put the paper aside. A big fare!

The passenger seemed so agitated and in such a devilish hurry that the driver had some doubt as to whether he ought to take him. He looked like a criminal, a man who had just robbed someone or committed a murder. It was the eyes of the man that seemed most strange. Later, in court, it was only by the eyes that this driver could identify Kral.

He drove out of Aix. But he had not enough petrol for the route. When he stopped at the *octroi* to fill up he saw that the passenger was in a great state of consternation. He hid at the back of the car so that no one in the street should see him.

Off they went again and the cabby drove hard. It was a dark night and there was a howling wind. The cabby was frightened, more than frightened. Perhaps he was driving some desperate character who would spring on him and murder him. He kept giving a backward glance, driving as fast as he could, but keeping an eye on his fare. By the glow of cigarettes he saw the man's eyes. Whenever they passed a car coming from the other direction Kral huddled into the back of the car as if to avoid being seen or to give the appearance that the taxi was empty.

The driver was relieved when they got to Avignon. Kral did not want to be driven to any particular address. In an empty street he made signs to the chauffeur, who stopped. Then Kral got out and handed him two hundred francs. The cabby gave him some change, which he did not count. He walked off quickly. The chauffeur, with a weight off his mind and good money in his pocket, went off for a drink. Kral found the railway station, where he had not long to wait for a train coming from Marseilles. He took a ticket for Paris. He skulked at the far end of the platform till the train came in. No one noticed him. He got safely into the train unobserved and found an empty compartment, where he stretched himself out and pretended to sleep. The conductor came and punched his ticket. No one else paid him the slightest attention.

But he could not sleep. The panic of Marseilles was still in his blood. The headlines of the newspaper he had seen seared his eyes. He was not overjoyed that the King was dead. The deed which he had been told would be glorious was now no more than murder. His only interest was to save his own skin. Kelemen—he had got used to calling Vlada the Chauffeur Kelemen—must be in prison, probably being tortured to extract the truth. Kelemen would not dare betray Pavelich, but he might denounce Kral, because Kral had run away instead of throwing his bombs.

But it was not to the interest of Pavelich that Kral should be arrested, perhaps tortured and made to confess things. Kral still had faith that the *poglavnik* would save him. He remembered advice given him in Paris: "If you are in any difficulty, come to the big café near the Opera House." He now clung to the hope that at Paris, at the Place de l'Opéra, he would see someone, perhaps Kramer. He steadfastly thought of Kvaternik under the name of Kramer as he had been instructed. Kramer had said "Au revoir!" He must be looking after Pospishil.

He arrived in Paris in the morning. The police were not watching the arrivals from Marseilles. The Gare de Lyon had its workaday air, everyone going about his business. The newspapers had sensational captions, but there was no sensation. People were not gathered in groups discussing the murder, as Kral had imagined they would be. He could not read French, but he bought a paper to look at the pictures. There were two photographs with the name Petrus Kelemen, one of him as a smart businessman taken from his false passport, the other the dreadful distorted face of the dead murderer taken from the morgue. Kelemen was dead. Kral was not horrified. He was actually relieved because dead men tell no tales. And the French believed his real name was Kelemen!

Kral felt better in Paris. The great city seemed to shelter him. There were so many people that the interest in individuals was divided down to nothing. He watched for a bus marked Opéra and hopefully boarded it. Then he had his morning coffee and *brioches* like a citizen of the world at the café at the old table. But no one came to greet him there. He felt lost. Fear began to surge back on him. The place to go to was not

Paris but Fontainebleau. Pospishil and Raich were there. But they would be leaving that day. He paid his bill. He watched for a bus marked Italie. If only that bus were going to Italy and not merely to the Place d'Italie where the buses started for Fontainebleau! But no bus for Italie came along. Panic got him again. He jumped into a taxi and surprised another cabby. "Fontainebleau!" he cried.

He waved money at the taxi driver and told him to drive to Fontainebleau, to the *gare*. He knew that much French. The Parisian cabby at once suspected he was a crook and notified the police after he had set down his fare and taken his money. Kral, at Fontainebleau railway station, took a second-class ticket to Évian on the Swiss frontier and then he disappeared. The police had some difficulty finding him. They did not imagine it was an accomplice of the assassin of Marseilles and they did not take much trouble. Kral had to satisfy himself that Pospishil was not in the town before he set off alone for Switzerland. In a town of 18,000 inhabitants that was not too easy and he could not go to hotels and ask. That would be inviting suspicion. The police, baffled, became more alert in the evening and telephoned Paris that there was a mysterious foreigner lurking in Fontainebleau. Paris replied that all strangers must be identified. Paris was sending three detectives; they would arrive in an hour. At nine o'clock a gendarme found Kral, who had returned to the station to wait for the train. Kral turned pale, but he offered his passport for inspection with a steady hand. The passport seemed to be in order. The photo tallied. The name was given as Malny. But when the gendarme made a movement to search him he bolted. It was dark. Kral had a good pair of legs and was running for his life. He was soon clear of the town and into the forest. The Forest of Fontainebleau is extensive. One can easily hide in it.

The difficulty, especially in the month of October, was to find something to eat. Kral slept out and it was bitterly cold. All next day he concealed himself, only coming into the open after nightfall. He wandered far from Fontainebleau and then tried to find a wayside shop where he might buy food. But he had no luck. The shops in this region are mostly in the villages. There is not such a thing as a coffee-stall or an inn on the dark narrow roads between the high trees. Kral became weak through hunger and being weak became confused. He did not use his compass to any purpose. He might have traveled by night like those escaping war prisoners who traversed hostile Germany and got to the Dutch frontier during the Great War. He might conceivably have got that way to Italy, picking up food where he could at night. But he wandered in circles in the forest. On the fourth day he came to a main road and decided to keep to it. He slept the fourth night in a ditch by the side of the road. On the fifth day he was so hungry he became reckless and trudged along in the daylight. To be arrested had become a lesser calamity than to be starved to death. He saw by the guideposts he was on the way to Paris. He did not care. He still had seven hundred francs and if he could get to the big city he had a better chance of hiding away. He might find a compatriot who would befriend him.

On the afternoon of October 15 there was a telephone message to the police at Melun. The message was that a suspicious-looking character had been into a bar at the crossroads for Corbeil. He had paid two francs fifty for coffee that only cost sixty centimes.

That was the suspicious circumstance which betrayed Kral. Police were sent out and, a quarter of an hour later, they brought the man to the police station. Kral made no resistance. He was happy to be under arrest. They fed prisoners, didn't they? That was all he wanted —food. He was ready to talk, tell a long story. He had spared the women and children of Marseilles. But give him food.

Meanwhile Pospishil and Raich had been arrested at the Swiss frontier. Kelemen had been identified from Sofia as Vlada the Chauffeur. As soon as the portrait of the murderer appeared in the Sofia papers the talk went round. Many people recognized the face. The Italians arrested Pavelich and Kvaternik in Turin, a precautionary arrest. They did not keep them in prison long and they refused extradition. They took care that no incriminating documents fell into the hands of the French police. In due course Pavelich and Kvaternik were secretly removed to quarters known only to the Italian authorities. They did not expel them from Italian territory. What happened to the blonde lady, Maria Vudrasek, no one knows. But the story is that she is on some obscure island with the other two.

CHAPTER V

MAN AND KING

THE murder of Alexander shocked Britain and America. It caused consternation in France, grief and rage in Serbia, chivalrous regret in Bulgaria. It plunged Kemal Ataturk into Oriental sorrow. It awoke an echo of Pan-Slavism in Soviet Russia, where Stalin is reported to have said that 150,000,000 Russians stood behind Yugoslavia. It was not entirely unexpected in Germany, but it was regarded as unfortunate. For the Germans, a brave man, a fine soldier, and a possible friend had perished. Germany had clean hands. She could, without reserve and with complete sincerity, pay homage to "our old but heroic enemy." Italy and Hungary had known that the murder was possible and had expected it. They expressed official sympathy: "The assassinations at Marseilles have profoundly wounded the conscience of the civilized world," but only in these lands was the removal of the King an unqualified relief.

The political significance of the death of Alexander was something concerning which men could have varying opinions. There were even those who honestly believed it would help Yugoslavia, giving her the chance to revert to a democratic regime. But about Alexander the man no one could honestly speak an evil word. In many ways he was a model. Fathers could place his life before their sons as an example. There were no skeleton cupboards, no moral blemishes. To the English he would be a gentleman, but he was better than that. He had something of the quality of Abraham Lincoln, though he was not so wise, something of the quality of Wolfe, or Gordon.

He had had a father whom he could admire. We are used to thinking of King Peter as an old man, the King Peter with the burly weather-beaten face of the old campaigner, the man who had to be carried on a stretcher through the snows of the Albanian retreat. But he also was a hero. He shouldered a rifle in the Great War like a common soldier. He had fought all his life for freedom. He believed so much in freedom that he translated John Stuart Mill's *On Liberty* into Serbian, from the French. The cause of France seemed to him the cause of liberty and he volunteered for France in the Franco-Prussian War. He joined the Foreign Legion, was wounded, and later taken prisoner. But the same night he was captured he broke away from the Germans, swam the icy Loire, and got back to the French Army. The rheumatism which he had in later years is said to date from that night. The French decorated him for bravery. That was in 1871 when he was twenty-seven. Four years later he appeared in disguise in Bosnia and Herzegovina, and raised the standard of freedom. These provinces were still under Turkish rule. As Peter Mrkonich, he organized armed bands of rebels and helped to free Bosnia and Herzegovina from the Moslem. He was unable to incorporate these provinces in Serbia. Austria-Hungary coolly assumed a protectorate and later annexed the lands which Peter had helped to set free. But Peter became known to the Serbs as the "Liberator." After he came to the throne he fought the Turks again and liberated Macedonia and southern Serbia. But despite his glorious career he never became proud or arrogant or set himself high above his people. He was brother in arms to every Serb.

But it was not until 1903 that he was called to be King. Until then the Obrenoviches ruled in Belgrade. For the greater part of his life Peter was an exile, but never embittered, always living for his country and freedom.

In 1883 he married the eldest daughter of King Nicholas of Montenegro, the Princess Zorka, and he went to live opposite the palace in the little house where Alexander was born. Zorka bore him five children, first Elena, who lived to marry the Grand Duke Constantine of Russia, then Milena, who died in childhood. Prince George was born in 1887 and Alexander in 1888. The fifth child lived only three weeks and the Princess Zorka died in childbirth. Alexander became an orphan at fifteen months. He grew up without a mother, a sad experience for any child. Prince Peter Karageorgevich had to be father and mother in one. He did not marry again and no other woman came into his life to share his family care. He might have had much help in Cetinje from the willing household of King Nicholas, but he renounced that when his wife died. He was not on the best of terms with his father-in-law. Peter was too democratic in spirit to countenance the royal caprice he saw in Montenegro, and he was too honest not to despise the financial operations of the poet King.

Almost immediately after the death of Princess Zorka, Peter moved with his children to Switzerland and took furnished rooms in Geneva. He was very poor, but was not oppressed in spirit because of that. He even added to his family by adopting another baby. His brother Arsène, married to Princess Demidov, had a baby son, Paul. He added little Prince Paul to his family in Geneva. Of course he had a nurse to help cope with these tiny children—some cousin—but as soon as the boys were old enough he helped teach them to read. He was a strict and solemn schoolmaster and ruled his household with a rod of iron. Woe betide any of the children who were late sitting down to meals!

But there was a backyard, or rather an interior yard, where the children romped. Toys were sent to them, especially by Aunt Helen, who was very fond of Sandro and sorry that the children had gone away from Cetinje. Sandro was Alexander's pet name. They had even a toy horse and carriage, very handsome, and Alexander could sit astride the horse while Prince Paul sat in the carriage.

Alexander was fonder of Paul than he was of his elder brother George or of his sister. And this childish attachment was a thing that persisted. Long afterwards, when Alexander became King, he still must have Prince Paul near him. He did not crave the presence of Elena or of Prince George. But his cousin Paul must be his neighbor at Bled, in Slovenia, and at his palace outside Belgrade.

October 24, 1896, was a great date, when Aunt Helen married the heir to the throne of Italy and Peter took the children, all except Elena, to Rome for the festivities. Elena did not have enough marks at school and was punished by being left behind.

Alexander grew up speaking French, went to an elementary school in the town, and sat with Genevan boys and girls of his own age, working sums on a slate, poring over history books, learning geography and drawing maps, though he was never asked to draw a map of the Balkan Peninsula, that part of the world not being thought sufficiently important for Swiss children to study. Only older pupils learned about the Balkans. Little Sandro was a good boy, better behaved than his elder brother George. He was a favorite with his teachers and sometimes obtained better marks than his father thought he was entitled to. But he was a typical schoolboy who went every morning with his satchel on his shoulders. He played games in the playground and the street, and was popular with the other boys. At home a Serbian lady called each day, generally in the evening, to teach him his own language. His father taught him Serbian history, showed him Serbia on the map of Europe, showed him Bosnia and Herzegovina, the places where battles had been fought. The children grew up to be proud of being Balkan and Serb.

It was a poor household in Geneva. There was no wealth, no luxury. There was not so much food as at Cetinje. King Peter could almost live on black coffee only. He brought up his children to be most frugal, a habit that remained with Alexander all his life. He never was much interested in eating and drinking.

But there was ambition. The father believed in the future of his family, a future in the service of the Slavs. He enjoyed some influence through the Montenegrin Court. Montenegro was small and insignificant, but the daughters of King Nicholas were connected with the grand world. Zorka had married Peter, an exile, and that seemed a poor match. But Helen had married the heir to the throne of Italy. A third married the Grand Duke Nicholas, the uncle of the Russian Tsar. Montenegro enjoyed an intimate friendship with the Russian Court and church. The Russian connection was still the strongest hope of the Slavs, other than their belief in themselves. Peter kept up a correspondence with Russia and decided to commit his children to the protection of the Romanovs. When Alexander was ten years old he must say good-by to Geneva and his playmates and go to school in St. Petersburg. The École des Pages accepted the young prince.

Sandro made the long journey but he did not go alone. George and Elena went to Russia to be educated also. Prince Peter was left to his clubs and his newspapers and political friends in Geneva. But he kept young Paul with him. His own children never returned to Geneva, but he went to Russia at Christmas and Easter and sometimes in the summer to be with them in the holidays. It was a holiday for him also. Russian hospitality was boundless and he and they were more comfortable in Russia than in Switzerland.

The boy Alexander learned Russian. He spent over eight years of his youth in Russia between 1898 and 1908. There seemed every likelihood of his becoming more a Russian than a Serb. But that did not happen. He never really submitted himself to Russian influence. The only thing Russian about him in later years was his accent sometimes when speaking Serbian. Although he may have been somewhat mollycoddled in the company of Russian princes, he remained the hard Serb. He did not become sentimental or write poetry, he shed no tears. No one ever saw Alexander weep after he was ten years old. He did not become a philosopher or an intellectual. On the other hand, he got no bad habits. When later he was a military cadet he did not indulge in heavy drinking or get involved in any disturbing love affair. He managed to find Balkan company in St. Petersburg and seemed to prefer it to that of Russians.

At school he shone in mathematics. He seemed to show a scientific bent. He had no flights of fancy or

KING ALEXANDER IN CHILDHOOD AND YOUTH

imagination. His mind grasped readily the limited and defined. What was always interested him more than what might be. A young realist! Under the circumstances, although he was a frequent and welcome visitor in the palaces of Nicholas II, where the talk was perhaps too much of prayer and miracle, he never became a fanatic in matters pertaining to religion. He was not freethinking, but he was tolerant. He very definitely did not believe that there were miracles in modern life. A man must fight for what he believed and back the rightness of his cause with a strong right arm. And he never had repentance moods or grieved over sins, but that was natural because he seldom did anything which could trouble a reasonable man's conscience.

Did the Romanovs guess, when they adopted the Karageorgevich family, that one of these princes would play a great part later in Serbia? They gave the sons the freedom of the Winter Palace; they planned for Elena marriage to a grand duke. It is probable there was political calculation. They were confident of the future of Serbia, and, alas, of the future of the Romanov dynasty. But Elena might not have made that exalted marriage had not Prince Peter been called to the throne.

Alexander Obrenovich had made an unpopular marriage with Draga, a widow and the daughter of a shopkeeper. She had been childless by the first marriage and it seemed likely she would be childless by the second. In Serbia, a childless marriage is considered punishment by God, a childless queen a disgrace. King Alexander Obrenovich was also unpopular for other reasons. A military conspiracy formed against him, and one night a band of armed men burst into the old palace in Belgrade, shot both Alexander and Draga and threw their bodies into the street, an appalling double murder that caused the name of Serbia to suffer for many a long year.

Peter Karageorgevich had no part in this crime and was not privy to the conspiracy. It was as much a surprise to him as to other people living in Geneva. The grandfather of Alexander Obrenovich had killed the original Kara George, the first liberator of the Serbs. Grandfather had killed grandfather, but there was no blood feud. Prince Peter did not lust for the blood of the Obrenoviches. But as he profited by the murder, some have thought erroneously that he bore some of the guilt. In 1903 he was, by popular election, made King of Serbia. George and Alexander were then withdrawn from the École des Pages and continued their studies with private tutors in Belgrade. But Prince George was heir to the throne.

Prince George exhibited a very different temperament from that of Alexander. He was exuberant, whimsical, given to fads and violent preoccupations, whereas Alexander was obedient and studious. In the Serbian family what the father ordains is law. The son dare not set himself against it. But King Peter soon had much trouble with Prince George, who was of an unruly temper that did not brook opposition. He behaved as if the heir to the throne were above the law. Men's lives were in danger from his passions. It is possible that he had some physical defect which would have rendered him childless. He has never married. King Peter never explained adequately why he disinherited him. But in the wild condition of Serbian politics, with freedom from the Turks only half won, he was probably justified. His successor must be one who could carry the burden of leadership without estranging the people over whom he ruled.

King Peter told his elder son that he would have to renounce the succession and he renounced it. There was no rebellion. On March 27, 1909, at the age of twenty, Alexander became heir to the throne. Prince George loathed Prince Alexander because he had taken his birthright. But he never contrived anything against him. He remained loyal. He fought in the Serbian Army during the war, going to Paris and London after the Albanian retreat, subsequently living as a country gentleman near Nish. After the assassination at Marseilles he said, "I regret him as King but not as brother," showing that he did not forgive. But King Peter's orders could not be disobeyed.

Alexander had completed his Russian education in the previous year. He now occupied himself with military maneuvers and affairs of state. The youth of twenty fast became his father's right-hand man. It was characteristic of King Peter that he shared his confidence. He did not jealously guard his position. He was a king who walked the streets of Belgrade without a bodyguard. He was not above sitting in a public restaurant or café. In his bearing he was completely democratic. But he preferred the company of soldiers to all others. Soldiering had first place in his mind. And in that neither he nor Alexander was idle. The little army was raised to a state of excellence. The capacity and character of officers were gauged. King Peter was always preparing. There were Serbians yet to be freed from the Turk, and he would strike again.

Until the outbreak of war with Turkey, in 1912, Alexander's advance in rank was slow. In 1905 he was a corporal. When he became heir to the throne, in 1909, he was made second lieutenant. King Peter was not the sort of monarch who thought his sons must of necessity be generals. He conceived of soldiering as a hard trade and had a contempt for dandy officers who had not yet smelt gunpowder. Alexander was a smart young subaltern. The face of the young man was much more alert than that with which the world became familiar later on. It was a face which could be read by anyone: it contained no mysteries. There were the eagerness and obedience of a well-trained but mettlesome horse.

But he was not wanted for cavalry charges. It was not enough to be brave and intrepid. King Peter was not entirely satisfied with his Russian training. In the millionfold army of Russia the responsibility of the individual officer was naturally much less than in the army of a small state. In Serbia every officer of ability must be prepared for the eventuality of very large responsibility. Alexander was deliberately prepared for taking command in the field. At the outbreak of the war with Turkey he was only a colonel. But he was very soon commander of the 1st Army. He won his first fame at the battle of Kumanovo, where his army routed the Turks, and he made a victorious entrance into the royal city of Skoplje.

In that battle he showed great valor and fought in the very front ranks of his own army. He pleased his father tremendously, for Peter liked a brave soldier. Alexander showed then, as ever afterwards, that he had no fear of death. That being killed was a tragedy never entered his mind.

But it would be a mistake to think that the strategy of Kumanovo was conceived in the mind of the young prince. It was not on his initiative. He was merely in agreement with Putnik, Stefanovich, Mishich, his father, and the rest. Serbia had not found a young Napoleon. Serbia has a talent for war. Her officers throughout the Balkan wars of 1912–13 and in the Great War with Austria, Germany, and Bulgaria, showed outstanding ability. There were no duds. There never was one-man leadership in any campaign. The responsibility was divided and the glory ought to be shared with many men. Alexander was a capable officer like the rest. But the outstanding fact is that he was very young. At the age of twenty-three he commanded a victorious army in the field and did himself and Serbia the utmost credit.

In the following year, 1913, the Bulgars made a treacherous attack on their allies and began a foolish war without ultimatum or declaration. They had become discontented with the terms of peace which were being arranged. For in the arbitrament the Tsar Nicholas II of Russia leaned more toward the claims of Serbia than those of Bulgaria. The Bulgars thought there was the opportunity of securing for themselves by a sudden military coup the greater part of coveted Macedonia. It should be said that before declaring war on Turkey the Balkan League had promised Bulgaria a much larger share of the spoil in case of victory. But natural disappointment could not justify the murderous attack on "brother Slavs."

On the night of June 16–17 the Bulgars assailed the Serbian 1st Army. But the young commander was not taken off his guard. He counterattacked and drove the Bulgars back, over their old frontier, in confusion. That success, perhaps more than Kumanovo, showed the older generals that the heir to the throne was of worth to them in the field. White-bearded, resolute Putnik, with his massive face; the bold *voivod* Stefanovich, with long, white rolling moustache; acute and intellectual Mishich, all men of sixty or over, came up and congratulated the stripling, the tiny Prince with features of a falcon. Alexander smiled modestly, the faint smile of a youth who would minimize his own exploits but is pleased to have the praises of the old men.

When in August, 1913, the victorious army returned to Belgrade, the capital was delirious with excitement. The modest Prince bore himself well: the cheering did not turn his head. King Peter saw that the people had accepted the heir as sincerely as it had him. Let the crowds rally round Alexander! Peter was sixty-nine and in poor health, but he had support in his old age. In June of the following year he virtually allowed Alexander to be King. The young Prince became Regent. In all but title he became King of Serbia.

This was decreed on June 11, 1914, little more than a fortnight before the world-shaking catastrophe in Sarajevo. The successes of the Serbian Army had inflamed the imagination of the Slav youth in the provinces of Bosnia and Herzegovina. The Slavs there still languished under the rule of Austria-Hungary. There was a conspiracy in Sarajevo, aided and abetted certainly by some Serbs in Belgrade though not by the King or the Regent. And the world was set on fire. The plotters succeeded in killing the heir to the Austrian throne.

At the very outset of his regency Alexander had to cope with the effects of this assassination. The Austrians sent their monstrous ultimatum, couched in such terms that it seemed no other settlement but war was possible. Behind the young head of Alexander was the long head of Pashich, one of the cleverest politicians of his day. Guided by him, Alexander and Peter examined the document and instead of flatly refusing its terms extracted everything with which they could possibly comply. The world was surprised by the humility of Serbia's answer. Any other state but Austria-Hungary would have discovered in it a basis for argument. But Austria was bent on war. She had been the passive enemy of Serbia throughout the two Balkan wars, and the success of the Serbs was a blow to the realization of her plans for extension in the Balkans. Serbia must be beaten while she was weak. She must not be given time to organize herself to become a menace.

Alexander remembered his friendship with the Romanovs. Before answering the ultimatum he sent a telegram to the Tsar, Nicholas II. He said he was willing to make an investigation and to punish any Serbian subjects found to have had any part in the Sarajevo crime. But he pointed out that the demands Austria made were so humiliating that no self-respecting state could submit to them all. Only forty-eight hours were allowed for an answer and the Austrian forces were already concentrating on the frontier. He told the Tsar he would do what Russia advised, and begged him to take the kingdom of Serbia under his protection.

The Tsar replied at once that his only desire was to avoid bloodshed. He said he would use every effort to calm the Austrians and avert war. He advised Alexander to do everything in his power to make his, the Tsar's, task easier, everything compatible with Serbia's honor. The Tsar would work for peace to the last. But if, in spite of his most sincere wishes, he did not succeed, the Tsar assured the Regent that he would not remain indifferent to the fate of Serbia.

But the Austrians would not be mollified by Serbian

humility. Serbia must drink the hemlock cup. The Minister was withdrawn; the order of invasion was given.

Nicholas II prematurely ordered the Russian mobilization. A terrible surprise was in store for the bullies of Vienna and Budapest. The Serbs were less prepared for war but they were tried. They were nationally homogeneous and not a horde of rebellious races. Their troops were braver, their officers superior in intelligence. But no one knew that in advance. It seemed a foregone conclusion that Austria would overrun little Serbia with the greatest ease and exact the maximum penalty, probably annexing the country. The Russians were concerned. The Tsar was stirred by Alexander's appeal. He called up his men from the utmost limits of his empire. It took a long while to mobilize that great Russian Army. But in reply the Kaiser mobilized also and with the swiftness of lightning. France then must mobilize. Germany, without waiting the outcome of events, decided to raid her old enemy, France, and plunged across Belgium instead of going to the assistance of her ally, Austria. World war was enkindled. Apart from the Battle of the Marne the first big victory of the Allies was a Serbian victory.

There had been little compulsion upon Serbs to join the army, no Prussian militarism. They were rugged mountain folk, independent and disinclined to recognize anyone as master. In general they were ready to fight when work on their farms was slack, but while fighting they never forgot their land and cattle in the background. King Peter announced that any man who did not want to fight could go home. But Alexander was the new generation, with a more realistic outlook. He believed that victory could be won, but he called every Serb to defend his country.

The Serbs were in no position to defend Belgrade against the Austrian onset. They had but little heavy artillery and were uninterested in fortress war. They could not spare a garrison to fight to the bitter end in a beleaguered city. The defense of the capital was left to a few gendarmes and volunteers. The main army at once retired to a more advantageous terrain. Its possibilities lay in the open, in free and rapid movement. The Austrians were flattered by the ease with which they crossed the Danube and the Sava, but when they attacked south of Belgrade they encountered a very stubborn resistance. But the Serbs must have been appalled if not frightened by the tremendous and sustained bombardment from the Austrian artillery, at that time some of the most powerful in the world. Their own petty field guns were soon silenced. The Serbs realized they were fighting a more redoubtable foe than the Turk. But they fought back day and night: they shot away the greater part of their ammunition. It was a war of big guns versus rifles.

Alexander was tireless. He was always at the front and in the most dangerous sectors, encouraging everyone with his presence. The bursting of shrapnel in his vicinity moved him not a whit. He was as cool and calm as in a drawing room. No nerves! His little head never made involuntary movements to avoid splinters of shell. He never quaked even when men were blown to bits within his sight. In the midst of awful war he was at home. But his face was grave. He did not make jokes with the men. The Serbs do not like people who make jokes at serious moments. Only when he seemed narrowly to have missed death men would see a gentle smile on his lips. Death and he were on quite friendly terms.

The Serbian Army slowly retired in the face of tremendous odds, dug new trenches. Old King Peter, rifle in hand, was in the trenches fighting like a common soldier. Late summer had gone. It was the rainy, muddy season. In a short while the heavy guns of the enemy would be in difficulties. Alexander and his generals were resolved on a counterattack, but awaited fresh supplies of ammunition. The enemy had not yet met the Serbs man to man. They underestimated the capacity of the Serbs to fight back. Suddenly, at the end of November, the whole Serbian Army struck, and struck furiously, and all the little field guns were barking again because ammunition had come up. At the first blow in the center the Austrians began to retire, but the orderliness of this movement was compromised by another even more violent attack from the left flank and a panic flight of divisions through divisions, the greatly extended line doubling up in confusion. That was the moment for the Serbs to show their quality. They had the enemy on the run, an enemy that greatly outnumbered them but whose very numbers were a source of bewilderment. The fighting army of Alexander drove on, never allowing the Austrians a moment to recover their wits. The whole vast punitive force which was to thrash little Serbia was in ignominious flight, throwing away weapons and equipment as it went and not stopping till it reached the Danube whence it had come —320 officers and 42,000 men surrendered; 142 heavy guns were taken and 60,000 rifles, 4,000 horses, and vast quantities of ammunition, to say nothing of field equipment and provender. In its headlong flight the

Austrian Army did not fire back. Old King Peter, in a ramshackle car, went ahead of the Serbian Army shouting, "Faster, faster!" to the chauffeur. He was one of the first to enter Belgrade. He went first to the cathedral church and then to his palace. Some student had pulled down the Austrian flag from the palace and he handed it to King Peter. The old man threw the black and yellow rag onto the ground, trampled on it, and spat on it.

Prince Alexander and Prince George also entered in glory. Father and sons celebrated a great victory. The first campaign was ended. The enemy did not fight back, having no further stomach for conflict with the Serbs. The Regent was in high spirits. Soon it was his birthday: he was twenty-six. Congratulations—not on his birthday but on the victory—showered in from Russia, France, and England. The Serbs had wrought a great service which was appreciated. Alexander himself took a larger view of the war than did either King Peter or Pashich. All that King and statesman hoped was that the Austrians would finally withdraw and leave Serbia to develop in peace. That was the time when it was confidently predicted that the war would be over by Easter. It already seemed something of a stalemate. But Alexander began to think of the disintegration of the Austrian Empire and the liberation of the Croats and Slovenes.

There was a long lull in the war. Something even worse came to decimate the Serbian population, and that was the frightful typhus epidemic of 1915. The wounded recovered or were invalided out. The hospitals became full of typhus patients. Alexander was less a soldier than an inspector of hospitals. All his energy was given to combating the disease. His own health was not very good. He had a grumbling appendix and chronic violent indigestion. About the same time he began to notice that he was getting shortsighted. But he had no time to attend to these troubles. He did not admit that there was anything the matter with him.

Except that he had become rather heavier in the face, he looked very well. But when the war was resumed on this front it put a very heavy strain upon him.

Secretly the Austrians were trying to get a separate peace with Serbia. It is a pity it was not arranged, because one separate peace must infallibly have led to others. Russia had no cause for quarrel once the independence of the Balkan States was guaranteed. France and England, though becoming embarrassed by secret treaties with Italy and Russia, did not wish to prolong the bloodshed one day longer than was necessary to obtain an honorable peace. But the Serbs could not seem to desert their allies, least of all Russia. On August 23, 1915, at Nish, the Serbian Parliament voted for the continuance of a war of liberation and thereupon the government rejected the Austrian overtures for separate peace.

Not the Austrians but the Germans answered that renunciation, the German general staff, the redoubtable Mackensen. If the Austrians could not cope with the wretched Serbs the Germans would take the matter in hand. At the beginning of October, Mackensen launched his great offensive. The Bulgarians saw their moment to take revenge for their humiliation in 1913, and they allied themselves to the Central Powers, attacking Serbia in the flank and rear. The Serbs were compelled to make an immense strategic retreat from the Danube to the mountains of Albania and Montenegro, fighting delaying actions, rear-guard actions

against the Germans and Austrians on the one hand and
against the Bulgarians on the other. They put up a brilliant defense that evoked the admiration of the Germans themselves. There never was a rout or panic flight.
The main army withdrew intact, shepherding the Parliament, the diplomatic corps, the Allied missions, the
nurses. But it did seem to the higher command of the
enemy that the army had retreated merely to perish in
the snowy wildernesses of Albania, perish, or surrender
en masse.

Alexander, King Peter, Putnik, and the other generals decided to plunge to the Adriatic shore across the
mountains. Neither Putnik nor King Peter was fit.
They had to be carried most of the way along precip-
itous narrow trails, sometimes in blinding snow. There
was intense frost and scarcely any food. The Albanians
shot down the stragglers. Hundreds of men perished
of exhaustion and frostbite.

The Regent Alexander was also most unwell. He
could hardly ride for pain. But he did not admit it.
Where so many others were suffering it was not for him
to complain. He rode ahead of the army. Perhaps he
hoped to get to some hospital in time. Only when he
was nigh falling off his horse did he receive medical attention. He was taken to a little house and operated
upon at once. That was at Lesh. He continued the retreat with unhealed wound, borne on a stretcher at the
head of a body of troops.

The Serbs did not know whether there was pursuit
and they could not be sure that even when they reached
an Albanian port on the Adriatic they would be saved.
The weary trek to Durazzo continued. How exhausting
it was for Alexander no one could tell, for he never
complained. Those French and English accompanying

the army were astonished at such endurance. They advised that the Regent be put on the first boat and taken away to be nursed, to Italy or some island. King Peter was also in favor of that. "Even if the worst befall us, let not the enemy have the triumph of capturing the heir to the throne!" But Alexander replied in a weak voice, "We must have ships for all. I shall not leave till the last soldier has embarked."

These words have been more quoted than any others Alexander ever spoke. He would stand by his people to the last extremity and nothing could move him. He had developed under the stress of war and had become a very stubborn man. He was of very different mettle from King Nicholas of Montenegro, who had also evacuated his country and got to Durazzo. King Nicholas got away to safety on the first boat.

The situation at Durazzo seemed pitiable in the extreme. There were no supplies, no transports. The Allies had failed in their promises. They had assured Alexander that there would be adequate assistance, but that assistance had devolved upon Italy, who was jealously perturbed by the presence of the Serbian Army in Albania.

The Regent, now commander in chief, but very ill, lay in bed at Durazzo and, thinking of the desperate plight of Serbia, had recourse once more to the Romanovs. His mind went back to happy days in St. Petersburg and his conversations with the Tsar. He trusted Nicholas II and knew him to be a friend. So from his sick bed he dictated a letter to the Tsar:

In hope and faith that on the Adriatic shore we should receive succor promised by our Allies, and the means to reorganize, I have led my armies over the Albanian and Montenegrin hills.

In these most grievous circumstances I appeal to Your Imperial Majesty, on whom I have ever relied, as a last hope and I beseech Your high intervention on our behalf to save us from sure destruction and to enable us to recoup our strength and offer yet further resistance to the common enemy.

To that end it will be necessary for the Allied fleet to transport the army to some more secure place, preferably Salonika. The famished and exhausted troops are in no condition to march to Valona as designated by the Allied higher command.

I hope that this my appeal may find response from Your Imperial Majesty, whose fatherly care for the Serbian people has been constant and that You will intervene with the Allies to save the Serbian Army from a catastrophe which it has not deserved, a catastrophe otherwise inevitable.

No one stirred to save the Serbian Army till the Tsar got busy. The governments of the West paid little attention to the Serbian exploit, which only became famous after the war was over. It needed a sharp note from Sazonov to spur the Allies to activity.

Tsar Nicholas replied:

With feelings of anguish I have followed the retreat of the brave Serb troops across Albania and Montenegro. I would like to express to Your Royal Highness my sincere astonishment at the skill with which under Your leadership, and in face of such hardships and being greatly outnumbered by the enemy, attacks have been repelled everywhere and the army withdrawn.

In compliance with my instructions my Foreign Minister has already appealed repeatedly to the Allied Powers to take steps to insure safe transport from the Adriatic. Our demands have now been repeated and I have hope that the glorious troops of Your Highness will be given the possibility to leave Albania. I firmly believe that Your army will soon recover and be able once more to take part in the struggle against the common enemy. Victory and the resurrection of great Serbia will be consolation to You and to our brother Serbs for all they have gone through.

Then the French and British began to send food through a supply station at Brindisi. The transport of the troops was delayed all through December, January, February, and March. The Serbs believed that the Italians sabotaged the efforts of the French and British, but all three powers were dilatory. The fate of Serbia was merely a question of extra man power. Were the rags of the Serbian Army worth salvaging for service on other fronts? Fortunately the Bulgarians did not decide to raid Albania. The Germans withdrew their main forces for other activities and the Austrians were idle. The Serbian Army was not subjected to any further attack. But it was a long time before it was entirely removed to Corfu. Alexander remained to the last. Peter went prematurely to Salonika.

Pashich and the Parliament and the greater part of the army were on Corfu. There was relief and rest and then spring sunshine. Alexander completely recovered after his long and painful convalescence. But he was not content to have his forces left stranded on the Greek island. He must have uniforms, rifles, ammunition, equipment, plan, and direction. He left Corfu and set off to convince the Allies that a real offensive from Salonika must be organized and that the restored Serb Army must be sent there. That had been King Peter's conviction. That was why the old King had gone there right away.

The Regent visited Rome, Paris, London, to present his case, and found many people willing to give him lunch but few to listen to his plans. General Dimitrievich describes his efforts in London: "It proved hard to convince the British higher command. Prince Alexander sits at a large table surrounded by staff officers. The table is covered with green cloth to which is tacked a large map of Europe. Alexander has to explain the strategic significance of the Salonika front and to con-

vince them that an offensive there would help to win
the war. It is difficult. The British higher command and
the specialists cannot see it. The Regent's plea is that
a successful blow struck from Salonika into the center
of Serbia would relieve the pressure on the other fronts.
The British position on the western front is not too
bright. They are hard pressed. At length they agree that
there is something valuable in the Salonika plan, not
only for Serbia, but for the whole Allied cause."

The Prince Regent achieved his mission. There remained but to buy a few French books to take back to
Corfu and to have his eyes tested. In Bond Street he
bought those rimless glasses without which he was seldom seen again in public. He ordered a dozen pairs: he
intended to be well provided.

Some ten thousand men had been transported from
Albania to the French colony of Tunis. They also were
brought to Corfu, where the man power of the Serb nation was concentrated, some 160,000 men. They were
having a holiday of a kind, but drilling all the while.
They were ready to resume the fight whenever the Allies were ready to transport them to a scene of action.
In the summer of 1916, some three months after the
arrival at Corfu, the reëmbarkation for Salonika commenced. Salonika was no longer to be merely a side
show. French, British, Russian, and Italian contingents
were also designated for that front.

The coördination of the efforts of this mixed force
was no easy matter, subject as it was to the changing
moods of Western politicians. But the little Serbian
Army was a compact unit and soon went into action.
In the early autumn it was again on Serbian soil, fighting the Bulgars. On September 30 it stormed Kaimak-
chalan. On November 19 Alexander drove into Monas-

tir (Bitolj), which had fallen to the Serbian Army. That was, however, all. There was no winter offensive. The forces in front of Alexander were too great. During all the following year the Salonika armies marked time. The aspect of Europe at war changed because Imperial Russia collapsed in revolution. The fall of Nicholas II was naturally a great blow both to King Peter and to the Regent. They believed in freedom but had no illusions as to Lenin and Trotsky.

King Peter said, "We Serbs are all peasants, but free peasants. My grandfather was a peasant and I set more store by that than by my throne." But that did not mean he would ever fight for a dictatorship of working-class politicians. Both Peter and Alexander had an unpleasant experience of politicians, whom they regarded as the necessary parasites of a state.

Then America entered the war and it was the signal for great numbers of Serb, Croat, and Slovene immigrants to volunteer for the Salonika Army. In June, Alexander edited a manifesto to the effect that he was fighting for a free Yugoslav state combining the three peoples, Serbs, Croats, and Slovenes, in one.

All through the following year the Salonika Army grew. In September, 1918, the great offensive began, British, French, Italian, Russian, Serb contingents and armies at length coördinated and fully equipped. Marshal Franchet d'Esperey was in command, but the spearhead of the forces was the army of Alexander. The time had come. The Germans had shot their bolt. Bulgars, lacking support, withdrew, crumpled up. The army of Salonika struck and triumphed. It made an end of the war. Before the last of the month an armistice was concluded with Bulgaria. On October 29 Alexander marched into Belgrade once more.

The war was won and in a short while the empire of
Austria and Hungary died. Serbia took possession of
Bosnia and Herzegovina, Dalmatia, Croatia, and Slo-
venia, and a part of southern Hungary known as the
Voivodina.

CHAPTER VI

HEIR OF LANDS AND TROUBLE

ALEXANDER was not wounded in the war and he came out of it in good health, in the prime of life, unshattered either in body or nerves. He had become experienced in handling men and in getting his own way. His will had developed. He was not a man who was in two minds about anything. But victory had not given him a swelled head and his temper was equable.

He had become a moderate pacifist, one who did not wish the Great War to be repeated or continued, but who knew nevertheless that the army must be kept in a state of preparation for any eventuality. He was ever conscious that soldiers and not civilians, least of all politicians, had won the war, and had an instinctive knowledge that soldiers guaranteed the peace. The members of the Serbian Parliament, even those who were young and able bodied, never shouldered a rifle. They had some hardships, removing with the army to Corfu, but they regarded themselves as privileged persons. It was not easy for him after the Armistice to become a civilian and a mere politician, and he did not try. It was a long while before he had himself measured for civilian suits and when he did possess mufti he was seldom seen in it. Military habit had become ingrained and the soldier prince in due course became the soldier king.

When the war was over he continued to live under

discipline. He did not relax and have a good time. He ate sparingly, as if the rations were still limited. Perhaps unlike a soldier he indulged in no hard drinking. A small glass of wine with his lunch and another with his dinner were all he asked. Dimitrievich told me that he reckons that if one put together all the *rakkia* that Alexander drank in his lifetime it would not amount to more than a liter. And yet the royal *slivovitsa* made at Oplenats is about the best in the country. But the Prince Regent had one weakness: he smoked endless cigarettes.

He gave his uniforms to be cleaned and repaired, for he disliked wearing anything new and was fondly attached to old garments. He did not wear things once and then throw them aside. The mentality of a frugal family remained. To the end his handkerchiefs were darned. He ordered the old palace to be cleaned and the rubbish the Austrians had left to be taken out and burned. But when it was cleaned he would not live in it. It must be prepared for King Peter; he would not usurp his old father's hearth. He went to live in a one-story house across the way, but a little up the main street of Belgrade, an old-fashioned stone house with a great backyard. He ordered in straightback chairs and solid tables, his old camp writing-table, and soldier's bed.

The royal guards were on sentry outside the house, but it was an unpretentious beginning. There all the day and half the night he received generals, politicians, delegates, with coffee and cigarettes endlessly relayed. It was decidedly a bachelor's establishment. No woman helped. Few women were received. For there was no feminine interest in the life of Alexander.

The war and the revolution in Russia had destroyed one possibility for Alexander. He would not marry into the Romanov family. It is said that he had a long-standing romantic attachment to one of the Tsar's daughters, who was murdered at Ekaterinburg, and that the young Grand Duchess once gave him a ring which he cherished. That is probable, for King Peter had spoken to Tsar Nicholas II about it and in January, 1914, Pashich, visiting St. Petersburg, made a formal proposal and the Tsar said he would regard such a match with favor.

Prince Alexander was thirty years of age in December, 1918, and it was important for the Karageorgevich dynasty that he should soon find himself a wife and obtain an heir. Thoughts of marriage did not naturally occupy his mind very much, but Pashich was insistent. His father's advice must be sought. But King Peter had not returned to Belgrade.

King Peter did not take part in the campaign of 1918, nor did he make a state entry into his recovered capital. He remained behind in Greece and grew a long white beard. It was only in September, 1919, that he returned to Serbia, first going to a hotel at Arangelovats and then slinking into Belgrade practically unobserved. He would not live in the old palace because he preferred to think that he was not a king any more. People saw him in the street and did not recognize him. He had a calm and benign face and looked like a saint. Two years of rest and peace had smoothed away the lines of care from his old face. But then he cut off his flowing beard because his people knew him better without it. He went to live in a villa on the hill of Topchider, a few miles from Belgrade, and he lived there to the end. His voice was heard occasionally, criticizing this and that, but he took no real part in affairs of state.

Father and son did not live together as might have

been expected. But the Karageorgeviches are not a clan. They rarely gather in numbers under the same roof. The larger family feeling does not exist. Prince Arsène, King Peter's brother, elects to live in Paris, avoids Serbia. Alexander's sister Elena lives in voluntary exile in Switzerland. Alexander and George were not reconciled. King Peter went away to live by himself at Topchider. The only relative who remained comparatively intimate with Alexander was Prince Paul.

Prince Paul was left behind at Geneva when the other children went to St. Petersburg. He remained with Peter. When Peter was elected King, in 1903, he brought Paul back with him to Serbia. Paul had private tutors. During the war he went to Oxford and completed his education. He never had to serve in the army. He returned to Serbia and became Alexander's only confidant within the royal family.

King Peter, however, was drawn nearer Prince George, his elder son, whom he had disinherited. He had always seemed more fond of George than of Alexander, even at the time of the removal from the line of succession. Prince George was often in attendance upon his father during the campaign, especially in 1914, bringing munition boxes for the old man to sit on, adjusting his binoculars, furnishing him with rounds of ammunition when the King wanted to fire. He was a tall and handsome fellow. When the war was over he had fewer medals than Alexander, but he looked a proper figure of a man. Any father would have been proud of him and it is likely that King Peter was a little sorry for him, too. Prince George, moreover, had the merits of the defects of his temperament. He might be extravagant of phrase and action when in a rage, but he was sensitive and had sympathy, while Prince Alexander had a dignified reserve and was always the same: cool, easy, and polite, a man with a smile but no store of laughter or tears.

The Regent emerged from the war more a European than a Serbian. His father reverted to type and was sheerly Balkan. But Peter had no reason to regret giving Alexander the conduct of affairs. He would make the sort of monarch the new triune kingdom required. If only he would find a Slav wife!

King Peter would have been content had his son chosen to unite himself to a Serbian lady, but Alexander thought that would give some family too much influence in affairs. He was stubborn; he had developed a long chin. Not even his father could argue with him for long. And King Peter was in his second childhood: he was not very reasonable.

In the summer of 1921 Alexander made a visit to Paris and while he was there the old King died. The only person with Peter at the end was his disinherited son, Prince George. His death greatly agitated Alexander, who became suddenly ill, was confined to his bed, and ordered by his doctor not to travel. The funeral in Belgrade took place without him. Prince George was chief mourner.

When Alexander returned he submitted himself to Parliament for formal acceptance and was proclaimed King. Within a year he went to Bucharest and sought the hand of Princess Marie, the daughter of King Ferdinand of Rumania. The match was a surprise for many Serbs, but Alexander must have known his mind for some time. He was going to make alliance with the European dynasties because his country had joined the West. Princess Marie seemed a good choice because she had some Slav blood, being on one side descended from Tsar Alexander II of Russia. Perhaps he prized more the fact that she was also descended from Queen Victoria. The young and beautiful Marie was very English. Prince Paul and she got on famously. He also was very English.

This English connection had some importance later because the children of both Alexander and Paul were brought up in an English atmosphere and were sent to English schools.

Of course King Alexander was rapturously congratulated on his marriage, though some may have wished he had married a Slav. But when, in 1923, Queen Marie gave birth to a son and heir, she attained great popularity. A woman does not mean much in Serbia till she has a child. She means more if she bears a son. Queen Marie bore two more sons, no daughters. She became ideal.

Normally before marriage there ought to have been the coronation, but the King was opposed to that. He said it was too expensive for his poor country, but it was really because he hated ceremonies. He was never crowned. He was a king who never wore a crown.

The King had given orders that a new palace should be built alongside the old palace in the main street in Belgrade. It was finished in time for him to receive his Queen there. At first they made their home in the midst of the city. It was spacious but almost as simply furnished as the little house he had been inhabiting across the way. His rooms there were still those of a soldier and rather Spartan. But the Queen introduced the feminine touch in the reception rooms, showing her great taste for handicraft and embroidery. In a sense the sovereigns lived apart in their home. The King was not uxorious. He did not allow the Queen to have any influence upon his decisions. "The Queen," said he, "has no part in affairs of state. I admire her because she is devoted to her children and seeks no other sphere of interest." But they found one another companionable. The King took her to his farm at Oplenats. They went on many picnics and behaved among the peasants with complete freedom from embarrassment. Wherever Alexander traveled Marie went with him.

But the finding of a suitable consort could only have been a minor problem in the early years following the war. The peace, reconstruction, reparations, consolidation of the new territories, occupied Alexander's mind to the exclusion of other considerations. First there was the problem of the terms of peace. Europe in war had been noisy but the Babel of peacemaking was even noisier and no one understood anyone else's language.

The issue in Europe had been greatly complicated by America's entry into the war and the fourteen points of President Wilson. The making of peace was also a conflict. The view of France was that spoils go to the victors; the view of Italy was that the Allies should respect the deal which had been made with her when she went into the war. Italy had come in on a contract. The view of Britain was that all future enemies should be eliminated. The view of America was that the nations of Europe should go into committee as friendly powers. England gave lip service to the right of self-determination for small nations, but she had signed away in advance some of the territory which is now Yugoslavia. The future of Serbia was a very considerable problem.

Was Serbia to have Dalmatia? A large portion of it had been promised to Italy. Was Serbia to have Croatia? It had always been understood in London that the Croats would have the right of opting what they wanted to do. Was Serbia to have a slice of Hungary? Was she to

language, may be considered one with the Serbs. They elected to dethrone King Nicholas and cast in their lot with the new state. Bosnia and Herzegovina were glad to escape from Austrian rulership on any terms. Only the Moslem element asked for guarantees. The one Slav region which did not want to be linked to the destiny of greater Serbia was Croatia. The Croats had not foreseen the downfall of the Austro-Hungarian Empire and though discontented were unprepared for it. The Croats in Alexander's Army had been mostly volunteers from America, not from Austria. Desertion of Croats from the Austrian Army had not been so marked as that of the Czechs and the Poles. They fought as well as any other units in that multinational army—perhaps because they were used almost entirely against the Italians who had claimed their lands. The collapse took them by surprise. They had to make their minds up in a hurry as to what kind of political future they required. Many would have preferred to inaugurate a new state, a Croat republic, imitating the Czechs. Some even talked of a "Great Croatia" which would have taken over Serbia. Zagreb was unscathed by war and felt highly superior to ramshackle Belgrade. But the Western Powers would not hear of setting up yet another state. Some politicians were ignorant of the existence of the Croats. The Croats had not advertised their cause like the Czechs. But self-determination was the order of the day and if these Slavs had chosen to be incorporated in Hungary or united to Italy it is possible that their claims would have been considered sympathetically. Italy was ready to present the peacemakers with a *fait accompli* by occupying the country. The Croats were in a panic. They dared not unite their destinies with that of the defeated powers. On the other hand, they were afraid of being absorbed by

victorious Italy and forced to become Italians. And racial pride rendered it intolerable to become governed by
the Serbs, to whom they felt superior in culture, man-
ners, cleanliness, and religion. "We once had a king of
our own," they wailed; "he was called Tomislav." But
the only Croats who wanted a kingdom were the partisans of the Hapsburg dynasty. More were in favor of a
republic. Only immediate occupation by the Serb Army
prevented the setting up of a peasant Communist state.
It went against the grain to have to acknowledge a Serbian king. But the Croats had no real choice. The Serbs
had liberated them and they had to take the consequences. On November 24, 1918, the Zagreb National
Majority appointed a commission to negotiate with the
Serbs, demanding that the question of the seat of government, what should be the national flag, and what form
the new state should take, should be decided by free
vote. A constituent assembly was to be called to settle
these fundamental matters, but until that assembly had
completed its work the Croats agreed to acknowledge
King Peter and his Regent Alexander.

The general election did not take place for a year and
then produced surprising results. The Communists, generally considered negligible, won 58 seats. Radich's
Peasant party won only 50 seats. The Slovenes, under
Dr. Koroshets, a Roman Catholic priest, won 27 seats.
The Moslems voted for themselves and won 24. The
Serbian Radical party got only 91; the Democrats, made
up of Serbs and Croats, 92. Pashich, now president of
the assembly, deliberated and intrigued and argued for
eighteen months before a settlement was reached. Then
the St. Vitus' Day Convention was agreed and the Kingdom of Serbs, Croats, and Slovenes was ratified and had
a constitution. Alexander took oath to abide by this con-

stitution, and for better or for worse Croatia was incorporated in the new state which in time was to be called Yugoslavia. But from the first there were strongly disaffected elements in Croatia. The flame of separatism was never extinguished. Great Britain had her Catholic Ireland; Great Serbia had her Catholic Croatia.

The new kingdom had seven frontiers, those of Albania, Greece, Bulgaria, Rumania, Hungary, Austria, Italy. It ought to have been strong internally to face calmly so many possibilities of external difficulty. At the commencement of the peace era only one of the countries bordering on Yugoslavia could be said to be definitely friendly. That was Rumania, and that was one reason why Alexander chose to ally himself with the family of King Ferdinand by marriage. Hungary, despoiled of the Voivodina, where there was a large Magyar population, remained an enemy, biding her time. Austria retained a contempt for the Serbs, a barbarous race which, through the help of strong allies, had profited by the dismemberment of the empire. Vienna, as a center of news service, was able to distribute disguised propaganda to the world. Bulgaria smarted from defeat and the final loss of territory which she had held and coveted so much. With peace, Italy had ceased to be an ally and had become an enemy. She was bitterly opposed to the extension of Serbia across the Balkan Peninsula and unwilling to recognize a kingdom of Serbs, Croats, and Slovenes. She was assimilating half a million Slovenes in her new territory and intended that they should be Italians without the possibility of appeal to an outside power. Italy regarded the whole of the Dalmatian coast as historically Italian and only waiting to be restored to the scepter of Rome. She considered that she was cheated by the peace treaties and thereupon commenced that strange policy of

identifying her interests with those of the defeated powers. Albania, in which persisted a tribal hostility to the
Slavs, became an unofficial Italian protectorate and a
potential base for an invasion of Dalmatia.

Throughout his reign Alexander strove to mitigate international jealousy and enmity. He may have failed to
solve the internal problem, which was well-nigh insoluble, but he had more success in foreign policy. Very
fittingly, at the spot on the Cannebière in Marseilles
where he was murdered black stones have been inlaid
in the roadway to make the word PAX. He sought peace
and security on every hand. There was no sword waving
or provocation. He resented the legend that wars began
in the Balkans, endangering the peace of the West and
European civilization, and it was his object to show that
his country was a force on the side of peace and in no
sense a menace to any neighbor.

He lived to see the Germans desiring economic part-
nership—perhaps friendship. He assuaged the bitterness
of Austria. He won over the Bulgarians. Two states
alone baffled him, Italy and Hungary. These countries
exploited the differences between Serbs and Croats and
tried by financing and organizing terrorism to weaken
the fabric of this new, weak, loose, and unconsolidated
state. Italy was the leader. Incident followed incident,
outrage followed outrage throughout the reign of Alexander.

CHAPTER VII

DEMOCRACY FAILS

DEMOCRACY depends for its life upon political freedom, and political freedom depends on individual freedom, freedom of the mind and will. But democracy is not a gift. President Wilson could not give it to the small states he championed. In a sense it is inherited. Generations work for it: men die for it. It is won by fighting and it is bequeathed. It is not possible to take a savage tribe, or some primitive race or backward, undeveloped nation, and make it democratic overnight.

But that was the assumption of the peace treaties. Wilson strove to make the world a superstate on a universal democratic basis, all nations respecting the rights of others and coöperating to obtain fullness of life and expression. It was fine, but it could not be realized by appending signatures to the covenant of the League of Nations. It was like a voice saying, "Let there be Light!" but it was only the voice of Wilson, not of humanity as a whole.

The assumption was that individual states would preserve free institutions and that their representatives at Geneva would be the voices of the democracies of the world. The assumption failed: therefore the League failed. But a paradox remained. States like Yugoslavia could be ever loyal to a moribund League while domestically they had been forced away from freedom and democratic government.

The races composing the state known afterwards as Yugoslavia had very little experience in democracy. The Serbs were a violent race escaping from centuries of thraldom to the Turk, dedicated to national freedom. They had at least fought for freedom. But it was national freedom. If, in the war with Austria, some of them consciously fought to liberate the Croats it was because they believed that the Croats were Serbs also. The Serbs had the most experience of parliamentary and constitutional government. Milan Obrenovich was obliged to grant a liberal constitution in 1889. When his successor, Alexander Obrenovich, tampered with the constitution he was murdered and the Serbs invited the man who had translated Mill's *On Liberty* to be their King. He was king by popular election and was obliged to respect the political freedom of his subjects. That obligation happened to coincide with his personal inclination. He removed his son George from the succession lest political freedom be endangered by the unruly disposition of the heir. Alexander was not quite so democratically minded as his father but he also, upon accession, submitted himself to parliamentary election.

In the peace era after the war the Serbs at least understood the practice and mechanism of parliamentary government. A parliament had even sat at Corfu and deliberated throughout the tragic years when Serbia was said to be nonexistent. It was a group of turbulent Serb politicians which had been elected by Serbs and it naturally came back thinking of itself as Serb rather than Yugoslav.

In the empire of Austria-Hungary Croatia lay under the jurisdiction of Budapest and was governed by a Hungarian viceroy. From a status resembling that of a conquered province it had been moving slowly toward self-responsibility. The Croats had well-organized parties, a political press, and other prerequisites for using the political forms of democracy; and the Diet controlled a wide range of domestic activities. But the franchise was limited to less than a twelfth of the population. In 1918 manhood suffrage was granted by Austria-Hungary, but that was a war measure designed to stem the tide of revolution. The Diet was not entirely elective. It was composed of nominated officials, landowners, clerics, and a number of Croat representatives elected on the limited franchise. The Croat population was one of the many racial oppositions in Austria-Hungary, but they had been so long in subjection that few dreamed of emerging from the empire as a free and separate national community. The fall of the empire was a surprise. The Croats had suddenly to decide what they were and what they wanted. Many were acutely conscious of themselves as Croats. None thought of themselves as Roman Catholic Serbs. Only a few were ready to call themselves Yugoslavs.

But the Serbs also were not certain what the Croats were—a conquered enemy, or a sort of Serb, or "brother" Slavs like the Bulgars. King Alexander had had no contact with the Croats and at the outset knew little about his new subjects. He was obliged to accept the Serb assumption that Serbs and Croats were one people. He sent his army at once to occupy Croatia. The downtrodden Croatian peasants were rising to make an agrarian revolution against their Magyar and German masters. He stopped that. At the outset he was obliged to control Croatia, not a very auspicious opening for a democratic regime. But then the Croats themselves had little experience. The masses were more ready for an agrarian revolution than for democracy.

Bosnia and Herzegovina, after four hundred years' servitude to the Turks, went under the government of Austria-Hungary and had even less experience of democracy than Croatia. The people were extremely backward. Not only were the peasants illiterate, but about a fourth of their number were serfs. Slavery lingered on there after it had been abolished from the rest of Europe. There was no freedom of press or speech, and the provinces were most rigorously governed. There was a large Moslem population of Slav extraction, not Turkish. These people thought of themselves first as Moslems and only secondarily as Serbs. It proved very difficult to persuade them to think of themselves as Yugoslavs. In southern Serbia the people had quickly to set aside the Bulgarian language and speak Serb. As their native dialect is something between the two that was not so difficult. But they thought of themselves as Macedonians. There was a Moslem minority which was unchangeably Turkish.

In the Voivodina there were large Hungarian and German minorities who had no inclination to identify themselves with the new state. This province had sent representatives to the Hungarian Parliament, but the peasant masses were without votes.

The Slovenes were better prepared than most, having enjoyed adult suffrage since 1907. They sent a compact body of Slovene representatives to the Austrian Parliament and had attained a higher degree of political development than the Croats. They proved in the upshot more capable of assimilating the political conception of Yugoslavia.

It is not surprising that when the representatives of all these races and sections came to Belgrade, confusion was worse confounded. The reverse of the Pentecostal miracle was achieved. They spoke with tongues and none could understand them. Parliament was a collection of minorities unwilling to cohere to obtain ends which they had in common. Speeches were loud, emphatic, and unrestrained. No one was able to convince anyone else on the floor of the house. From the first Alexander was exasperated. What a contrast to the *esprit de corps*, the unanimity, the ordered purpose of the army! Politicians are the soldiers of peace, but they showed themselves as untrained men, far less efficient than the soldiers of war. The soldiers had been first class: the politicians were no class at all.

But still the political experiment was begun honestly. The elections were free. There was no interference on the part of King Peter or of the Regent Alexander. The framing of the new constitution was left to the elected Parliament. "Make your decisions, whatever they are we will abide by them!" There were many plans, each supported by a sectional majority but outvoted by the other minorities *en masse*. At length, after several crises, when it seemed that the parliamentary system would not work at all, the largest minority, the Serbs, bought the Slav Moslems by agreeing to compensate Mahometan landlords for confiscated lands. The Moslems then agreed to the Serb draft of a constitution and it was voted over the heads of Croats, Slovenes, and the rest. All the others had wanted federal systems but had been divided as to details and they had not learned to compromise. The Croat *bloc* declared roundly, in 1922, that the constitution had been obtained by fraudulent means. They had been tricked by the wily Pashich. Even the representation in the constituent assembly had been weighted in favor of the Serbian regions.

The new constitution granted representative government and freedom of religion. But power was centralized in Belgrade and there was not adequate guarantee for individual rights, freedom of speech and of public meeting. It gave the government of the hour extensive power of control by police. In the Balkans, when political persuasion fails, the gendarmerie is the standby of authority.

The new constitution was the 1903 constitution of Serbia, reëdited to embrace Croats and Slovenes. Even Pashich was conscious that a federal system would have been better. On a free vote Parliament would have chosen to have a republic, making Alexander the first president. It had the great example of the Czechs and Slovaks, who seemed happier under Masaryk. If Alexander had agreed to it there would have been a republic. But he was for kingship and the dynasty. Had he allowed a republic it might have swiftly developed into a Soviet republic and the dictatorship of the proletariat. He was not going to allow his country to follow in the destructive course of Bolshevism.

It was a confused time. The Parliament of 1920 camped among the stones of Belgrade. Trams had not begun to run. The cafés were lighted by oil lamps at night. Newspapers had only just got started again. Gossip and rumor ran unchecked from café to café. The menace of Communism and revolution was the bogy of the time. Fifty-eight Communist members! That was the first turnip lantern in the Belgrade night. Communism must be put down.

Very soon after the assembly of the first Parliament a decree was promulgated dissolving all Communist organizations and prohibiting the Communist press. That decree was carried into effect with violence by the police, and was answered by violence by the Communists. On the day of the promulgation of the St. Vitus' Day Constitution an attempt was made by a Communist to assassinate the Regent. A bomb thrown from an unfinished building missed its mark, becoming entangled in telegraph wires: the man was arrested and sentenced to life imprisonment. Two months later the Communist party was pronounced illegal and debarred from having representatives in the Skuptschina. The first Parliament of 1920 had 58 Communists; the second, in 1923, had none. In July, 1921, the Minister of the Interior, Drashkovich, had been killed by a young Communist, and that murder together with the attempt on the life of the Prince Regent had caused violent animosity against the Marxists. But in the 1920 elections the Communists had polled as many as 200,000 votes. These voters were mostly in the poverty-stricken areas. The war against the oppressor had been won and the underdog wished to raise his head. This underdog has, to this day, remained a political problem in Yugoslavia. There are too many people on the verge of beggary. But the members of the first Parliament did not stop to consider the consequences of banning any one political party. Democracy's chances of development are impaired once a certain political creed, no matter how abhorrent, has been made illegal. What is more, the dispersal of the Communists by gendarmerie gave a precedent for dragooning other political parties and disposing of the personal liberty of difficult politicians. There never was another election in Yugoslavia free from police interference.

After Communism, the next trouble of Alexander was the Croat *bloc*, which emulated Gandhi and refused to coöperate. In vain Alexander addressed to the hostile Croats comfortable words: "Separated for centuries but not alienated from the one family, separated by the brute force or cunning of the mighty empires of Rome, Byzantium, Vienna, and Stambul, but never broken in spirit, we have faithfully preserved the holy traditions of bygone generations. For centuries we have endured under difficult historical conditions and under the influence of varying faiths and we have developed where and how we could our mutual or individual traits, always remembering, always knowing that we are brothers and that we are one. . . ." The Croats did not intend to be at one with the Serbs unless the Serbs accepted their programs.

Stephen Radich was the leader of the Croat *bloc* which won 50 seats in the election of 1920 and 71 seats in the election of 1923. After Nikola Pashich, he was the most remarkable man in the new country, the uncrowned king of Croatia, having a position among his own people similar to that enjoyed in Ireland at one time by Parnell. He was not a great statesman. A weathercock in politics, it is difficult to systematize his views without disclosing a mass of contradictions. But he owed his fame to a gift for sentimental oratory. He spoke a language that even the most illiterate could understand. He was always like a father telling fairy stories to his children. He was beloved by the masses, and tiny tots in the streets sang songs about him, a legendary personage even before he died.

This Stephen Radich is a key person in the study of the reign of Alexander. His life was united to hope for the new country: his death was a tragedy that led to further tragedy. The murder of Radich in 1928 must be connected historically with the assassination of Alexander at Marseilles in 1934. It gave Italy and Hungary their opportunity to organize racial revenge. That King Alexander had been a firm friend of the Croat hero was no hindrance. Radich was the figurehead of the Croats and the Serbs could be advertised as the eternal enemy. The murder of Radich made the problem of Serbo-Croat conciliation almost insoluble.

Radich was forty-seven in 1918, a plump little moon-faced man, always smiling, not Balkan in appearance but surely Slav. He might have been a Russian. The Serbs do not like facetiousness and playfulness and with diffi-culty tolerate a waggish politician. They could not un-derstand why he exercised such overwhelming influence on the Croats. But he had not grown up among the Serbs and they did not know him.

He was a man of the people, one of eleven children of poor peasants on a seven-acre farm near Sisk. He and his brother Ante seemed clever and went to school in Za-greb, the rest stayed on the land. Stephen's political ad-ventures began when he was sixteen. He was sent to prison for shouting in a theater. He had cried out, "Down with the Viceroy!" The Hungarian police could not tolerate even a childish demonstration in the Opera House. When he was set free he found himself rather a hero among the other boys. But his headmaster advised him to keep away from the school for a while lest the authorities demand his expulsion. He must not lose the right to matriculate.

With time on his hands Stephen decided to go to Russia. He became very enthusiastic for the Russians and rapidly learned the language. He had an extraordi-nary facility for languages. When he returned to Zagreb he told his schoolmates that they must learn Russian and began a private class, teaching them himself. This at once provoked suspicion and he was placed under police surveillance, on suspicion of being a Russian military spy.

The behavior of this feather-brained lad seemed so peculiar that it was decided to arrest him again and he was placed in a home for mental deficients. Three official doctors examined him and reported that he was mad but harmless. The authorities banished him from Zagreb and sent him back to work on his father's farm. But he continued his studies and passed his matriculation as an external student a year or so later.

He obtained permission to reside in Zagreb and was entered at the university, where he at once began to organize a political movement among the students. He edited a patriotic Croat protest, was arrested, and sentenced to four months' imprisonment. There was no trial or sentence: he was just seized and jailed. He was fed by political friends through the prison bars and amused himself by learning Czech. He prepared himself to go to Prague and study law. In the following year he was arrested in Prague and then banished from that city. He went to Budapest, learned Hungarian, and entered the university there. That was at the beginning of 1895: he was only twenty-four.

He was a good-natured youth, capable of getting quickly excited but not of violence. He never struck anyone in his life, did not carry firearms, and was not interested in the bomb as a political instrument. Wherever he went he carried a village guitar, *tamburitsa*, about with him and sang to it. Being a Croat rather than an Austrian or a Hungarian, calling for a Croat king, demanding a Croat flag, and the official use of the Croat language, all this was to him a game. He was not a fanatic. When traveling between Budapest and Zagreb he infallibly quarreled with railway officials because his ticket was printed in Magyar and not in Croatian. On one occasion a conductor pushed him off a train because of this. He organized demonstrations to burn the Hungarian flag, unfurl the Croatian flag, and cry "Long live the Croat king!" though there was no king of Croatia.

Once more in Zagreb he was arrested by the Hungarian authorities, tried for sedition, and sent to prison for six months. By that time he had become popular and was already a well-known personality. When he was liberated he was sent under police escort to his village, but he could not be hidden there. He was resorted to. Already he was a leader. But he wanted to go to Russia again. The money for the journey was subscribed and in June, 1896, he set off for Moscow.

In Moscow he entered the university and continued his studies. He had his banjo with him and one cannot think that he studied very seriously. He had become a rolling stone. He stayed only five months and then went to Paris. He had not enough money to enter himself at the Sorbonne, so he quitted Paris for Lausanne, where he resumed his education. He was at home in every city and every university, speaking all the principal languages in Europe. But, after all, he finished his education in Paris at the school of political science and received the title of Lauréat des Sciences Politiques. Then his life as a journalist began.

He returned to Zagreb, again took part in demonstrations, was again arrested, and again sentenced to six months' imprisonment. When he got out of jail in February, 1903, he was at liberty for little more than a month before he was arrested again and kept in durance till August. In the following year he helped to organize the Croat Peasant party, the party which he eventually represented in the Parliament at Belgrade.

The police left him unmolested for some years. He wrote articles, pamphlets, books. He went to Prague again. He was now married to a Czech. He met the delegation from the first Russian Duma. He was always greatly attracted by Russians.

In 1908, when Austria annexed Bosnia and Herzegovina, Radich approved. He did not share the Serbian indignation. He did not like the pretensions of the Serbs, certainly did not regard the Serb as "big brother," but rather as some sort of wild cousin. The annexation added territory to the hypothetical "Great Croatia." In St. Petersburg he explained this view to the Russians and urged them to recognize the annexation. Austria was not grateful. A period of arrests and imprisonments followed. That his wife might have a means of living while he was in jail, he started a Slav bookshop in Zagreb. He was a member of the Diet, leader of the Peasant party which gained increasing influence, but the immunity of members did not save him from imprisonment. Repeatedly after he was elected his election was annulled.

When the Archduke Ferdinand was assassinated in Bosnia, Radich condemned that as he condemned all terrorism. But he welcomed the war, out of which he believed would come a new Austria and a betterment of the position of the Slavs in the empire. He foresaw a Triune Kingdom of Austrians, Hungarians, and Croats. The Croats would be masters of annexed Serbia and then "Great Croatia" would be realized. Radich caught the war fever. He wrote poems in praise of Franz Joseph. When in December, 1916, Franz Joseph died, he wept over him as a wise man and a martyr and the father of his people. But he had no illusions concerning the new emperor, Karl I. He continued to be loyal as regards the war, but in opposition to Hapsburg politics. The Russian revolution and the democratic appeals of President Wilson made a strong impression on him and he obtained a new vision of the outcome of the war. When the Germans began to fail he was already a defeatist. Very soon he became a republican. He visited the Bulgar Minister in Vienna and implored Bulgaria to cast in her lot with all the southern Slavs—in a republic.

His following in Croatia was peasant and working class. There was a strong opposition from Pribichevich and the Serbian minority in Croatia, from shopkeepers and the professional classes, and what may be called the representative men in Croatia. Practical-minded people saw that with the Serbs winning by force of arms their King could not be removed by Croat sentiment. The Croats would have to make a deal with the Regent Alexander. Radich opposed. He would not accompany the executive delegation to Belgrade. He appealed to President Wilson for a peasant republic in Croatia. But the Serbian troops had occupied the province. In March, 1919, Radich was arrested by the Serbs for his subversive propaganda and was sent to prison for eleven months. Other leaders, including Dr. Machek, were imprisoned also. A popular agitation resulted and 167,000 people signed a petition to Wilson. Radich called that the "first republican reflector," light shining out of darkness. At the end of February, 1920, Radich was set free, only to be arrested again within a month and sentenced to two and a half years' imprisonment. So at the very beginning, the treatment of the popular leader was unfortunate and it seemed to the peasant masses that they had merely exchanged one tyranny for another.

In June, 1920, while Radich was in jail, Alexander made a state entry into Zagreb and the townspeople gave him a great welcome, though these demonstrations for the Karageorgevich were highly deceptive. Although Radich was only amnestied from prison on the day of the first election, his party managed to win 50 seats. In the next election his became the second strongest party, with 72 seats.

Parliamentary democracy was maimed because this compact body of Croat nationalists refused to coöperate. But Radich was not so much to blame as Pashich and Pribichevich, who took no steps to conciliate the Croat leader. They underestimated his significance and did not foresee the influence of Radich upon the whole destiny of Yugoslavia. Otherwise they would not have been so rash as to make a martyr of him by imprisoning him.

But there was still a chance of reconciliation because Radich was so good-natured. No amount of persecution could make him bitter. He had something of the quality of George Lansbury—an undying sweet-tempered pacifism. He did not wish strife, not even verbal strife. "We are opponents: we are not enemies," he said of the Serbs. He believed that the Serb peasant could be made to see that monarchy was just an old wooden plow and that they would find a republic more practical. King Alexander regarded him with tolerance. It was not on his orders that the police watched Radich so much. The country was police ruled. The police were sheep dogs who must keep the flock together. Radich had no objection to keeping in the flock, but let the flock be a republic, not a monarchy. Radich said flattering things about Alexander, but the King could not intercede for someone who wished to push him off his throne. King Alexander bore himself well as the sovereign of three peoples, and showed no preference for Serbs or antipathy to the Catholic Church. The imbroglio of Belgrade politics cast no shadow on him and his popularity with his new subjects grew steadily. He had proved himself a brave soldier and a patriot and he was an honest man.

The stigma did not fall on him but on the Serb politicians.

Radich slipped off abroad in July, 1923. First he went to London, and although he was not received by prominent politicians he was much influenced by the British point of view, especially by the arguments of Wickham Steed. He was told that his idea of a republic was fantastic and that he had much better work for the establishment of a limited constitutional monarchy such as obtained in England. The king to be the symbol of unity! He went from London to Moscow and told the Bolsheviks they were wrong. They ought not to have a dictatorship of the proletariat, but a peasant republic. But the English impression remained. He said he was no separatist. The Croats would coöperate in the state of Yugoslavia and work for a republic. He was still harping on the republic after he had secretly resigned himself to monarchy. He allowed the Croat Peasant party to take part in the debates in Belgrade. Things were moving in the right direction.

But the Serbs still did not understand him and they nearly wrecked the state again by pressing for the proscription of Radich's party. Soon after he returned from Russia the party was declared illegal. The government proceeded to deal with it as they had dealt with the Communists. Radich had said to a French journalist on October 17, 1924, "We will take the oath of allegiance to the King. King Alexander is honored in Croatia and beloved in Serbia. We want to make him ever more honored and beloved." But in December Radich's party was declared illegal.

On January 2, 1925, Dr. Machek and other leaders were arrested. Radich hid himself in a recess behind racks of books in his bookshop, but the gendarmes in their

For one thing the Queen much preferred talking to Radich than to Pashich, whom she could never understand.
The Queen had learned some Serbian but Pashich spoke
a dialect that was nearer Russian than Serb, and he could
not speak in any other language that Queen Marie could
understand. "All I remember him saying to me was,
'That is that,' " said the Queen. But with Radich Her
Majesty talked in English, which she regarded as her
mother tongue. The intimacy of the royal family and
Radich may be gathered from the following words of
the Queen: "You know he had become almost blind. He
really could not see to eat his food. Often when he came
to lunch I would take his plate and cut up his meat for
him so that it would be easier for him. He was often with
us, and my husband and I were very fond of him."

And Radich as Minister made no revolutionary inno-
vations. He found posts and pensions and sinecures for
many Croats. That was the privilege of ministers and in
that respect he was no better than the Serbs. But he
started a campaign against corruption. There was much
corruption in high places and the exposure was good
propaganda for his party. He went on the stump in
Serbia, visiting districts which had previously been forbidden to him, and he carried his slogans to the Serb
peasants, merely dropping the word "republic." He was
still out for a state founded exclusively on the require-
ments of the peasantry. He preached a hatred of town
influence. "God made the country; the devil made the
town," said he. "Christ was born in a village; He was
crucified in a town!" He trusted the people, but from
the term "people" he excluded townspeople, shopkeepers, manufacturers, financiers. Otherwise he spoke like a
true democrat. "When I am with the people I am bath-
ing in the ocean," was another characteristic utterance.

There is no doubt that he continued to irritate the old guard of Serb politicians. He made new enemies by his charges of corruption and newspapers attacked him with unbridled vehemence. The withdrawal of the freedom of the press was a measure of the subsequent dictatorship, but it should not be forgotten that when the press was not gagged it comported itself badly, demanding blood. It provoked murder and was morally irresponsible. The press earned the repression which followed at a later date.

The epithets flung across the floor of the house were as insulting and violent as those used by journalists. In English "parliamentary language" implies a certain restraint of phrase. In Belgrade it would have to imply the very opposite. The Skuptschina was a sort of zoo where some of the animals were uncaged. One may call it democracy, but it was not a pleasing spectacle. The debates passed from one unnecessary crisis to another. Members seemed to think they were elected to evoke passions rather than to find a common ground or proceed wisely about the country's business. Radich himself was disgusted and was soon telling the King that he ought to send a posse of troops and make a Pride's Purge.*

* How the country suffered from parliamentary intrigue may be judged by the records of the Ministries of Agriculture and Agrarian Reform. The most pressing need after the war was the adjustment of the land systems and the reorganization of agriculture. Serbia owed all to the peasants and had a duty to them. And the people in most need of help in Croatia, Slovenia, Bosnia, and Herzegovina were the farming stock. Yet less was done for the peasants than for any other class of the community. A competent Serb authority remarked that the peasant has not improved his position since the days of Kara George. The cause of the tiller of the soil should have been placed above politics. But no coördinated effort was possible when the responsible

Radich survived several parliamentary pandemo-
niums. He even dared to take part in the accusation of
corruption leveled against Pashich's son. There was no
doubt that the hands of the younger Pashich were not
clean, but it was a dreadful humiliation for the ancient
Prime Minister, then turned eighty years of age, and a
humiliation to the Radical party itself. But Radich and
his Croats were necessary to Alexander for the work of
unification. It was unthinkable that Radich should be
sacrificed. That would have meant a renewal of Croat
disaffection. Pashich resigned in April, 1926, and he
died before the end of the year. The Cabinet was recon-
structed under Uzunovich and Radich retained his ministerial post. Crisis followed crisis. The Cabinet was re-
constructed six times in one year, but Radich remained.

But in April, 1927, a Radical intrigue succeeded.
Vukichevich made alliance with Dr. Koroshets and his
compact Slovene party and decided to drop the Croat
votes. At the general election which followed Radich
made a counteralliance with the Democratic party and
together they won 122 seats, almost enough to outvote
all other parties combined. He then decided to be reconciled to his old foe Pribichevich who, as leader of the
Independents, had 20 seats. The Radicals were enraged

---

ministers were changed every few months. From 1918 until the
dictatorship there were some twenty changes. The first Minister
for Agriculture lasted a month; the second, four months; the
third, two weeks; the fourth, four months; the fifth, three
months, when a Minister for Agrarian Reform was also appointed. But the heads of the two ministries were constantly
changed and the only man who could stand by his job for more
than a year was Krsta Miletich, who lasted from July 18, 1921,
to January 6, 1923. It will be clear that nothing resembling a
five-year plan for agriculture could be made when there was no
prospect or even desire for continuity of office.

by this opportunism and their administration obviously would not last. The King was ready to dismiss Vukichevich and offered to make Radich Prime Minister. But Radich advised a temporary dictatorship. The King had better send a general and make a clean sweep of the old gang of politicians. Radich in Parliament threatened the government with a general. Alexander must have been startled by the suggestion of a military *coup d'état* and rejected the advice, though he kept it in mind. He had long since lost patience with the politicians, who by their eternal wrangles stopped progress and spoiled his reign.

Then happened the momentous tragedy second only to that of the assassination of the King at Marseilles— Stephen Radich was murdered.

Parliament assembled on April 26, 1928. Radich, leading the opposition, declared for General Zhivkovich. "We approve the idea of a general as prime minister. For that would mean that the King obtained the position which is his due, arbiter among us. What more natural than that the King, who is the glory of the monarchy, should become the arbiter of our destinies and make the necessary compromise. And it would then be natural to have here a general who was not a partisan but the representative of the King." This and succeeding speeches of an obstructionary nature on the theme of a military administration caused uproar at every session. There were shrieks of "Blood fiends! Butchers! Bashibazuks!" One Belgrade newspaper declared that Radich and Pribichevich should be murdered for Yugoslavia's good.

If you call the devil he will come. At the session of June 20 a wild Montenegrin deputy, a member of the Radical party, arrived with a revolver, determined upon execution. This man, Punisha Rachich, already highly embroiled with the Croat group in Parliament, opened

fire on Radich's supporters. With his first shot he
wounded Pernar, from whom he had demanded apology
for obstruction; with his second he killed Dr. Basarichek; with the third he shot Stephen Radich in the
stomach; with the fourth he wounded Granja; with the
fifth he killed Paul Radich. Only then was he overcome
and the weapon taken from him. The wounded were
removed to a hospital, the dead remained.

One can but repeat the Shakespearean phrase: "Then
you and I and all of us fell down!" This was a greater
blow than Austrians, Germans, Bulgarians, Turks ever
struck at Serbia. It was also a blow at the King, an affront, for Radich had been his favorite, the man the
King delighted to honor, a favorite without favoritism.

Stephen Radich was mortally wounded and King
Alexander was overwhelmed by grief—grief and consternation. He hurried from the palace to the hospital
and sat at the bedside of the stricken leader. Radich was
in great pain but fully conscious. He clasped both hands
of the King together in one of his. "All will yet be well,"
he whispered. "Thanks to God and to you. I'll recover. I
have so much to do."

Alexander said comforting words. He sent for his
own doctor. He bade Radich hope. "Vukichevich is re-
signing. I want to proclaim you Prime Minister. All
power shall be in your hands," said he. A man between
life and death must have something to live for. The King
put the premiership before the leader's fading eyes. But
Radich shook his head. He still thought it would be better to have a general.

The bullet was extracted. The wound healed. There
seemed prospect of Radich's recovery. He was sufficiently recovered to be removed to Zagreb. But at the
Croat capital complications ensued. He died on August

8. His death was peaceful. All his last words were directed to averting strife and ill feeling. He did not ask revenge. All he asked was that the peoples live together peacefully. But these last Christian wishes have seemed to be in vain.

His body was carried to the house of assembly of the Peasant party, where it lay in state and hundreds of thousands of people filed past to look for the last time on the lineaments of the uncrowned king of Croatia. Death had put the seal upon the man's greatness. One might have doubted while he was alive, but it was certain when he was dead. The burial place of Radich in Zagreb has become a Croat shrine, not perhaps what Radich would have wished. It is an altar of Croat nationalism, not an altar of Yugoslavia.

With a heavy heart King Alexander tried to regulate the position in Parliament. The Croat deputies decamped to Zagreb and did not return. The only thing possible was a national-front ministry drawn from all parties who would serve. As the outrage upon the Croats had taken the form of an attack by one of the Orthodox Church upon Catholics, the King would not appoint a Serb prime minister. He chose for Premier a Catholic priest, Dr. Koroshets, the leader of the Slovenes. But with racial passions inflamed and 85 deputies refusing to appear in Parliament there seemed no promise of political peace. As Alexander said, parliamentarism was not functioning except as a negative force causing daily more dissension in the land. Radich's advice remained with him. Some of Radich's last words had been, "I am afraid for the country. Now there is only the King and the people." On January 6, 1929, King Alexander dismissed the Parliament and made General Zhivkovich his Premier, thus infringing the constitution. In a statement to the people he declared that the preservation of unity was the greatest aim of his reign. Parliamentarism remained his ideal. But it had for the time being failed and other methods would have to be tried. Thus the dictatorship was inaugurated.

claque, was organized to disprove the statement of
Radich that the Croats were unanimous in their opposition to Hungary. No man of strong convictions joined
the Frankists. The Croat members of the party were
sheerly opportunist, out for what advantages might be
obtained for themselves by selling Croat nationalism to
the Hungarian masters.

The result of the war was not what any Frankist
would have desired. Hungary ceased to dominate the
Croats. The Slavs of the Balkans raised a new banner
of Pan-Slavism, with the conception of a state of southern Slavs. The Frankists were forced into a paradoxical
position. They had to forget that they had been opposed
to Croat nationalism because that nationalism had become so valuable as a means of cultivating dissension
with the Serbs. The Frankists had to work for an independent Croat state under the protection of Hungary.
The hope of beaten Hungary lay in the weakening of
the new Slav state. Unlooked-for help was forthcoming
from ex-enemy Italy. Italy bitterly resented the formation of the kingdom of Serbs, Croats, and Slovenes. It
was too big and threatening. She wished the Slav territory of Austria-Hungary parceled out in petty states
so as to be able to divide them and dominate them.

From the time of the making of the peace treaties
Italy began to have a common ground with Austria and
Hungary. All three states resented the emergence of
Yugoslavia. And this resentment may explain why Italy
determined to support the cause of revisionism. But
Italy, despite complaints, had done well out of the peace
settlement. She had taken extensive territory inhabited
by Austrians and Slovenes. No program of strict re-
vision for all parties concerned would suit her because
she had decided to give nothing back to Austria. But

she supported Hungarian revisionism because it was directed in part against Yugoslavia. If the Voivodina could be restored to Hungary, and Croatia detached from Serbia to become a satellite state, Italy would have a free hand to take over, colonize, and assimilate ancient Illyria, the whole eastern shore of the Adriatic.

The Frankists in 1919, with their pockets empty, shorn of power and position, were allotted a new and ultimately lucrative task. They must foment ill feeling between the Serbs and the Croats, bring about an armed rising, and achieve the disintegration of Yugoslavia. The theory was that the new kingdom of Serbs, Croats, and Slovenes was not a homogeneous entity but a conflict of hostile races, religions, and interests. It would task the genius of a Bismarck to unify it. Italy was confident that it could not hold together. Hungary was encouraged by Italy. Austria, perplexed by her own problems, was less interested, but those personages who hoped for a restoration of the Hapsburg dynasty worked secretly in coöperation with Italy and Hungary. The Frankists were well posted both at Vienna and Budapest. But they were impoverished after the war. They were short of funds and could do little unless financial support from Italy were forthcoming.

That Italy was willing to go to some expense was proved by the encouragement she gave to the partisans of the Montenegrin monarchy. Hundreds of Montenegrin monarchists had been afforded shelter in Italy, placed in camp, armed and drilled with the object of using them for an attack upon Yugoslavia via Albania. That little army of rebels had been demobilized and dispersed before Mussolini came to power, but the Italian attitude was not improved after the Fascist march to Rome. The Italian answer to the formation of the Little

Entente was a project for the establishment of a central European Catholic state comprising Austria, Bavaria, Hungary, and Croatia. It became increasingly urgent to detach Croatia from Yugoslavia. Why not recruit an army of rebellious Croats, similar to that of the insurgent Montenegrins? The assassination of Radich and the establishment of the Serb dictatorship were highly favorable circumstances. The Croats had reverted to noncoöperation. They were bitter. Racial feeling ran high and the Church could be used to increase it.

The principal leaders of the Frankists were the Croat, General Sarkotich, who had remained an Austrian subject, Colonel Perchevich, late of the Austrian Army, Ante Pavelich, Gustave Perchets, intelligence officer in the Hungarian Army, and Branimir Yelich. Of these the one of most intelligence was Ante Pavelich, a lawyer and member of Parliament. Radich said that the Croats regarded these persons with shame and humiliation, and that no party based on Hungarian or Italian intrigue could find backing except among the more ignorant or demoralized. Dr. Machek became the leader of the Croats after the demise of Radich, but he never dreamed of leading the Croat Peasant party into the Frankist adventure. The existing political parties could not be used by Italy and Hungary. At best they could only be provoked or stampeded into civil war.

The Croats are on the whole a passive people. They have more culture than the Serbs but they have less taste for violence. They do not take naturally to arms. That is demonstrated by their history under Austria-Hungary. They were always in a ferment but there was never an armed rising. This is a race which has been tamed by centuries of subordination to a superior culture. They do not naturally resort to violence to win their freedom:

they must be goaded into it. They were not fitted for the role which Italy and Hungary cast for them, unless the idea was that they could be *forced* into a civil war with the Serbs.

Still there was discontent, there was unemployment. There were disgruntled persons and criminals. There were young enthusiasts whose careers had already been compromised by arrest, young people who had been expelled from schools for their political opinions. There were those who could be secretly enrolled in an army of independence if someone were willing to support them and pay them wages. But such an army could not be organized on Yugoslav territory. Even if it escaped the vigilance of the police it would be denounced by the Croats themselves. The army must be organized either in Italy or in Hungary. The Hungarian government put no difficulty in the way of establishing training camps for such an army on its territory, near the Yugoslav frontier.

Pavelich planned to organize a raiding army on the Hungarian side of the river Drava, something similar to the army of Bulgarian bandits which raided Serbian Macedonia. The Internal Macedonian Revolutionary Organization was the terror of southern Serbia. When later it was dissolved it was found to be in possession of over ten thousand rifles with an immense reserve of bombs and ammunition. The I.M.R.O. was no amateur society. If murders, robberies, and outrages similar to those the Bulgarians had organized could be committed on the northern frontier the authority of the Yugoslav government would be shaken and there would be constant encouragement for disorder.

At first, however, nothing more was done than to appeal to Croat youth and obtain membership for the secret society. All that members had to do was to take an oath of obedience. There was nothing to pay, no membership dues. The ritual of taking the oath was picturesque, something to appeal to youth. The Croat flag was spread on a table. On it was placed a knife and a revolver and on these a cross. The candidate spread his open right hand on the cross and repeated a formula: "I swear before God and all that I hold sacred that I will observe all the laws of this society and will execute without conditions all that I am ordered to do by the supreme chief. I will scrupulously preserve all secrets entrusted to me and will betray nothing, no matter what it may be. I swear to fight in the Ustasha Army for a free independent Croat state under the absolute control of the supreme chief. Failing in my oath, I shall accept death as the penalty. God help me, Amen!"

This also had to be signed. It sounded dangerous and therefore may have been attractive to very young men. Sometimes such societies are formed in a moment of exaltation, but one never hears much more of them. Pospishil, who was later sent to kill the King, was one of the first to be sworn in. He says there were a thousand who joined on that seventh of January, 1929. He probably exaggerates. In any case, if there were a thousand it proved extremely difficult to collect them later on and persuade them to wear the Ustasha uniform. But names were wanted more than men. Pavelich, the supreme chief, had a good enough list to present. If he seemed to have the men it would be easier to get the money. Having formed his secret society, he went to Vienna.

In Vienna he met various Frankists and Italian agents. At that time Italy was lavish in her financial support of the Heimwehr and of those persons upon whom she

could reckon for support against Germany. She was still
a determined opponent of *Anschluss*. That did not concern Pavelich. He required support for his own political
venture, the army he proposed to raise.

He met Gustave Perchets and Yelich, who had formally expatriated themselves by taking out Hungarian
passports in Budapest. That was the first service of Hungary. Hungary was prepared to give Hungarian national
passports to any members of the Ustasha for whom they
might be required. But Italy was not absolutely convinced that Pavelich meant business. He must first make
alliance with the Macedonian Organization in Bulgaria,
study its methods, and plan something on the same scale.
Italian agents in Bulgaria had sounded members of the
organization and found them ready to coöperate. The
Bulgarians sent a delegate to Vienna to confer with
Pavelich and Perchets. This was Nahum Tomalevsky,
an important member of the organization.

It is considered probable that the Italians supported
the Macedonian Organization, but it is certain that
Nahum Tomalevsky was privy to Pavelich's plans,
knew of Italy's part in the plot, and of the help promised in Hungary. He became the unfortunate possessor
of dangerous secrets. At a later date, after the Macedonian Organization had broken into factions, he was
murdered by the same man who later killed Alexander.
Dead men tell no tales. But in the winter of 1929 he
brought an invitation to Pavelich and Perchets to come
to Sofia.

The three men set off together by way of Hungary
and Rumania. They naturally avoided Yugoslav territory. The members of the Macedonian band crowded
the railway station at Sofia and gave the two Croats an
uproarious reception such as might have been accorded

royalty. Pavelich made a stirring speech in answer to the address of welcome, telling the Macedonians that he had come to make a common front. "Now is the time for brother Croats and Macedonians to work together for the liberation of our peoples reduced to slavery," said he. "Long live free Macedonia and Croatia!"

For these and similar utterances he was tried for high treason in Belgrade, found guilty, and condemned to death on July 15, 1929. But of course he did not make an appearance at the trial. He was not seen in Yugoslavia again.

Ivan Mikhailov, who was the head of the Macedonian band, admitted the two Croats to many of the secrets of the Macedonian Organization, explained the organization, and reviewed its activities. Gustave Perchets was shown a bomb factory and had explained to him the mechanism of infernal machines. It would appear that he made a careful study of the latter, for he started making them when he got back to Vienna. Pavelich was not shocked by the record of Ivan Mikhailov's band, the many murders and incendiarism. Mikhailov's men dashed across the frontier at night and raided farms in southern Serbia, shot down the peasants, set fire to houses, plundered, rode back. Vlada the Chauffeur, who afterwards killed King Alexander, was a typical bandit in the employ of Mikhailov, driving out in a fast car on a moonless night, waylaying Serbs, murdering and robbing them. The whole border had been terrorized. According to Mikhailov, the ultimate effect of this would be that the population would soon rise in revolt and make common cause with their brethren in Bulgaria.

The Serbs had been forced to send great numbers of troops to guard the Bulgar frontier. Bulgaria was caged

in Serbian barbed wire. Conditions prevailed that almost amounted to a state of war. But subsequently
Mikhailov's band was checked by Lazich, governor of
the Vardar province. He wrote to King Alexander, giving some remarkable advice. He said that the Macedonians of south Serbia had not the least desire to be
united to Bulgaria. "Let the King authorize the arming
of the population, send us 200,000 rifles, and the people
themselves will make peace." The timid politicians in
Belgrade were scandalized by the suggestion. "Give the
Macedonians arms? Why, there would be a rebellion
at once, and these people would make common cause
with Bulgaria." Lazich, who was a native of these
parts, said, "No, you do not understand, they are ours.
They will never turn against us." King Alexander said,
"That's the man for me. He understands his people
and trusts them. I will trust them also." The King au-
thorized the distribution of arms and ammunition to
the farms. Lazich became a great local hero. The cut-
throats from over the border had a very hot reception
next time they raided. And they were cowardly. They
did not come again. King Alexander congratulated
Lazich. He had found one of the new men he wanted
to serve him under the dictatorship. Lazich was soon
made Minister of the Interior.

But in 1929 there was no prospect of failure for
Mikhailov. He was so powerful that the Bulgarian government itself dared not interfere with his activities.
Pavelich and Perchets were impressed. What Mikhailov
had done they could imitate. They could achieve even
more because Croatia was more vital to the existence of
Yugoslavia than Macedonia. They felt they could convince the Italians. That was even more important than

any immediate success because the Italians had the money. As exiles from Yugoslavia they had no means of subsistence unless the Italians supported them.

So they left Sofia for Varna on the Black Sea coast and took boat to Stambul. At Stambul they transshipped for Athens. At Athens they got on an Italian ship and sailed for Rome. At Rome they were received as plenipotentiaries of the Croat people but none the less secretly. Their arrival was not even observed by spies. Great secrecy was required and they were not admitted into the presence of Mussolini. They were interviewed privately by a number of leading Fascists who endeavored to form an estimate of their character. That Pavelich was condemned to death in Belgrade impressed the Italians favorably. The man could never return to Yugoslavia till the existing regime was overthrown. That made him secure: he was not likely to betray Fascist plans. The Serbs must think him both important and dangerous: they took him seriously. He had been a member of the Parliament: he was a representative man. He might be raised eventually to be the Duce of a new Fascist state in Croatia. With an army behind him he might one day make a march on Zagreb, imitating Mussolini's march on Rome. Both men were sounded on their Fascist views and expressed themselves sympathetic. They would do all in their power to advance Italian policy. It was well understood that in the event of Croatia's gaining her independence she renounced all pretensions to Dalmatia. In the event of a break-up of Yugoslavia, Italy would annex the Adriatic coast from Fiume to Cattaro.

There was no written contract. It was a "gentleman's agreement." Such agreements are made when the mutual interest is sufficient to make a signed document superfluous. For Pavelich and Perchets this agreement was a gamble. They would be well paid as long as they proved serviceable, but at the whim of their employer they might be cast off into an inhospitable world. They must constantly show results in order to insure continued financial support. They gambled on two possibilities: either they would make enough money in five years to retire from the business, or war would break out between Yugoslavia and Italy.

The Fascists decided to have Pavelich domiciled in Italy and gave him a villa on the Viale Castelfidardo, at Pesaro. They showed their habitual lavishness in the funds they placed at his disposal. The struggling lawyer, who had never known what it was to be free from financial worry, became a rich man. Perchets was given ample credit at Vienna and would receive his subventions through an Italian agent there. He would be able henceforth to indulge his taste for luxurious night life.

Neither of the men abjured his Yugoslav nationality, but Pavelich obtained an Italian passport under the name of Antonio Serdar and was quite free to use it to make journeys to Budapest, Vienna, Berlin, wherever he wished. He was not debarred from leaving Italy, because his masters knew he was bound to return. Perchets obtained a new passport from the Bulgarian Legation in Rome and became Matthew Tomov, a Bulgarian journalist.

It was believed that Pavelich had begun to enroll an army in Croatia and he was told that he must transport it to Italy and recruit it further by all means in his possession. Some years of preparation were necessary, for Pavelich would not be able to march on Zagreb with a mob of raw levies, least of all against the intrepid Serbs. For the moment Italy was not interested in Hungarian assistance and was not willing that the main army of invasion should be merely in the service of Hungarian revisionism. The Magyars could strike when the time came and cause a diversion, making the Serbs fight on two fronts, but the first object in the adventure must be the acquisition of Dalmatia for Italy. Land near Brescia was allotted to Pavelich for the formation of the first armed camp.

Orders were given for the manufacture of uniforms for this army, something distinctive. The men must not resemble Italian soldiers. Quarters would be prepared at the Brescia camp. Rifles and ammunition, bombs, explosives, targets, would be sent.

Perchets must make his headquarters at Vienna, organize an international press campaign against Yugoslavia and do all he could to keep King Alexander nervous while the army of invasion was being prepared. He volunteered the information that he had made a close study of infernal machines at Sofia and that in his belief the maximum disturbance would be achieved by blowing up trains in Yugoslavia. They must fulfil their promise to the Macedonian Revolutionary Organization and keep northern Yugoslavia in a frenzy through terrorism. His program was approved.

King Alexander, being dictator, was more vulnerable than if he had a ministry responsible to Parliament. All outrages would be considered as protests against a Serb tyranny, at least they could be so interpreted abroad. And if the Serbs lost their heads in repression it would give Italy a pretext to intervene to restore order. Perchets would make liaison with Colonel Perchevich in Vienna and with Branimir Yelich and would keep in close contact both with Rome and Budapest.

So the two leaders of sedition separated for the time.

Pavelich went to Pesaro and Perchets went to the Austrian capital. Pavelich had more responsibility, but Perchets had more scope for luxurious living. As Matthew Tomov he took a spacious apartment on the Wiedner-Gurtel, sumptuously furnished. He became lavish in his expenditure and began to live the life of one of the new rich. He might be seen every night at expensive cabarets and obviously had money to burn, the richest Bulgarian journalist ever seen in Vienna.

He lived with Yelka Pogorelets, a dark Croat girl whom he had first adopted and then seduced. She was a gipsyish creature, with the meager ambition of wanting to become a cabaret artist. She liked music and dancing, and the sparkle of night life in Vienna made her think that being a turn was a career. She was Perchets' dancing partner. But she was capable: she could run an apartment, supervise servants, and she could do secretarial work. Perchets made her his housekeeper and also his secretary. He was somewhat idle: he could not attend to all his letters himself. Considering the secret and dangerous career on which he was embarked he was very rash. This untutored girl was capable of curiosity.

Perchets never stinted her with money. She could buy what clothes she liked. Vienna fashions were at her disposal. She could expend what she liked on cosmetics and beauty treatment. He did not supervise the household bills. Yelka wondered where all the money came from. When she asked him the question he was angry, but when she had to handle his correspondence she soon discovered that her lover and almost everyone else connected with him was in the pay of either Italy or Hungary. As she understood that Perchets was going to marry her she became anxious. She would loathe having a spy for a husband.

At first Yelka did not realize that her lover was going to make bombs and blow up innocent people on trains. She was ready to work for a free Croatia and liked to think that the men who visited the apartment were patriots, but it was a shock to discover that they were in the pay of a foreign power. She kept her counsel: she did not at first quarrel with Perchets. Perhaps she was too much in love with him. She even showed a smiling countenance to the Italian press attaché, Moreale, though she knew that most of the money came through him. He was at that time the agent for financing the Heimwehr and was in close contact with Prince Starhemberg.

CHAPTER IX

LONELY DICTATOR

THUS, at the same time that Alexander became dictator the plot to destroy his country was hatched. The plotters failed to destroy Yugoslavia, but they were able, after five years, to destroy the King. As King Alexander became the one man, the state, the only authority, it became more practical to destroy him than to invade Yugoslavia or to foment a civil war. A greater blow could be inflicted upon the new state by striking down the one prop of its government. King Alexander had moved out of the company of responsible politicians into a dangerous loneliness. Did he not make a mistake?

When he assumed dictatorship King Alexander became more aloof, more hedged in majesty. He was far removed from the mood of King Peter, who said, "We are peasants. My grandfather was a peasant." A king needs a Parliament if only for the sake of company. The behavior of the politicians had been outrageous, but the hush from the Parliament house was disconcerting. King Alexander never moved as freely among the people as King Peter had done. He was a stage removed from the source of his power. King Peter had been called to be King: his son inherited kingship.

> Princes and lords may flourish or may fade,
> A breath can make them as a breath has made!

Peter Karageorgevich was made King by the breath of the people and never forgot it. He never had pretensions to greater power than was given him by Parliament and he was ready to relinquish the power he possessed as soon as the task appeared too heavy for him. King Alexander, united by marriage to European royalty, had more sense of permanence. Instead of being subject to the will of his people, he took the destiny of his people under his personal responsibility. His suspension of the constitution was praised at the time, because the common man was at the moment tired of the political wrangle and it was felt that the dictatorship would bring the King into closer personal contact with the masses. The politicians had done little or nothing to right the many grievances of the common people.

The King's appearance went against him. In Serbia men with hirsute faces are always popular. That was part of the secret of Pashich. When Stephen Radich at length shook hands with Pashich he held the old man's fingers in his hand a long while and gloated on that face with its long beard. "Elijah!" he exclaimed. King Alexander not only grew no beard or side whiskers but shaved off his little black moustache. He ceased to look like the characteristic Serb of his age and resembled more an American. In civil attire he looked like a college professor from the Middle West. In short, he was rather a foreigner.

He deliberately went away from Serbism. As King of Yugoslavia he must not appear too much of a Serb. Henderson, the British Minister at Belgrade, said he was the only real Yugoslav he ever met. He sought to portray in himself a new type, a man who was not Serb or Croat or Slovene, but Yugoslav. He was aided by the fact that through upbringing he was already cosmopolitan. He was more European than his subjects. Child-

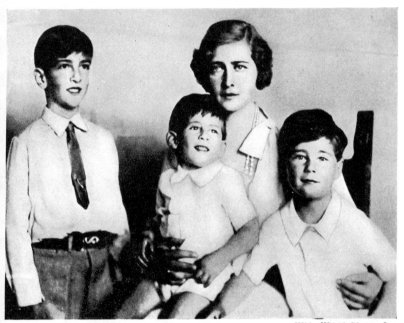

QUEEN MARIE OF YUGOSLAVIA WITH HER SONS, CROWN
PRINCE PETER, PRINCE ANDREI, AND PRINCE
TOMISLAV

hood in Geneva and St. Petersburg had denationalized him.

With a view to making himself as much King of the Slovenes as of the Serbs he had taken up summer residence at Bled in the Julian Alps, on the confines of Austria and Italy. The diplomatic corps followed him there and were thankful for the comfort of modern hotels and the pleasant odor of old Austria. Bled was utterly non-Balkan. A Serb there must feel he is abroad. The shopkeepers speak German by preference. Croats and Slovenes talk German there to show that they are cultured. For these races, although politically abjuring the old Austria, have an inferiority complex and must talk German in order to affirm that they are really Europeans and not barbarians from the Balkan Peninsula. Alexander, with his wife and children, spent the happiest and most carefree part of his life at Bled.

His cousin, Prince Paul, took a villa twelve miles from Bled, beside the romantic lake of Bohinja. He lived there with his wife and family, often entertaining relatives of the Greek court, Prince Nicholas, Princess Helena and their daughter, the Princess Marina, who afterwards married the Duke of Kent. There was an English governess. Everyone spoke English. Alexander and Marie were frequent visitors, and as the Queen of Yugoslavia preferably spoke English there was a strong British influence in that corner of the realm. It was decided to give the King's sons an English education. Curious how Alexander, who had no affiliation with Great Britain, pursued the same course as Nicholas of Russia had done. The court language in St. Petersburg was also English. But otherwise Prince Paul did not have much influence on the King. It is doubtful whether

Alexander ever sought his cousin's advice on political questions. He was fond of him. They had romped together as children. But until he nominated him to be Regent, in case of his sudden death, he never meditated allowing him to share in the responsibilities of government. He acquired for him a villa at Dedinje and had it put in order so that they might be neighbors in Belgrade also, but Paul and his family did not spend much time there, much preferring Bohinja to the capital. He lived as a private citizen and was, indeed, too poor for his position. The King also was poor. There was not much money in the royal court. Alexander employed Prince Paul to go to London and raise money on the King's life insurance so that he might have the capital with which to exploit a gold mine that had been discovered. Prince Paul kept in touch with British political trends and kept the King informed, but he was not used for diplomatic missions.

Prince Paul was the only royal personage upon whom the King could have called to relieve him of some of the burdensome functions of state. Paul's father, Prince Arsène, lived a carefree existence in Paris and had renounced court life and politics. The King's sister, Elena, was a widow, living in Switzerland. His brother, Prince George, was "put away." The monarchy, as far as the Karageorgevich family was concerned, lived in isolation. As if to accentuate this isolation the King, in the same year that he became dictator, removed from the center of Belgrade to a hill on Dedinje, outside the suburbs. Till then the kings and princes of Serbia had lived on the main street of Belgrade behind the fine sentries in their boxes, behind the gilt-topped railings and flower garden of the Stari Dvor. Peter, when he was invited to become King, in 1903, had to inhabit the apartments where Alexander Obrenovich and Draga had been murdered. He said he could not sleep: the ghosts of the dead sovereigns haunted the place. He ordered the palace to be pulled down. That original palace stood in a square which is now in summer a luxuriant flower garden. Peter built himself a new palace. That palace looked like a left wing of an unfinished building. He left it during the war and never returned to live there. Alexander wanted him to live there after the war was over. But the old monarch thought he would merely be in the way; he preferred to go into complete retirement in a modest villa far from the center of the city. Alexander had been obliged to build himself another palace, a right wing, similar in design and balancing the older house where his father had held court.

But Alexander did not like the trams hurtling past his home, nor the swarms of people sitting at tables on the pavement at the corner of the street, nor the forming up of unofficial delegations outside the palace gates. Neither he nor the Queen liked living in constant publicity. He gave orders for another palace to be built at Dedinje, some miles away, amid the Topchider uplands. In December, 1929, he removed to Dedinje and never again inhabited the palace on the main street. So the people lost some of the sense of possession which comes from having the sovereign living in the midst of them.

"The time has come when no one should stand between the people and the King," declared Alexander when he annulled Parliament. But in a physical sense he contradicted himself when he moved out of Belgrade. It is difficult for an autocrat to combine being King with living the life of a country gentleman. Politically he was not nearer his people. A Parliament, be it ever so rowdy, combines the people with the throne. The rise of General Zhivkovich, acting for the King and speaking in the King's name without any popular mandate to do so, made the King seem farther away. It made the monarch lonely. It also made him a target for abuse, even a target for the bullets of assassins.

For three years, without intending to do so, Zhivkovich usurped the King's position, put him into partial eclipse so that the people could not discern who was running the country or what was the King's part in government.

Peter Zhivkovich was a cavalry general, commander of the King's guard, with headquarters in the vicinity of the royal palaces at Dedinje. He was not in the same category as the heroes of the war, Putnik, Mishich, Stefanovich. His soldiering did not undergo the test of a command of an army in the war. A guards colonel, he was only promoted to the rank of general in the year 1924.

He belonged to the faction of the Serbian Black Hand which, in 1903, conspired to murder the Obrenovich King and Queen, Alexander and Draga. The officers of the Black Hand remained under a cloud during the reign of King Peter, and though Zhivkovich dissociated himself from its activities, the connection may account for his slow advancement. He served throughout the Balkan wars and the Great War, and was in the retreat through Albania; yet he attained only the rank of colonel. The Black Hand, after the accession of Peter, became a more secret organization: its aim was to keep the control of the dynasty in the hands of the army. It was finally liquidated at Salonika in 1917, after an unsuccessful attempt on the life of the Regent

Alexander. Colonel Zhivkovich came into prominence
after that event by organizing a bodyguard for the
Regent on the Macedonian front.

His career up to the time he became prime minister
had no national significance. He was no politician. His
name had not been associated with achievement of any
ᴋind. He had not been even a man behind the scenes.
He had not been intrusted with any important tasks
even of military administration. He had absolutely no
experience in government, but he was the King's friend.
An intimacy had sprung up between the sovereign and
the general. The commander of the royal guard was
constantly in contact with the King. And Alexander
liked him.

King Alexander had a penchant for men of good
character but not much brain. In a country of so many
opportunities and so much corruption the King, when
he found an honest man, "grappled him to his heart
with hoops of steel." Zhivkovich was a man who lived
simply on his salary, contracted no debts, was shy of
using influence, and possessed a childlike loyalty. He
was stout, the sort of man who slept o' nights, not a
lean Cassius. He had a ready and engaging smile. His
conscience was always clear. So, when plagued by politicians, Alexander would ask his opinion and obtain a
manly, soldierly comment on affairs.

As a personality the King found Zhivkovich refresh-
ing. That must account for the frequency with which
statesmen being received at the palace found the general
there, a tacit listener to the conversation. Except for
Stephen Radich, most of them resented the soldier having any opinion on affairs of state. It was recognized
that the army was strictly nonpolitical and could never
be brought in as the arbiter between the parties.

But there were no accidental ties binding the King and Zhivkovich. They shared no hobbies. The King went shooting regularly and was an excellent shot. Zhivkovich confessed to me ruefully, "I went only on one hunt with His Majesty. I am no hunter." One may surmise he was a bad shot. Alexander was fond of a rubber of bridge, but the general did not play cards. The King was a bibliophile, but Zhivkovich seldom looked at a book and did not know French. He could not share the King's literary interests. And he was no military strategist: he could not discuss campaigns with him. Yet Alexander called him by his Christian name and for many years he was the nearest person to the King.

It was remarkable that the democratic Radich should advise the King to make Zhivkovich Premier, that a Croat should desire to see a Serbian general in control. The Croat leader had intimate converse with Zhivkovich only in the fatal year 1928. Their first important meeting was on the occasion of the baptism of the King's second son. On January 19, Queen Marie had given birth to another boy, and King Alexander, as a compliment to the Croats and perhaps at the suggestion of Radich, decided to name the child after the legendary king of Croatia, Tomislav. Another gesture to show he was a true Yugoslav and that his children were as much Croats as Serbs! Radich was enchanted. Suppose the heir died, there would be another Tomislav, King Tomislav the Second. The name Tomislav is a rallying cry of the Croats.

Radich's praise of the King might seem fulsome or indiscriminating, but not to Zhivkovich. He approved a man who spoke so highly of the sovereign. And in any case he knew that Alexander liked Radich. So he invited the Croat politician to visit him at Topchider. They met again and talked much of the army. Zhivkovich recalled an incident when the Russian contingents arrived at Salonika in 1916. The Russian officers did not like the promiscuous way Serb colonels and majors, and even generals, would eat and drink together with the rank and file. A Russian colonel spoke to him about it. But Zhivkovich said that Serb officers could not sit down to eat while the men went hungry. They must look after their men before they looked after themselves. Old King Peter did not mind sitting in a trench and sharing rations with private soldiers. "You see, the Serbian Army is truly democratic."

Radich was impressed. The Austrian and Hungarian officers had had a lofty disregard for their men, as if without rank a man was a mere animal. "I think," said Radich, "the army has a truer instinct for democracy than any of the political parties striving for power in Belgrade." When Radich talked to him of the violence of some leaders, the venality of others, Zhivkovich showed a cheerful noncommittal ignorance. The general had a fresh and invigorating personality, just the man to teach the politicians that country comes first. So Radich began to advise the King to impose a dictatorship with Zhivkovich in control. Not till after Radich was assassinated did that advice mature in the King's mind.

But it was too easy a way out. Alexander, who was a shrewd judge of character, must have known that Zhivkovich was merely a "yes man." Whatever the King arranged the general was likely to approve. He would not stand up for his own opinions, because he had no opinions. All he required to know was the King's mind on any subject and that would guide his actions and utterances. King Alexander moved on the assumption which is common in Yugoslavia that the state is a small one without pretensions to be a great power or to have influence in Europe, a peasant-cum-army state. But what had been possible in little Serbia was not practical in the aggrandized kingdom of Yugoslavia. He had inherited the complication of politics of the Austrian Empire and it was imperative that he should find men of talent to cope with it.

Radich's advice had been, "Find capable men outside the antagonisms of politics and appoint them to the ministries!" He wanted the King to make a clean sweep of the senior politicians. He approved Zhivkovich for Premier because the general was completely outside politics and therefore likely to be impartial. At the same time he was a man who could not be bought and would not push his own material interests. But it was not easy. The system in Yugoslavia does not allow men of talent to shine. It is no land of opportunity. There is no publicity for the achievements of young men. No one who is at all young is considered of importance. The seniors keep him severely in the background. There is no quick way for men of parts to come to the front, and Alexander is not to be blamed if in this respect he cannot be said to have known his own people. He could appoint Zhivkovich but he could not give him a supporting ministry drawn from capable men who were outside politics.

There is no doubt that, dating from January 6, 1929, when the King announced the dictatorship, the people began to sulk. His popularity was still unimpaired. But everyone was expecting inspired personal leadership and the dawning of a new era. The public was also tired of the old gang of politicians. So the disillusion was great when Zhivkovich's Cabinet was announced. Uzunovich, Marinkovich, Koroshets, the professional politicians, had returned. The only difference was that this Cabinet was responsible to the King alone and was to be allowed to govern without the check of parliamentary criticism.

The ministers were even more subservient. They had to do what they were told. The King and General Zhivkovich sat in conclave. They ran the country without being capable of doing so to the advantage of the country. The supporting ministers drew their salaries, appointed their relatives and friends to posts, accepted the usual presents from contractors and manufacturers, and could not be brought to book because there was no Parliament and because criticism in the press was forbidden. Those who defend the King's action in this conjuncture say he had no other course open to him. He had to use the men he knew. After the assassinations in Parliament in 1928 and the subsequent deadlock it was manifest that the constitution would not work. The King was a realist in politics. If one system failed he must try another.

Zhivkovich's outlook seemed refreshingly simple and hopeful. The country was tired of the political wrangle, shocked by the murders, distrustful of party politics but endlessly devoted to the sovereign. It desired peace and unity more than anything else. The King must first make unity and then free institutions could gradually be restored. Unity must be imposed from the throne. So unification became the main plank of Alexander's domestic policy. It is clear that the King was very trustful with Zhivkovich and that the two soldiers together were more naïve than they were apart. "They wept like anything to see such quantities of sand." Serbs, Croats,

Slovenes, Bosnians, Montenegrins, Herzegovinians, Shumadians, Macedonians, must be swept away for a country of Yugoslavs only.

In October, 1929, came the first fruit of the new regime. Yugoslavia was proclaimed and the country was divided into a set of new provinces with new names. In order to get rid of local patriotism and sectionalism, Croatia became the Savska province, Slovenia became Dravska, Montenegro and Herzegovina were lumped together to become Zetska, Bosnia became Drinska, Macedonia became Vardarska, the Voivodina and part of Serbia became Dunavska. Some wit remarked of Serbia, "Once you were a principality, then you became a kingdom, but now you are merely a province."

The King hoped that in time Croats would forget they were Croats, the Serbs that they were Serbs, the Slovenes that they were Slovenes, and upon being asked what they were would proudly reply that they were Yugoslavs.

The historic provinces and countries had been named after rivers, except Dalmatia, which had been named after the sea. It is as if, in Great Britain, Wales were named Severnia, Ireland Shannonia, and Scotland Clydea.

Serbia, which had fought its way to independence out of centuries of bondage and oblivion, ceased to exist as a political description. It was parceled out in various *banovinas*. The national flag of Serbia was removed to a museum of historical curiosities, and the Serb regiments were paraded to renounce the flag for which they had fought and to salute in its place the new flag of Yugoslavia.

Yugoslavia means the country of the southern Slavs, but it has the disadvantage of its meaning being never likely to be understood except in Slav countries. To the Western world the name was an ugly novelty, too like that of Czechoslovakia not to be confused. The name "Serbia" had the advantage of having won a position in the minds and hearts of many people. It was not new. It had won its place on the map. It had history and it had had an unforgettable part in the war. But the name "Yugoslavia" had to win recognition, had to get history and tradition. The change of name helped to reduce the significance of Alexander's kingdom. "One of the new mushroom states which sprang up after the war."

Zhivkovich, as Minister of the Interior, arranged for large deputations to come from the new provinces to express their loyalty to the King and their faith in his leadership. On December 17 Alexander received a large delegation of Croats from the Savska province and from Dalmatia, renamed Primorska. On December 25 he received the South Serbians and Macedonians from Vardarska. On the 29th, the Montenegrins and Herzegovinians; on January 19, 1930, a deputation of Bosnians and Slovenes and also of Serbs. In general the deputations were mixed so that it would be impossible for a spokesman to say "We—" anything else but "—Yugoslavs."

The changes were accepted calmly. There was the indifference of a dog who stands by when his master changes his name, indifference and some tail wagging. Since the inauguration of the dictatorship public opinion was very difficult to assess. The press, which had so shockingly abused its freedom, had been put under police control and any paper expressing a distasteful opinion could be confiscated forthwith. Editors must confine themselves to news. Opinions must be submitted.

In this anomalous position they printed photographs of Zhivkovich in uniform every day and hailed all as for the best. If a man's reputation could be destroyed by having his photo printed every day it must have ruined Zhivkovich. His face did not convince one as the answer to Yugoslavia's problems. I saw him about this time. He received me in general's uniform and looked magnificent. His first words were, "You know, we have come to look upon you people who write as very dangerous. I say nothing for publication." That was the military outlook. Journalists often give away secrets of strategy.

But it is not really very much use calling a house divided against itself "Harmony Home." The racial antagonism still remained. And there were other divisions. Yugoslavia is even more sharply divided by creed than by tribe. The Serb commonly calls his religion Serbian, identifying nationality and Church. But a Yugoslav may be anything—Orthodox, Roman Catholic, Old Catholic, Moslem, Jewish. The creeds could not be unified by proclamation.

The nation is also divided by alphabets. The Serbs and Montenegrins use Cyrillic letters, somewhat similar to the Russian and Bulgarian alphabets. The Church uses old Slavonic. The Croats have a Latin script with a set of accents of their own. The Moslems of Skoplje read Arabic. King Alexander meditated a bold step in 1929, the standardization of script. To show his impartiality he proposed to sacrifice the alphabet of the Serbs and adopt Croatian. But that was more than the Serbs would endure in the name of unity. The Orthodox Church resented the project. It looked like a step toward Yugoslavia becoming a Catholic country.

The King showed plainly that he had no manner of

bias against the Roman Catholic Church. He was ready to receive the blessing of Roman bishops and to go to divine service in their cathedrals. He decorated the Archbishop of Zagreb, Mgr. Bauer, with the highest order of the realm, the great star of the Order of Karageorge. Zagreb was worth a mass. He was careful not to attach an Orthodox father confessor to his person. He did not make the sign of the cross in the Eastern way for fear of offending those who made it in the Western way. He did not emulate the Tsars of Russia in religiosity. He showed no interest in miracles and did not seek out holy men for converse. The Serbs did possess one outstanding religious leader, Nicholas Velimirovich, Bishop of Ohrid and afterwards of Zhicha, a man to whom thousands flocked. But when occasion arose Alexander did not advance him to be Patriarch as was well within his power. He preferred the safer Varnava. The Orthodox Church must not be allowed to advance to a position of power as it had done in the old Russia. Both churches were in part supported by the state and Alexander understood himself as a King of both Eastern and Western Catholics. Rome could not be interfered with, but the Serbian Church was more dependent on the state, making it possible for the King so to arrange the election of the Patriarch that one third of the votes were at the disposal of the government. The Patriarch became the King's nominee. The Orthodox Church, which had preserved the nationhood of the Serbs through the centuries, was deliberately frustrated for the sake of Yugoslavia.

The King pursued a religion of good works and enlightened materialism. In a crisis he invited no one to pray. He was interested in the restoration of ruined churches and monasteries, but more as an antiquarian than a religious man. He sent money gifts to people in distress. He was limited but he was a man of his word. His loyalties were lifelong. He kept his promises. He told no lies. When asked a difficult question by an interviewer it was noticeable that he did not resort to euphemisms. He had a horror of ministers who used their position to enrich themselves, dismissed them when they were found out, and never reappointed them. He was perhaps too righteous for the people he had to govern. He felt that very few got a beating from the police who did not deserve it. He was not cruel, but he had a rough-and-ready way of dealing with politicians who thwarted him.

Svetozar Pribichevich, who led the "Independents," the Left wing of the Democratic party, declared for a republic. He was a Serb, but a Serb of the old Serbian minority in Croatia, an ex-Austrian subject. He had not fought in the ranks of Serbia and was not united to the monarchy by the sentimental ties which bound the Serbs of Serbia. He was a man of intellectual honesty, probity, and ability. He was recognized as a front-rank man and held the post of Minister of Education for several years. He was also a leader of the more intelligent journalism and his newspaper, the *Retch*, attracted some of the best writers of the country. The *Retch* was liberal, rather like the Russian *Retch*, which was its inspiration. It stood for the liberty of the subject and free, untrammeled democracy, and in due course it was suppressed.

The greatest achievement of Pribichevich's career was his alliance with Stephen Radich. The truly democratic elements had made a common front combining both Serbs and Croats. But Radich came to have a much stronger faith in Alexander than Pribichevich

ever had. In hospital Stephen Radich wrote a funeral
oration for Paul Radich and Basarichek, who fell by the
assassin's hand in Parliament, and he gave it to Pribichevich to read at the grave. He said, "We believe in our
people as the people believe in us. We believe that the
King at this moment faces a very difficult problem, but
King and people will solve it together."

That King and people would solve it together was
not apparent in the regime set up on January 6, 1929.
Pribichevich had some angry converse with the King,
being quite capable of browbeating the monarch. Having a strong will and stubbornness of character, he was
as difficult to move as Alexander. He remained in intimate contact with the Croats, whose tendency, since the
death of Radich, was also republican. "The people must
decide," was his bedrock. Pribichevich came to the conclusion that the main hindrance to a unity of Serbs,
Croats, and Slovenes was the dynasty. Despite Alexander's effort to be a colorless Yugoslav, he was the
symbol of the hegemony of the Serbs. The military
and the police directed from Belgrade controlled the
whole country and there was no prospect of freedom
while these forces had no Parliament to check them.
That Parliament had failed to work did not impress
Pribichevich. It would work if not subject to interference from interested parties. It would function as
it should if there were a republic and an elected president.

Pribichevich was interned, taken from his home to a
place far from his supporters, placed under house arrest,
and subjected to police surveillance. He fell ill, but that
did not mollify Alexander and Zhivkovich. He remained behind the barbed wire of the police. President
Masaryk then interceded for him, appealing to Alex-

ander to send the liberal leader into Czechoslovakia, where they would care for him. The King acceded, but Masaryk's request was humiliating. The Czechs thought highly of this man even if the Serbs did not. Svetozar Pribichevich disappeared from the political arena of Yugoslavia and ultimately died abroad. It was a loss.

The first ministry under the dictatorship started without Croat support. There was only one Croat in that Cabinet and he resigned during the following April. There was only one Slovene, Dr. Koroshets, and there were no Moslems. The Democrats were represented, both Right and Left wing, but it was predominantly a Serbian Radical Ministry. A number of Croats willing to serve for the ministerial salary were found later, but they were all ministers without portfolio. The first of these, Mirko Najdorfer, signed on on May 5, 1930. He was afterwards murdered by one of Pavelich's terrorists so as to deter other Croats from taking government posts.

Dr. Koroshets, the leader of the Slovenes, resigned in September, 1930. He had been moved from the Ministry of Communications to the Ministry of Forests and Mines, hardly the place for a priest. His ardent religious nature craved higher responsibilities. He had been Premier, but in the Cabinet of Zhivkovich he had but little weight. Although his place was taken by a member of his party, his secession was a manifest weakening of the cause of racial unity. He swayed the opinion of the whole of Slovenia.

The King prepared a new constitution to take the place of the St. Vitus' Day constitution enacted on June 21, 1921. That he had sworn to abide by the original constitution did not deter him. Constitutions do not naturally derive from monarchs, but from a people as a whole. No doubt, had the King lived he would have promulgated yet a third constitution. He did not consider constitutions holy. If one did not work, it could be changed. His new plans did not appeal to the man in the street or rank-and-file politicians. But the King took complete responsibility. Bogoljub Yevtich, Minister of the Court, read the text of the revised constitution to Zhivkovich and he replied that the results obtained were due to the initiative of the King alone.

By royal command a Senate came into existence. Ministers who by the original constitution had been responsible to Parliament now became responsible to the King alone. The ballot ceased to be secret and voluntary and became open and obligatory.* The authorities must be able to check for whom a citizen voted. The power to introduce new laws was largely the privilege of the King and his Cabinet, the Houses of Parliament merely having the power to confirm them or explain them, but such laws must be voted by both houses or they became null.

On November 8, 1931, a general election was held but only one party was allowed to take the field. The election was a demonstration of what the new constitution really meant, an all-powerful government with the backing of a sham popular representation. This was a curious election. There were no posters. No one was even allowed to scribble political slogans on walls. Newspapers were not allowed to voice opposition to the government list. All who had the franchise were ordered to exercise it whether they wished to or not.

* The new constitution left the question of the secrecy of the ballot dependent upon subsequent legislation. The King, according to Yevtich's account of their last conversation, intended to restore the secrecy of the ballot.

Croats had to vote for Serbs. The Serb, Croat, and Slovene peasantry were shepherded to the polling booths by the police. But even upon compulsion half the people in Croatia, Slovenia, and Dalmatia did not vote. Out of 3½ million electors in the whole country some 2,325,245 men were persuaded to record votes. All the 306 Members of Parliament elected were supporters of the government and there was no opposition whatever. A one-party utopia was realized.

The King pretended to be pleased with the result, but it is known that he had sleepless nights and had become irritable. The return of parliamentarism, even of the one-party kind, renewed the turmoil of 1928. The one party, calling itself the National party, began to murmur against the continued presence of a general in the Cabinet. They had nothing personally against Zhivkovich, but the spurs of a cavalry officer were out of place in politics. They wanted the removal of even the semblance of military dictatorship. "Back to politics!" was the cry. In January Zhivkovich ceased to be Minister of the Interior. In April he ceased to be Premier. He wanted to get out. His pride was touched. "I am a soldier," he confessed; "I am not a politician." King Alexander was angry. "I'll remove your rank and you can remain Premier as civilian," said the King. But Zhivkovich preferred his military rank. That humility or pride seems to have shocked the King and he neglected Zhivkovich for the rest of his reign, even failing to nominate him as a regent in case of his death. But the general was fortunate in not having to shoulder the responsibility of coercing those who refused to accept the new constitution.

Both Croats and Slovenes demanded a reconsideration of their position in the state. They said they had

joined Serbia in 1918 on certain agreed conditions.
Their leaders refused to keep silence. Koroshets, for
the Slovenes, proposed Catholic home rule in the West.
The King considered his statements treasonable and
had him interned on the island of Hvar, off the Dalmatian coast. Suffering from diabetes, he obtained permission to go to a sanatorium at Split, where he remained till the King's dead body was brought on a
warship to that port, when he joined the procession of
mourners and was informally pardoned. Prince Paul, as
Regent, promoted him to be Minister of the Interior.
Such are the ups and downs in a politician's life in
Yugoslavia.

Dr. Machek, who had become leader of the Croats,
was a lawyer and an intellectual, very different from
Stephen Radich. He had no link with the village and
the peasant, but he had inherited some of Radich's
glory. The King did not make a friend of him as he
had done of Radich. Perhaps he found him antipathetic.
Alexander was at home with soldiers and with naïve or
open-hearted politicians like Radich, men whose peasant origin was written in their faces. To please the
King there had to be something in a man which he could
identify as Balkan. There was nothing Balkan about
Machek. His face belongs more to Vienna and the West.
He opposed the new constitution even more vigorously
than Koroshets.

After the murder of Radich the Croats had to be
placated lest the breach between the races should become unbridgeable. Croatia made a cult of Radich. He
was the martyr who had died for his motherland,
Croatia. His grave is more visited and adorned than
the grave of any unknown soldier. Blood speaks and
the feud was expressed by three million people whisper-

ing against Serbia. Youth was continually in a ferment. There were demonstrations and parades. In order to hold a public meeting one had to have police permission, a restriction always galling to the Croats. Naturally enough, unauthorized meetings took place and they were dispersed by the use of the truncheon. When there was resistance the gendarmerie opened fire. There were harmless people killed and wounded and many arrests. And every affray with the police fanned the flames of racial animosity. There was no appeal, because the gendarmerie were above the law. The only means of countering brutality lay in secret agitation and in protest abroad. The scandal of popular maltreatment was aggravated by the murder of Professor Schufflai on February 18, 1931. In this it was considered that the Zagreb police were gravely compromised.

Dr. Machek was the quiet champion of a persecuted people. There was nothing aggressive in his behavior. He expressed his loyalty to the dynasty but demanded a decentralized state, with a large measure of home rule at Zagreb. He never gave the slightest encouragement to Pavelich or let him think that it was possible to foment an armed rebellion in Croatia. But to him the new constitution of September 3, 1931, was a scandal. The Croats had been cheated. They had accepted unity with the Serbs and Slovenes on terms which had been communicated to the Western Powers and approved by them. Serbia had acquired her extensive new territory after the war subject to guarantees of racial self-determination. The Croats would never have agreed to come in on the terms of the new constitution. Great Britain and America would not have sanctioned such treatment of the Croats. In November, 1932, Dr. Machek framed a resolution condemning the hegemony of Belgrade and demanding a return to the open position of December, 1918, restoring to the Croats the right of self-determination. The resolution was signed by six politicians besides himself and communicated to the foreign press in the form of interviews. Machek was arrested under the Defense of the Realm Act, tried, and sentenced to three years' imprisonment. He was amnestied by Prince Paul very soon after the death of the King.

It is, no doubt, vain to consider what might have been; but if the King could have come to an understanding with Machek the course of history would have been changed. It would have been made clear that Pavelich had no backing in Croatia and that to raise an army of independence on foreign soil was a waste of money on the part of the Italians. The King would have been able to stop the terrorism which was raging at the time, and he would have averted his own doom. Italians, Hungarians, and Austrian legitimists derived much encouragement from the coercion of Croatia.

But Alexander did not realize that. He dwelt in a fool's paradise and even imagined that in 1932 Yugoslavia was stronger and that, with the new constitution, the races were consolidated and presented a united front. The Foreign Minister and Premier, Marinkovich, who was in ill health and too old for his job, considered that Italy had been impressed by what Alexander had achieved. The Italian minister in Belgrade, Signor Galli, seems to have played a double part, assuring Marinkovich that the move toward Fascism on the part of Yugoslavia was highly acceptable to Mussolini, but at the same time sending the Foreign Minister in Rome exaggerated accounts of the spirit of revolt in Yugoslavia.

Galli, by combining natural and artificial phenomena, could present a picture of Yugoslavia on the brink of revolution. He could report the continued boycott of the government by the Croats; the discontent of the Slovenes; disaffection of the leaders, Machek and Koroshets. The dictatorship had even been deserted by its strong man, Zhivkovich. Possibly the army was no longer staunch. Many Serbs had become critical. Pribichevich had been forced into exile. Montenegro was restive. These were the natural phenomena. Add to them the list of outrages, the murders and bomb explosions, and the Italians could imagine that Yugoslavia would shortly fall to pieces. The outrages which began in 1929 were mostly artificially contrived. They did not take place as the result of the indignation of the people; but it just needed these blowings up of trains and explosions in barracks to make the general picture convincing to Mussolini.

King Alexander would have felt relief if Italian enmity could have been removed. He bore no grudge against Italy, nursed no grievances. It is to his credit that, despite unparalleled provocation, he never bore himself aggressively toward Italy, never threatened. He saw some resemblance between his own political position and that of Mussolini. Parliamentary government had failed in Rome and the Duce had stepped forward to save his country. Democracy had for the time failed in Belgrade and King Alexander had taken the necessary steps to unite all warring factions. "United we stand: divided we fall," was the motto of Fascism that Alexander had adopted when he created Yugoslavia. Grandi had said that Italy was ready for an understanding. "Come to us without the Little Entente and without France and we will see what we can do for you!"

Such terms were naturally unpalatable, but Signor Galli, in 1932, seemed to suggest something better, a general appeasement, the inauguration of a new era of peace. As a result of his opinions, freely expressed, Marinkovich had considerable correspondence with Grandi. Would it not be possible for the Duce and King Alexander to meet and deal with all their difficulties as man to man? But the Yugoslav Premier and Foreign Minister was very ill and was forced to retire from office on July 3, 1932.

Srshkich became Premier and Bogoljub Yevtich, who had been Minister of the Court in the previous administration, became Minister for Foreign Affairs. The Italian conversations still continued. Yevtich did not find the accommodating spirit that Marinkovich had led him to expect. He waited to know the pleasure of the Italian Foreign Minister, and was thus forced into the position of patient suppliant. His King wished to do homage to the great Duce. That showed the proper spirit. But Mussolini preferred to wait a little. He would not bolster up a tottering throne. He was certainly not going to sign away his presumptive right to Dalmatia over a cup of tea with the Serbian King. To the proposal for a meeting with the King he replied arrogantly. Alexander must first of all consolidate the internal divisions of his country, then if he would apply again Mussolini would consider it. "I wait at my window," said Mussolini.

That amounted to an affront. From that time on Alexander worked more vigorously to thwart Italian policy in the Balkans. But the phrase, "I wait at my window," was seen afterwards to have a sinister meaning. Mussolini was staging a revolt at Lika on the boundary of Croatia and Dalmatia. His window looked across the Adriatic. He was going to drop a lighted match into the supposed powder factory of Croat and Dalmatian disaffection and watch the effects. Perhaps Yugoslavia would be blown to bits. Then he could move in and impose Fascist order on the other side of the Adriatic.

CHAPTER X

INTERNATIONAL SABOTAGE

GUSTAVE PERCHETS made life more pleasant for himself and his companion by buying a car. Pospishil was his chauffeur. He was not such an addict of night life in the city that he could not break away and get the fresh air of the mountains. He visited the Brenner Pass. He met envoys from Italy at the frontier. He received consignments of ecrasite and tolite and brought back stores of explosives to the apartment in Vienna. Some two kilograms of that ecrasite went off very soon in a barracks of gendarmes in Zagreb.

But houses in Vienna, even those which enjoyed protection, were not immune from police search. So Perchets took a small farm at Klingenbach, in the Burgenland. It was a remote and quiet place near the Hungarian frontier. The explosives were transferred to the farm, which became a bomb factory. Perchets began to have a hobby, the making of bombs and infernal machines. He had a taste for the ingenuity of clock bombs. In Vienna he bought small striking clocks and altered their mechanism so that they struck only the half hours, then so that they struck only at a given time and then so that instead of striking they ignited a fuse. He brought the adjusted clocks and the required metal containers to Klingenbach and completed the machines. He had a trusty assistant, Franjo Shimunovich, and when he went away he left him in charge, to continue the work and make sure that no stranger got access to the farmhouse.

Meanwhile Pavelich had agents in Croatia, recruiting for his army, and those who had already sworn to obey him were called up. Only a few responded to his call but they were daring fellows. They had the option of going to Italy to train or of serving Perchets. There was no need for Perchets to have more than six tried men at his disposal: he was not raising an army and it was easy to keep him supplied. The most daring of the helpers of Perchets was Mio Seletkovich, who opened the campaign against trains by trying to blow up the Zagreb-Belgrade express at Strizivoina.

The first bombs made were rather cumbrous, suitable for placing on the permanent way, even more suitable for the blowing up of police headquarters at Zagreb, which was one of the early exploits. Perchets thought out something more effective for his attack upon the railway services. He had been successful, but according to Pavelich he was not weakening the morale of Yugoslavia. The Serbs could stand a lot of explosions: they had iron nerves. Something must be done that would really terrorize the population. Perchets had it.

A small type of infernal machine was made for use in railway carriages. These explosive clocks with a very quiet tick were contrived by Perchets. International trains were chosen for the outrages so as to discourage visitors to Yugoslavia. Few tourists would arrive if it got around that the trains were unsafe. It would help to advertise the instability of conditions in Yugoslavia. It seemed a good plan and had the advantage of being much safer for the men who carried the bombs. It was not necessary to travel into Yugoslav territory and run the risk of being arrested. The bombs could be hidden in the trains in Austrian territory, and timed to go off after they had passed the frontier.

Special attention was given to the Paris-Belgrade express, the train which leaves Paris at seven in the morning and arrives in Belgrade at nine the following night. This train emerges from Austria between dawn and daylight at the time when the weary passengers are snatching their last sleep before the breakfast car is hitched on. The station of Villach is somnolent, even in midsummer, when the early morning twilight is in conflict with the still burning station lamps. The train stops and seems to dream. Then slowly it trails out of the station in the gloom of the mountains to the last halt in Austria, Rosenbach.

Perchets' men, with their infernal machines in suitcases, commonly boarded the train at Villach. Sleepy but benevolent Austrian conductors punched their tickets and disappeared. Passengers would generally be too weary to pay the least attention to the doings of newcomers. The terrorists were able to find suitable hiding places for their clock bombs, set them, start them ticking, dispose of them, and then step off the train at Rosenbach.

This had the desired effect. The most appalling train explosions took place. Passengers were maimed or blown to bits—as often as not foreigners, for there are seldom many Serbs in the through carriages of that train coming from abroad. This form of terrorism got much more on the nerves of Yugoslav officials than the blowing up of buildings or attempts to kill police officers. They had to answer for the persons of foreign subjects done to death or injured on their trains. It was, moreover, sabotage of a kind that threatened tourist traffic. And no one could be brought to justice. Soon it became clear that the infernal machines had been placed on the trains while the latter were still on foreign territory.

As the Austrian government was at first incredulous, it proved a difficult problem to cope with. Passengers who were unaware of the extent of the outrages began to think that the Yugoslav police were losing their wits. The police boarded the trains at the frontier, looked under all the seats of all the carriages, examined the racks and packages hanging from hooks. They turned out the lavatories and then locked the doors. They inspected the hot-water pipes. But when they found bombs they did not advertise the fact. No one knew. The press were seldom told anything. One can imagine with what detail and circumstance such outrages would be reported in the British or American press. Yugoslavia was dumb. The government would at least deny the satisfaction of publicity to the terrorists. The news went by word of mouth but the Serbs received it with their usual imperturbability. If they had a fault it was that of being too little shocked.

But secrecy and preventive measures failed. The police did not find all the hidden bombs. More explosions occurred, some of them far from the frontier. There was a sensational explosion at Zemun, where a certain Professor Brunetti was traveling to Belgrade with his wife and children. His wife and infant son were blown to bits before his eyes. The professor and several others were mutilated. At Zemun, on the other side of the Danube from Belgrade! Perhaps the bomb was really timed for the Danube bridge.

This was also an international train and still stronger measures had to be taken at the Austrian frontier. The through carriages from France and Switzerland ceased to be through carriages. At Jesenitse all passengers from abroad had to get out of their compartments onto the platform. Then the train was shunted into a siding and a new train which had not been abroad would be backed into the station and passengers continued their journey in that.

At the same time spies were sent into Austria to find out who was responsible for the crimes. At last they were able to provide the Austrian government with a list of names. An indemnity was claimed for damage done and the Austrians were asked to place the terrorists under arrest. The Yugoslavs never got any indemnity. But the Austrians had to pay some attention to these demands. Perchets and his collaborators enjoyed too high a protection to be put in prison. The Austrians did what they could. They requested Perchets, Seletkovich, and the others to leave Austrian territory without delay. Perchets had to pack up and go to Budapest. The others went to training camps in Italy.

Colonel Perchevich, who was not incriminated, remained in Vienna and became Pavelich's chief agent in Austria. He had established a press agency at his house on the Karolinengasse. From this center damaging news about Yugoslavia was disseminated to the world. Like Riga for Russian news after the revolution, Vienna became the source of innumerable lying or tendentious telegrams. The object of this press campaign was to deprive Yugoslavia of all political sympathy in the West and prepare the way for British and French indifference to her fate should she become the scene of civil war.

In 1930, despite their manifold activity, there were not more than thirty Croats associated with Pavelich. Hundreds may have sworn to obey him, but they remained quietly in Croatia. They might be ready to join in an armed rising, but they were not available for active coöperation. The number of recruits coming out of Yugoslavia was disappointing to Pavelich, clearly indicating that however much some Croats might yearn for independence they would not sell themselves to Italy and Hungary. Pavelich was forced to advertise and make propaganda. He obtained the money to start a series of newspapers. There were *Independent Croatia*, the *Croat Defense*, *Ustasha*, and, perhaps the most important, *Gritch*, published in German, French, and English. Besides these he found the money to print many pamphlets. None of these publications brought in any revenue. For the most part they were distributed gratis and one is obliged to remark on the enormous cost of these enterprises. Money flowed like water for Pavelich and his associates.

These were all printed abroad but were smuggled in bulk into Croatia and Dalmatia and distributed illegally. Those who received them probably read them but were quick to destroy them so as to avoid suspicion of being distributors. But they circulated freely outside Yugoslavia and were read by the emigrants, who were much in the dark as to what was happening in their country. It was easy to convince factory workers in Belgium or ranchers in South America that Alexander had caused the murder of Radich and that the Serbs were shooting down Croats like rabbits. And it was not difficult to persuade some of them that an army of Croat patriots was forming on Italian soil. They wrote enthusiastic letters to Pavelich from the most outlandish places. A few sold all that they had and repaired to Italy or Hungary to take part in the glorious work. "Say you have an army and you will get an army."

Pavelich soon had enough men in uniform to parade and make a show. He had himself and the first recruits photographed for propaganda purposes. That was very convincing and caused a glow of pride in the hearts of some ignorant emigrants. The men in uniform looked to be genuine soldiers, part of the great new Croat army of national independence. The Fascists, in their bureaus in Rome, also liked those photographs. They were deceptively convincing. It did appear that the Duce of the Croats was doing something.

In 1931 Pavelich sent Branimir Yelich to the Argentine, Brazil, and Uruguay, with ample financial credit and cases of printed propaganda. His mission was not to convince these distant republics of the rightness of the Croat cause, but to obtain recruits for the training camps. In South America the gathering of supporters for revolutions was nothing new, though Yugoslavia must have seemed a far cry. Yelich lived in style. The men he took over were offered wages from the moment they signed on. That was a feature of the Ustasha brigade. Everyone was paid. Some of the richer volunteers were squeamish about accepting pay, but they were exceptional.

Perchets ceased to be Matthew Tomov, a Bulgarian journalist, and obtained another passport. No use the police trying to trace Tomov any further. He became Emil Horvat, a Hungarian subject of independent means. Pavelich visited him in Budapest to discuss new plans. Perchets' base was now Hungary. No more terrorism could be launched from Austria. The time had come for Perchets to share in the major enterprise. Recruiting was looking up. Pavelich hinted of hundreds of new men flocking to the standard. A second training camp might be started in Hungary, similar to the camp in Italy. Perchets agreed to coöperate and he leased a farm at Yanka Pusta, near Drava River, four miles from the Yugoslav frontier and not far from the Zagreb-Budapest main line. He took this in the name of Emil Horvat. It was only a small property with two houses, one of which could be used as officers' mess and the other as a place for the men. But sheds for making bombs or for storage could be quickly erected or outlying cottages could be rented. The work which had been in progress at Klingenbach was transferred to Yanka Pusta. The protection given by the Hungarian authorities was more reliable than Vienna protection had been. If they could get the necessary recruits they could raid the Croat border with impunity. The activities of the Macedonian Revolutionary Organization could be imitated.

Perchets' method of recruiting, apart from sending agents to Belgium and France, was to beguile peasants from the Yugoslav side of the frontier to run into Hungary. Once they had crossed the frontier they were placed under arrest at Csurgo. Then they were imprisoned for several days before being confronted with Perchets. They were then invited to go to Yanka Pusta. If they did not agree to go they had the option of being returned to Yugoslavia, where they would be arrested, or returning to the Hungarian prison. They generally elected to go to the farm, where they took the oath and became little more than slaves of the commandant.

Yanka Pusta was not so successful as the camp at Borgotaro in Italy. The men were paid a small wage and they were fed and clothed, but there was continual discontent, insubordination. Perchets shot a man dead with his own hand. Several men took the risk of running back into Yugoslavia and placing themselves at the mercy of the police there. They denounced the camp as a fraud. Most said that they had been lured there under false pretences and gave a full account of the activities. The Yugoslav government was well informed but helpless. Helpless because the Hungarian government would not move for a long while and Perchets had high protection there.

The attempts to blow up through carriages on the Paris-Belgrade expresses ceased. The trains from the Hungarian frontier to Osijek and Vinkovtsi received attention. Attempts were made to blow up several small railway stations. Nothing really daring marked these enterprises. It seems peculiarly mean to leave an infernal machine under a seat in a waiting-room and then get on a bicycle and pedal off into obscurity. All that such acts strove to demonstrate was that the Belgrade government was incapable of protecting its people and that it was not safe to travel by train. Rather more spectacular was an attempt to blow up worshipers as they were going into an Orthodox church in Zagreb and an explosion in a barracks full of soldiers the same day. No terrorist dared to go to Belgrade and make an attempt on the life of General Zhivkovich or upon any ministers of the crown.

The making of infernal machines had become a hobby. The methods of Catherine de Medici were imitated. Thus an attempt was made to kill a Zagreb judge by the present of an interesting book. Tolite or some other rapid explosive was secreted in the binding. The book was rather stiff to open, as some new books are, and to read parts of it freely the cover had to be bent back. At a certain page a tiny fuse ignited and the reader would be blown to bits. This book was sent to the judge by post but it was opened at the frontier. Its pornographic contents and pictures were a fatal snare. A group of frontier police looked over the shoulders of an inspector who was turning the pages. Suddenly the volume exploded. The inspector was killed and two policemen were maimed for life.

More serious was the transport of arms and ammunition into Yugoslavia and the establishment of secret arsenals, on similar lines to those affected at a later date by the Fascists in France, though on a much smaller scale. A number of flat-bottomed boats for use on the frontier river Drava came into use for gun running. This river had to be watched day and night by the Serbian armed patrols, but although on one occasion they fought the raiders they were unable to stop the whole of the traffic. There must be stores of arms and explosives still undiscovered on Yugoslav territory. There was a terrific accidental explosion of one of these secret arsenals in October, 1933, and the dead body of one of terrorists was found near the place. He was Krobot, one of those who had been recruited in Brazil.

The establishment of secret arsenals in Croatia and Dalmatia was Pavelich's provision in case of a rising. The rebels must be able to get arms quickly or they would be crushed before they had time to assert themselves. Perhaps Pavelich had convinced himself that the people were ready for civil war. A curious effect of propaganda is that it sometimes convinces those who write it instead of those for whom it is designed. Pavelich must have boasted to Italian officers and high-placed Fascists that "the day is at hand."

Hence Mussolini's phrase: "I wait at my window." What was he expecting to see? That at the applying of a match the whole country would flare up? In the summer of 1932, when he said these words, he was supporting another camp at Zara, the Italian port in central Dalmatia. Zara is an isolated Italian possession in Dalmatia, a thorn in the flesh of Yugoslavia. There a band of men, mostly Dalmatian but with some Montenegrins, was being trained by a man called Servazzi, under the control of Ante Pavelich. They recruited from the Dalmatian peasants and fishermen, but all told never more than 200. They made free gifts of rifles and revolvers to people. A regular commerce grew up as peasants who had received free revolvers sold them for a hundred dinars and came back for more. Italy was informed that the coastal population was armed and was ready to rise. Mussolini had his fleet in readiness to make a descent when the time came. The French and British fleets seemed interested in what was afoot. At length the time seemed ripe for action and a raiding party was landed on the Lika coast, north of Zara. The people of the region had generally voted Independent and were sore at the treatment meted out to their representative, Svetozar Pribichevich. Now was the time for them to show their spirit and fan a local insurrection into civil war.

The raiding party, all in uniforms and bearing rifles, met with no resistance from coast guards. They commandeered donkeys to carry their ammunition boxes and baggage and then began a march inland to seize the railhead of Gospich. The peasants looked at them with mute surprise and did not seem to understand their cries of "Long Live Free Dalmatia! Long Live Independent Croatia!" No one joined them, but they were successful in penetrating nearly twenty miles. Then they began to encounter hostile demonstrations. Finally, nearing Gospich, they were mobbed by a mixed force of gendarmes and peasants, who sent them running back to the sea much faster than they had come. They left six cases of explosives behind and a great number of Italian cartridges.

Some of the raiders were arrested, but the majority got back to Zara. They were not decorated. Some of the Italians laughed at them and asked if they had been practicing for the Olympic Games. But it was not convenient to hold them long in Zara. They were shipped to Fiume and thence sent to Borgotaro and told to report to Pavelich.

Many exploits of terrorism were arranged from Zara, including the bombing of the 54th Infantry Regiment at Split. But there were no more attempts at invasion. Civil war was postponed. Better preparations must be made. Above all, more men were required. Pavelich hoped that Yanka Pusta would develop on a scale greater than his Italian recruitment. He visited the Hungarian camp and paraded the men. It was rather a disappointing turnout, only forty-five all told. Twelve of these had come from South America and another twelve from Belgium. There were some Bulgarians who had been sent by the Macedonian Revolutionary Organization. Had the opposite bank of the Drava been seething with revolt there must have been swarms of young men coming over to be sworn in to the Croat flag. But he still announced that Croats and Dalmatians would rise in revolt. He told the paraded men that Italy would soon declare war on Yugoslavia.

But perhaps he was beginning to doubt that. Italy's plan seemed to be to let Pavelich's men start the revolt without the employment of the Italian regular army. It might be due to his exaggeration of what he could do with his own men unaided. Some time or other he would have to make good his words. He dared not let the Italians know how pitiful was the force which Perchets had raised. The Fascists were paying much more than the services warranted. Still, he must continue to bluff them. His personal income and position depended on that.

Part of his bluff was to mint Croat money—five-*kuna* pieces with the words "Croat Free State" embossed. As there was no such money as the *kuna* recognized, these coins could not be changed into any other currency, though they might well be bought as curiosities. And they would not purchase anything, except at the canteens of the Italian camps.

There are signs that in 1933 the Fascists became discontented. Yugoslavia had not been obviously weakened by terrorism. There was no unrest, no political ferment. The various political parties remained passive under the dictatorship. The propaganda conducted in the foreign press had raised no agitation against the Yugoslav government. Great Britain had privately expressed her desire that Yugoslavia should return to democratic institutions, but she was too much occupied with other more pressing problems to take sides in Balkan politics. France was engrossed by the specter of resurgent Germany. Travelers to Yugoslavia heard little or nothing of the train wrecks and outrages. They reported an uncommonly peaceful country. Tourists swarmed to the Dalmatian resorts.

To make matters worse for Pavelich, his lieutenant, Perchets, became involved in several scandals. He had shot a man dead with his own hand. Another had committed suicide in despair. There was insubordination. One of the South Americans demanded the money for his passage back home. He declared that he had been brought over on false pretences and that the whole movement was a fraud. He had come to Hungary at his own expense and that may have accounted for his independent spirit. Perchets had him locked up in the camp prison. Several other men, led by Seletkovich, mutinied. Perchets sent some others to shoot Seletkovich. It looked as though civil war were breaking out in Yanka Pusta instead of Croatia.

But Perchets' men failed in their attempt on Seletkovich and it seemed for a moment as though Perchets himself might be seized and most likely killed. He rushed for his car and departed from the camp at full speed. In Budapest he sought military aid to quell the mutiny and a number of Hungarian soldiers were sent to restore order. The insubordinate men were overcome and sent under escort to Pavelich in Italy.

Perchets had been frightened and still expected vengeance. He changed his name and his address in Budapest and obtained another passport. He was now Joseph Steiner. When next he visited Yanka Pusta he had an armed guard all night. When he returned to Budapest he was afraid he might have been followed. He changed his name and his passport again. In order not to be traced he separated from his mistress and they had different lodgings. He kept Pospishil with him as bodyguard.

Then he had a quarrel with Yelka Pogorelets. He began to go about with another girl. Perhaps he did not want to be seen in cabarets with the striking Croat girl. Her presence identified him. Or he may simply have grown tired of her. It was a matter of jealousy. Yelka Pogorelets was attached to him in spite of his baleful activities, which she fully realized. But the presence of a rival was too much for her. After one or two scenes she decamped. He allowed her to slip out of his clutches. For a conspirator in a responsible position he was most remiss, for she got away with all the secrets, into Yugoslavia.

In order to secure her position with the authorities in her own country she told all she knew. The Serbs are slow at propaganda but this provided an opportunity too good to be missed even by them. She was encouraged to write an account of her life with Perchets and shortly afterwards there appeared a series of sensational articles in the Zagreb *Novosti*, showing him up, compromising Pavelich, Perchevich, Italy, Hungary. Her articles ruined the reputation of Perchets. It was weakly replied that she had been all along an agent of the Belgrade government, playing a double role. But Belgrade was not smart enough to have placed a pretty girl spy with a leading terrorist. In any case, what she wrote bore the stamp of truth and was believed by the Croats themselves. Perchets was obliged to efface himself. He disappeared in the late summer of 1933 and was not heard of again. Probably he remained in hiding in Hungary under yet another name. All the efforts of the police failed to connect him with the Marseilles crime. His chauffeur, Pospishil, disavowed any further connection with him. But of those who went ultimately to prison for the murder of King Alexander no one knows more than Pospishil. Perhaps at some later date his lips may be unsealed.

Colonel Perchevich became commandant at Yanka Pusta in place of Gustave Perchets. He lived at Vienna in the high society of the partisans of Otto Hapsburg. He had not much time for training soldiers. In any case, after the revelations of Yelka the Yugoslav government began to protest to the Hungarian government. The camp's existence was an international scandal. Early in 1934 Yevtich made a complaint to the League of Nations. Hungary must disband the terrorists whom she had been encouraging and sheltering on the Yugoslav border. There was damning evidence which could be set before the League. Rather than endure the humiliation of being called to order from Geneva, Hungary agreed to negotiate directly with the Yugoslav government for a settlement. As a result, the camp at Yanka Pusta was dissolved. Some of the men went to Italy. The others settled at Nagy Kanisza, six miles away from Yanka Pusta. No one was arrested. The situation was not entirely cleared up. The false Hungarian passports were not recalled. International sabotage continued but the instigators had received a setback.

CHAPTER XI

LITTLE ENTENTE AND BALKAN PACT

ALEXANDER never was perturbed by the frontier raids and explosions. He traveled freely in the trains, even on the dangerous line from Jesenitse. He avoided no personal danger and at the worst period of outrage he went regularly to shoot in the Julian Alps within a kilometer of the Austrian frontier. He did not hustle his Home Secretary to get to grips with the terrorists. Domestic and personal danger did not weigh with him. What did give him to think was the international aspect of these crimes. It was borne in upon him that Yugoslavia had serious enemies and that membership of the League of Nations was not a certain guarantee that he would not be involved in war. So far as the League was concerned he had bowed to the superior judgment of the West. Not for him to question the inspiration of America, the faith of Britain. The forming of the Little Entente had not been done on his initiative; it represented the thought of other minds, Masaryk, Beneš, Titulescu, Pashich. The League in its first conception did not seem to need the support of subsidiary alliances.

But it ought not to have needed the Locarno Pact. It ought not to have needed the Briand-Kellogg Pact. From the first the organism of the superstate did not seem to be healthy. A whole series of tonics had to be administered. And all the while its life force ebbed. It seemed to have been born old and an invalid. The small

nations were soon aware that the diffused support of
Geneva was not equal to the support of strong friends
in an old-fashioned alliance.

The Serbs missed Russia and nothing could make up
for the defection of the great Slav nation of the north.
King Alexander never forgot that Russia stood by
Serbia in the fateful moments of 1914. He was not
forgetful of the fact that Tsar Nicholas had, in 1915,
insisted on the transport of the Serb Army stranded on
the Albanian shore. He was grateful to the dead. But
the revolution was a blow to all the southern Slavs. It
left them without ethnic support, a branch cut off. In
the nineteenth century, Serbs, Bulgars, and even Croats
and Slovenes, and certainly Montenegrins looked to
Russia as a mighty force of Slavdom which gave them
the right to hold up their heads and believe in their
own future as Slavs, inspiring resistance to the Austrian
and war against the Turk. The proletarian revolution
put Slavophilism into the archives. The followers of
Lenin had enough to do to organize the new state. They
were not even faintly interested in brother Slavs unless brother Slavs followed their example and made a
Marxist revolution.

The political leaders of Serbia—and no doubt Alexander—were, in 1918, afraid that a revolutionary tidal
wave might come from Russia and engulf them. But
although there was persecution of Communists in the
early part of the reign there never was a virulent anti-
Bolshevik campaign. Distrust of Soviet Russia gradually faded as international interests came into align-
ment. The Slavs of the Balkans must look to Russia
even if she be red. Blood is thicker than theory. That
was why it was possible after the King's death for the

Moscow radio to proclaim that Soviet Russia was solid behind Yugoslavia.

Alexander gave shelter to the remnants of Wrangel's army and to thousands of refugees, but that was not a political act. It was merely the natural expression of gratitude to the old Russia. The Serbs did not forget their ex-allies. Of all nations of Europe they proved the best friends of the unhappy Russians. They not only took them in but gave them the means of living. Some they placed on the land, some they brought into the timber industry. Engineers from the southern railways of Russia were given a subvention and allowed to develop road transport. Professors were given chairs in the universities. Hundreds of Russians obtained posts to teach in the schools. Actors and producers were given the run of the theaters and produced ballet and Russian and Serbian plays, raising the stage to a European level. Architects and painters were used for the restoration of the monasteries and the construction of the royal church at Oplenats. Old frescoes were restored by the Russians. Facilities were granted for the education of Russian children. So the exiles found a second home in Yugoslavia.

These Russians have taken no part whatever in Yugoslav politics. Not one of them has ever come into the open to express an opinion. Only in their passivity have they been a political factor. Their very presence in Yugoslavia counted for something. They had no voice but they made it difficult for King Alexander to seek an understanding with Soviet Russia. He was only slowly brought to the view that ultimately Yugoslavia would need the diplomatic support of Russia. In 1932 and 1933 Alexander had to make up his mind whether

he was going to range his country with the powers of
the Left or with the powers of the Right. He could play
for the strong support of Germany or of Soviet Russia.
Mussolini's behavior turned the scale toward the Left.
The Little Entente, which had been a series of bilateral
agreements, must be changed into a stronger instrument.

He instructed Yevtich to sound the leaders of Ru-
manian and Czechoslovak policy and in reviewing the
situation Beneš was found to be strongly in favor of
an understanding with Soviet Russia. The mutual ob-
ligations of the Little Entente Powers were revised in
February, 1933, in a new pact. The three powers agreed
to vote as one on all matters of international importance.
They would give one another mutual assistance in re-
pelling an aggressor. They would not sign separate
treaties with other powers except by mutual consent.
Mutual consent appears to have been available in the
case of Soviet Russia.

Hitler had come to power in Germany in the previous
month and the whole outlook of Central Europe was
changed. A strong and dangerous Germany was arising,
determined to avenge the humiliations of past defeat.
The first ghost of the dead war to appear was Prussia.
The Little Entente and France soon began to call another shade out of the limbo of the past, Russia. Shrewd
commentators at that time said that all the war alliances
and the war fronts were to be renewed. Italy, not to be
behindhand, signed a pact of nonaggression and neu-
trality with Soviet Russia on September 2, 1933.

That seemed to guarantee that in the developments
of the following years Italy would range herself with
the powers of the Left, but the states of the Little
Entente did not ascribe much importance to this treaty.
Italy, aiding and abetting Hungary's program of re-

visionism, and drawn to Nazi Germany by a kindred political outlook, was not likely to line up either with democracy or Communism.

King Alexander had his own plan for securing peace in the Balkans, and peace in the Balkans concerned him much more than peace in Western Europe. He believed that a solidarity of the nations on the Balkan Peninsula was a first requirement. Let it become unprofitable for a Western Power to start a war there and impossible through diplomatic intrigue to set one Balkan State against another. He received assistance to that end in an unexpected quarter. The King of Bulgaria made a move to reconcile Bulgars and Serbs.

In August and September, 1933, Boris and Joanna, King and Queen of Bulgaria, went on a series of unofficial visits to Rome, Paris, and London. The Sofia press was in the dark, but hoped that "some political profit might result to Bulgaria." In London Their Majesties preferred to be incognito, a Mr. and Mrs. X at Claridge's. They were lonely sovereigns and the newspapers did not pay them much attention, though they were photographed often enough. In a Belgrade paper they were shown watching the sparrows snatching crumbs in Hyde Park. Boris at this time had a feeling of isolation. He was ready for friendships, but his country was under a cloud. Too many people had been murdered there. But he obtained advice and help in London. The kindly and peace-loving George V took a hand. Why should not King Boris, on his way back to Sofia, stop off at Belgrade and shake hands with King Alexander? A talk at Belgrade station while the train waited?

"The way to resume is to resume," said a famous American. And the French say, "It is the first step that counts." Yevtich, the Foreign Minister, was agreeably surprised when the message came through from London that King Boris would like to meet Alexander in an informal way as he was passing through Belgrade. King Alexander was not particularly enthusiastic. For a moment he was taken aback. He was never a man who was quick at the uptake when other people made suggestions.

"Yes, I'll meet him," said he, but his voice was almost a growl.

"Where? Shall we invite them to come to the palace?"

"No," said the King. "I'll do as he suggests, meet him at the railway station."

Yevtich was pleased. The few who heard in advance that a meeting had been arranged thrilled with a new hope. A commercial treaty with Bulgaria had been signed in the previous May. The Serbs began to whisper of a new era. One can tell the weather by the observation of the flight of birds, and when Boris and Joanna alighted in the capital of Yugoslavia the auguries were good.

There was one bond of kinship. Joanna was Alexander's cousin. She was the daughter of Princess Helena of Montenegro, now Queen of Italy. Alexander's mother and Helena were sisters and Alexander, when he was a child, was the favorite of Helena. Helena married the heir to the throne of Italy but never ceased to be very fond of Sandro. Her daughter Joanna had played with little Sandro as a child. But the war separated the families, and after the war Italy became hostile to the Serbs. A Queen of Italy has no influence in politics, otherwise Helena might have made possible the projected visit of Alexander to Italy in 1932.

The surprise of the meeting at Belgrade station was the rapturous greeting of King Alexander by his cousin

Joanna. "Sandro!" she cried and hugged him and kissed him as he stood there, cold and formal on the platform.

That human outburst of feeling made all the difference to the meeting of the sovereigns. Instead of being stiff, it was cordial. They walked along the platform to a sort of *de luxe* waiting room and drank Turkish coffee and smoked cigarettes and chatted like old acquaintances. Boris and Alexander had been friends but that was long ago, before the 1912 war with Turkey, when they were each heir to the throne of their respective countries. Rivers of blood had come to separate them. But suddenly there was not blood any more. They had shaken hands. They were sipping coffee together.

The possibility of real friendship and coöperation with Bulgaria had dawned on the mind of Alexander. Ruzhdy Aras had spoken to Yevtich at Geneva about a collective agreement in the Balkans, and he signed a separate agreement with Yugoslavia. Titulescu of Rumania took up the idea of a collective treaty. Alexander was already determined to form a Balkan Pact and the happy chance of the meeting with Boris yielded the new hope that Bulgaria could be persuaded to join. There was only half an hour before the train started for Sofia, but he talked international politics most of the time.

But King Boris would not promise to sign any agreements. The Mushanov ministry in Sofia was the most favorable to Yugoslavia that Bulgaria had had since the war, but it was still in peril from the Macedonian Revolutionary Organization, which pursued an anti-Serb policy guided by Italy. Boris was not almost an autocrat, like Alexander. He was a comparatively helpless monarch who wanted to rule in peace while extraneous political feuds raged year in and year out in his capital. All he could indicate was personal good will. When opportunity arose he would profit by it to make a real friendship between brother Slavs.

The station bell rang. The man who calls the names of stations was heard bellowing: "Train for Nish, Tsaribrod, Sofia, Stambul!" The royal party stood up and filed out from the waiting room. The King and Queen of Bulgaria were escorted to the waiting express and into their sleeping car. The barriers closed; the whistle blew and the heavy train began to lumber slowly over the rails. Boris and Joanna were at the carriage windows and waved back to Alexander like ordinary travelers. Joanna blew a kiss to her cousin Sandro.

King Boris had invited King Alexander to visit him on Bulgarian soil.

There is no doubt the commercial treaty had prepared the way for an entente. A Bulgarian minister said: "The new treaty signed on May 24 puts an end to an abnormal economic relationship which has been peculiarly disadvantageous to two peoples who are both neighbors and brothers. Almost thirty-seven years have passed since the last treaty of commerce between Serbia and Bulgaria . . . the new treaty inaugurates a new era of economic coöperation."

The Belgrade press, reduced to apathy by the lifeless politics of one-party government, was aroused by the arrival of Boris. Comment was restricted but it showed its interest by the prominence it gave the news. A new hope was born. The name Yugoslavia began to mean something more—Southern Slavia, that might also include the Bulgars. There is one desire which unites but also divides most of the peoples of the Balkan Peninsula: they wish to belong to something large. The phrases "Great Serbia," "Great Croatia" expressed that craving.

The name "Yugoslavia" is also an expression of it. Alexander merits praise for the steps he took to be reconciled with Bulgaria, but there is no gainsaying the fact that kings stood in the way of an even better policy. A union of Serbs and Bulgars in one state was devoutly to be wished. That is one reason why there is always a majority for federalism in Yugoslavia. The greater measure of domestic rights accorded Croatia, Montenegro, Slovenia, the more chance that Bulgaria would ultimately pool her national interests and come into a great union of free states. The Bulgarians have as much right as the Serbs to call themselves Yugoslavs and such a name is not distasteful to them, though they would never submit to be ruled by the Serbs. Some Bulgar politicians have been attracted by it, notably Stambolisky.

King Alexander had no such utopian plans. He merely hoped to strengthen Yugoslavia by uniting all peoples living on the Balkan Peninsula to resist interference on the part of the outside powers. The intrigues of Austria and Russia and the policy of Great Britain had caused most of the Balkan troubles of the previous fifty years. He was convinced that if the Western Powers could be forced to *keep out* there would be a sure and lasting Balkan peace. The menace in 1933 was from Italy. Italy, having established a base for Balkan intrigue in Albania, had announced in the spring of the year that the direction of her territorial expansion would be eastward. Perhaps Mussolini did not quite know his own mind at that date, for the expansion, when it took place, was not eastward but into Africa. But Greece and Turkey were apprehensive as to Italy's intentions. There is not one power that would welcome the Italian flag on the peninsula. President Kemal, who regarded Asia Minor as an extension of Europe and of the Balkans, was roused by the Italian threat and it was understood that he was willing to come to an agreement with Yugoslavia to conclude some sort of pact of mutual assistance.

Alexander promised to visit Kemal. He would have liked to have gone to him with Bulgaria in his pocket. But there was still the Macedonian Revolutionary Organization, the redoubtable Mikhailov ready to assassinate anyone who engaged Bulgaria in a pact with Yugoslavia. The Bulgarian government had to tackle Mikhailov before there could be the assurance of peace between the states. King Alexander decided to unite Rumania, Turkey, and Greece with Yugoslavia in his new pact, leaving Bulgaria to realize that there could be no advantage in being left out of a common understanding.

King Alexander had met King Boris on September 18. Before the end of the month he set forth with the Queen upon a series of visits designed to give royal confirmation to the terms of the pact to be signed in November. He ordered his destroyer, the *Dubrovnik*, to proceed to Constanza on the Black Sea. After calling upon his brother-in-law Carol, in Rumania, he would return the courtesy of Boris and Joanna by disembarking at Varna. Then he would continue his voyage to the Bosporus and hold converse with President Kemal. Thence to Greece.

The sovereigns were at Bucharest on September 30. They left Constanza on October 3, reaching Varna in the afternoon. Boris and Joanna had come to the Black Sea port and had arranged a rousing welcome, guns firing, flags flying, military music. For the first time since the war King Alexander set foot on Bulgarian soil. He was cheered by the Bulgarians in the streets of Varna. That was an event in the history of the two countries.

Cars were waiting and the royal party was conducted to the palace of Evksinograd, where it sat down to tea. The conversation of the Belgrade railway station was renewed and the reconciliation of embittered brother races was taken a step further. Alexander and Marie stayed to dinner with Boris and Joanna. The official bulletin said the meeting had been cordial. Perhaps, after all, the entertainment was a little dull. The King and Queen of Yugoslavia did not stay long. By half-past ten they were back on the *Dubrovnik*. Boris had pleaded for time for the consideration of the pact. It was encountering a secret but powerful opposition from certain politicians.

The *Dubrovnik* got under way and in the misty morning of the next day entered the Bosporus, with the wonder of Stambul on either hand. It glided across the still, green, shadowy water to face a white marble palace of the sultans. On the shores school children in masses had been paraded so that youngest Turkey might salute the King of Yugoslavia. They waved handkerchiefs to the *Dubrovnik* as it passed.

A little white yacht like a bird started from the palace quay and came to the Yugoslav destroyer. On it was Ruzhdy Aras in charge of three immense bouquets of flowers for the Queen. It was early. The Queen was not fully dressed. Alexander, in his admiral's uniform, descended into the yacht, which took him back to the palace leaving the Queen behind. A royal salute was fired. Out of the palace came President Kemal in top hat and frock coat. He was carrying white gloves and a walking stick. He stared at Alexander with an intense expression as if he would look through him. Kemal was curious: he was a judge of men. The King had the smiling indifference of one who seldom falls under the influence of another even though the other be a genius. But the Turk was pleased with what he saw—a real man, a worthy friend. According to Dimitrievich, who was present, he gloated on Alexander, following him about with his eyes. He embraced him many times and lavished oriental compliments upon him such as, "If Your Majesty were an apple I would place You over my heart."

Kemal led Alexander through the palace to his private Cabinet, across halls of alabaster and porphyry, glittering with crystal ornaments. There were gorgeous heavy carpets under their feet. There were modern French paintings on the walls. The Ghazi kept Alexander talking over coffee and Turkish delight till eleven, when he accompanied him back to the *Dubrovnik* to fetch the Queen. The King changed into civil attire and became a tourist. The Queen asked Kemal to free them for the rest of the day so that they could see the city. They would come to the marble palace for the entertainment in the evening.

So for the whole of the afternoon Alexander and Marie went sightseeing and visited museums and mosques and shrines. They were cheered as they entered the ancient cathedral of St. Sophia. Though Alexander was an Orthodox monarch he was not one of those who dreamed of restoring St. Sophia to Christianity. The Turks knew that. He was neither a Greek nor a Russian. They could cheer him wholeheartedly. He came as a friend, with no designs on the shrines of the Orthodox East.

The King and Queen were so taken up with the sights of Constantinople that they had to hurry back to the *Dubrovnik* to dress for President Kemal's banquet. That was going to be an event of oriental magnificence. King Boris' hospitality was pallid beside that of the Turks. At length the sovereigns arrived and met Kemal again

and Ismet Pasha and Ruzhdy Aras and the greater part
of the government, and the wives of the ministers, and
Kemal's own choice selection of beautiful women. It
was modern Turkey without veil and the women were
superb. A band played the anthems and then played
some of the hottest jazz. The dinner, in European style,
French cuisine, was served exclusively on gold and lasted
two hours. There was a magnificence quite unknown in
Yugoslavia and a mingling of the oriental and the
modern, but all in grand style. It was one of Kemal's
all-night entertainments. There was time for eating and
drinking, for dancing and card playing and for private
and confidential conversations apart from the many
guests.

Smoking long Turkish cigarettes, Kemal and Alexander played poker after dinner. The Queen took a
hand for a while, and then Ismet Pasha and the Foreign
Minister. The luck of the cards was with the King and
the counters piled up in front of him. According to Atsa
Dimitrievich, who was there, the King cleared everyone
out at last with a full house and then with a gesture
swept all the counters aside and said, "Nobody pays.
Let's talk of politics!"

Kemal was in great good humor and was ready to
enter into agreements even in excess of those contemplated by Alexander. He was convinced of the advantage of a Balkan Entente based on a similar treaty to
that of the Little Entente. He did not require to be
persuaded. He went further. He gave secret assurance
to Alexander of military assistance in the case of war
arising from an infringement of the independence of
Austria. In the event of a war with Italy, Turkey would
be Yugoslavia's ally.

It was quick work. The King and Queen returned to

their ship shortly after midnight. They were escorted by Kemal and a number of Turkish dignitaries. The stars glittered over Constantinople. The sovereigns were serenaded. Anthems were played. Then Alexander and Marie retired but Kemal and the rest returned to the Sultan's palace to continue festivities until four in the morning.

No one would deny that Kemal had an instinct for affairs. He was a man of greater force of character than Alexander, a genius, a sort of Turkish Peter the Great who raised his people out of Asiatic sloth and fatalism. He had cause for rejoicing because he wished Turkey again to play a part in European affairs. The West had concluded that Gladstone's phrase had been realized and that the Turk had been driven out of Europe "bag and baggage." But Alexander confirmed the fact that the Turk was still a Balkan factor and had an interest in keeping Western Powers out of the peninsula. And behind Kemal was Soviet Russia, bent upon thwarting Western capitalism. In joining forces with the Ghazi Alexander moved appreciably into the influence of Moscow. But the movement was not entirely of his own volition: it was a resultant of other forces and movements.

It was Kemal's plan that the Balkan Pact and the Little Entente should be unified and that both should obtain the support of Soviet Russia. The outstanding difficulty had disappeared. Moscow had no further pretension to the restoration of Bessarabia by Rumania. In the following year the Little Entente passed a formal resolution calling upon Yugoslavia to recognize Soviet Russia. This would have been done but that the murder of the King intervened. Prince Paul, whose mother was a Russian aristocrat and whose wife is a descendant of the Romanovs, became Regent and Yugoslav foreign policy was deflected into a different course. Otherwise Czechoslovakia in her understanding with Moscow would have been associated not only with the French Republic but with the Balkan States.

The King did not proceed from Stambul to Athens as had been expected but instead went to Corfu, where he dedicated a monument to the Greeks who fell in the war, and visited those places, like shrines to him, where the Serbian Army had encamped in 1916. He visited the many graves of Serb soldiers on the island of Vido. General Stefanovich and the Greek Vice-Premier Condilis were with him. He was deterred from conducting the negotiations for signing the pact by the stormy opposition of Venizelos. He left that to his Minister in Athens. The King was unable to understand what Venizelos and his partisans wanted, beyond getting back into power. Greece could not continue indefinitely playing a double game, supporting Italian policy, and at the same time professing friendship for Yugoslavia. And she must forget her furious enmity toward the Bulgars and the Turks. History could not be rewritten for the benefit of the Greeks. Fortunately the Premier, Maximos, was in favor of the pact, though he wished assurance that it did not mean conflict with Italy. The Yugoslavs pointed out that on the contrary it implied insurance against a conflict with Italy. If Italy had the Balkan Powers divided her intrigue for expansion at their expense would be facilitated. But if the Balkan Powers stood together the Italians would be frightened. Mussolini made much noise in 1933, but he was not so brave at that time as he became after the Abyssinian conquest and the alliance with Germany.

Alexander meditated including Albania in his pact,

but to quiet Greek apprehension he moved cautiously. He gave the Albanians secret assurance that Yugoslavia renounced forever any claim to Albanian territory and allowed it to be known that he desired to see Albania free and independent. The Italian protectorate over Albania was a thorn in the Balkan flesh, but it was also galling to the Albanians, who were ever restive under Italian control. Albania was a potential base for military operations in case of an Italian war. The danger impelled Alexander to seek friendship with Bulgaria. Because if the Italians could reckon upon a simultaneous attack from Macedonia and Albania, the whole of southern Serbia might be lost as well as part of the Dalmatian shore.

The Balkan Pact was signed at Athens on November 27, 1933, and simultaneously at Belgrade by Ruzhdy Aras on the part of Turkey. Bulgaria still delayed action.

But to avert disappointment at the caution of Premier Mushanov, Boris and Joanna paid a state visit to Belgrade early in the following month. Possibly the Bulgarian Queen had a hand in arranging that. Joanna wanted to see more of Sandro. This time the King and Queen of Bulgaria came as honored guests, not merely to be received at a railway station as in July. They stayed at the palace. Boris and Alexander went shooting. The promise of the reconciliation of the two nations which had been at enmity for twenty years remained. Both monarchs ardently desired it and worked to realize it, an example of kings having more power for peace than politicians. King Boris went far ahead of his government in carrying the olive branch.

CHAPTER XII

ATTEMPT AT ZAGREB

THE pact of the Little Entente was insurance against the revisionism of Austria and Hungary. The Balkan Pact was insurance against Italy. The overtures to Bulgaria were designed to show that the general peace would not be endangered by the Balkan Powers falling out among themselves. They had the further object of discouraging foreign interference and intrigue. The prospects of Italian irredentism were not very bright in the autumn of 1933. Mussolini was suspicious, perhaps jealous of Hitler. The new Germany certainly wished to incorporate Austria in the *Reich* and might have ultimate designs on Austrian territory lost to Italy, perhaps even on Trieste. Fascism was obliged to run counter to Nazism by lauding Bolshevism. But there was the prospect of Italy's becoming isolated in Central Europe.

Probably it was during the autumn of 1933 that Italy decided upon the conquest of Abyssinia. The European adventure was postponed because of the Balkan Pact. King Alexander stood in Mussolini's way. The Duce was angry but he did not intend to fight Yugoslavia. The little nations would beset him like wasps. Hitler would laugh at his legions setting forth to conquer Illyria and meeting with every possible mishap. Better to win renown on a safer field. De Bono assured him of a very easy victory in Abyssinia. Military achievement was needed to enhance the prestige of the army. For words

alone cannot make an army valiant. The Nazis must become convinced of the power of Fascism in arms. No
one really knew what the Duce had done for the Italian
Army, not even King Alexander. It had been mechanized
to such an extent that it was immeasurably superior to
the army which had fought in the war against the Germans. Any lack in fighting qualities had been more than
made up by increase in equipment, improvement in
weapons. Mussolini determined to make the Abyssinian
invasion a parade of his forces before the world.

But Yugoslavia was not ignored. Mussolini finds it
very difficult to forgive opposition or diplomatic success
scored at his expense. King Alexander had made himself
prominent in countering Italian schemes. He was therefore an enemy. Yugoslavia was a one-man country.
Remove this too energetic sovereign and it would be
helpless. The quarrels of incompetent politicians would
recommence and the disaffection of the Catholic races
would make for confusion. It was the opinion of a leading Yugoslav statesman that Mussolini wished to have
his hands free for his Abyssinian adventure so that he
would have no potential enemy waiting to attack him
when his armies were in Africa.

Pavelich was told by his "control" that he must arrange the murder of the King. His campaign of terrorism had petered out; for the year 1933 was unre-
markable in terrorism. Perchets had made a fool of
himself by allowing his lady secretary to run away and
publish her memoirs. Hungary was in danger of exposure before the League. The Croats showed no sign of
rising in revolt. Count Ciano must have pointed out to
Mussolini that there was little prospect of a return for
the money which had been lavished like water on Pavelich and his men. Pavelich had been presented with a

villa and received a large salary. The men in his camps
had to be fed, clothed, armed, paid. His journals had
to be supported, his many agents in Austria and elsewhere to be paid. And there was nothing to show for
the expense except some pitiful bomb explosions in
trains. Landing his army to start a civil war began to
look hopeless in the face of Alexander's activities. But
the Croat Duce could at least do one thing: he could
remove the one man who was thwarting Italy at the
moment. Among the many men at his disposal there
must be someone capable of a capital exploit, the murder of the King.

Pavelich's choice fell on Peter Oreb, a tall and powerful young peasant from one of the Dalmatian islands,
and as assistants he deputed two other young men,
Begovich and Pogorelats. They were all three well
trained in pistol shooting and the throwing of bombs.
Oreb was considered the best of the men in the Italian
camps, though he had never before attempted an assassination. It would have been the first murder in his career. But he was a strong fellow, active and daring, and
not likely to submit tamely to arrest. The scene for the
assassination was Zagreb. The King had announced that
on December 17, 1933, he would celebrate his forty-
fifth birthday at the Croat capital. Oreb and his companions must blow up the royal carriage as it passed
across the Yelachich Square.

There was deep snow on the mountains and the three
men were rigged out as skiers. They looked like typical
devotees of winter sports, the sort of youthful enthusiasts one may encounter anywhere in the Tyrol in December, whose skis were adequate explanation of their
appearance in any obscure village. With bombs and
pistols in their pockets they glided over the virginal

snow of the Julian Alps, slid from Italy into Slovenia unobserved, and then clattered into a third-class carriage of the first train and traveled to Zagreb. They had Hungarian passports, of which Pavelich had a store ready for any emergency. Each of them had two thousand dinars to spend and there was the promise of a very large reward if they succeeded. Oreb would have his freedom and capital with which to start life afresh. He believed what he had to do was easy.

He had never been in Zagreb, but he believed that everyone there hated the King. He did not ask himself why, if the King were so unpopular there, he ventured to visit it to celebrate his birthday. In the Italian camps they said Croatia was merely waiting for Pavelich's signal to rise in revolt, only waiting for Italy to declare war on Serbia. Pavelich had said to him that it would be easy to escape after he had done the deed because the people would be on his side and would save him from the police.

So they were a light-hearted trio in the Zagreb train. Only Begovich, in joking, told Oreb that he had orders to shoot him if he showed the white feather. Begovich was Oreb's policeman. But he was only twenty years old, a soured student whose life had been spoiled by politics. He ought to have been at a university but was a soldier in Italian pay, waiting for revolution to resume his studies. His playful smile masked a jealous watchful nature. He was chosen because he was the sort of weakling who would not let the strong man Oreb fail in his task. He would watch him like a cat.

Oreb was some years older, but in spirit he was younger. There was a certain devil-may-care irresponsibility about him. He had sworn to obey Pavelich and he had to go when he was ordered. But he was not taken

aback, made no protest, expressed no doubt as to his
ability to do what he was told. He was probably without imagination. At least he could not imagine the scene
in a great city when he would have to throw a bomb
at the royal car. He was an islander, something less than
a mere provincial. He had lived a life of crime, but it
was petty crime. Nothing spectacular characterized his
exploits on Korchula. The illegitimate son of a peasant
girl, he had to shift for himself at an early age. He had
worked for a smuggler. Then he became a smuggler on
his own account. He started with sugar. Owing to the
state monopoly the price of sugar in Yugoslavia was
almost three times the world price. By bringing over
contraband sugar from the neighboring Italian island of
Lastovo he made a meager living. From sugar he turned
to silk and any other Italian products waiting in the
boats in the channel. It was a night business and he
risked being shot by customs officers. There is not much
parley when Yugoslav customs officers run down a
smuggler. Oreb's life was constantly in jeopardy in this
hazardous business. But it is probable he took that risk
as lightly as he did that of going to Zagreb to kill the
King.

Later he discovered a more profitable line. Two of
Pavelich's agents appeared on the Italian island looking
for smugglers who would carry arms, ammunition, and
the newspapers *Gritch* and *Ustasha* into Dalmatia. They
had their receivers waiting on the mainland and this
traffic paid handsomely. It was easier. Nevertheless,
Oreb was caught at it. But he broke jail and fled, got
onto a boat, and took refuge on the island of Lastovo.
He was told he would be taken care of. All he had to
do was to join the army of independence which was
waiting to set Dalmatia free. He was taken on a boat

to Zara and then to Trieste. He was treated well. Just as a new recruit gets the King's shilling to buy himself a drink, so the poor smuggler, Oreb, was "treated" wherever he went. "Soup and a plate of meat and a bottle of wine for my dinner!" he exclaimed afterwards to the judge. He who had been used to wolf maize bread and rough mountain cheese, washed down with imitation coffee!

At Trieste he was met by Seletkovich, the man who had specialized in blowing up trains. Seletkovich did not seem to have been punished for his mutiny at Yanka Pusta. He was invested with Pavelich's authority at Trieste. Oreb was sworn in and took his oath of obedience to Pavelich, whom he had never met or heard of until then. He was then taken to Brescia. Seletkovich left him there and he was handed over to a sergeant and conducted to Borgotaro where he got onto an omnibus and reached the first camp. At the quartermaster's stores he received a khaki uniform and was marched to a small barracks where he found some sixty other soldiers, all in high spirits because the pay was good and the training nothing to affect anyone's nerves. Pavelich's soldiers were better off than the regular Italian Army. The food was better and within limits there was more freedom. He was told to say in the villages that he was a Bulgarian, a petty precaution lest the Yugoslavs get wind of the presence of an army of liberation upon Italian soil. Not that it was large enough to be called an army. Oreb visited other camps in northern Italy, at Bardi, Raffi, Gabrioli. There were not more than a few hundred men all told.

The Italian police never asked him any questions. These men in uniform went absolutely unmolested in this Fascist country where everyone is watched and con-

trolled. But privates in the Italian Army did not salute
Pavelich's officers and his men did not have to salute
Italian officers. Units of the Italian Army often passed
on the roads but exchanged no greetings. In the bars
they saw large pictures of Mussolini, but in their own
quarters they had equally large portraits of Pavelich.
He was their grand man. He inspected them on parade
and addressed them with high-sounding phrases as if
they were a host and not merely sixty men. Perchets,
Yelich, Perchevich visited them but they were more
aloof. Although their numbers were small there was
enough to make them feel that they were part of a
movement that was assured of success. Italy was behind them. When they had to fight, they would not
fight alone. And they were assured that the Croats and
Dalmatians would rise in their support. They would
rapidly be promoted to be officers when the war came.
There was much more *esprit de corps* than had ever obtained in the Hungarian camp. For Pavelich was a more
capable commandant than Perchets. He lived in luxury
but he saw to it that his men had good rations. There
were fewer risky exploits than were detailed to the men
on the Hungarian frontier of Yugoslavia.

They marched, they drilled, went to musketry and
bombing practice. They learned to fire with revolvers.
The life was that familiar to anyone who has ever been
in military training. Life was even monotonous. It was
only in November, 1933, after the signing of the Balkan
Pact that it was evident that something new was afoot.
Pavelich and the other officers had a number of private
talks with individual men. They asked questions. They
made tests of men's nerves. It began to be rumored that
some were going to be chosen for a special exploit. Pavelich seemed to take a fancy to Oreb, invited him to his

villa, flattered him, asked him his life story, wanted to know if he was ready to take a chance to make his fortune. "Half a million liras are waiting for someone!"

Half a million liras, one could live in comfort for the rest of one's life on that, take a wife, settle down. It appealed to Peter Oreb. He had never handled even a thousand-dinar note. But he had always been offered definite sums when asked to smuggle arms into Dalmatia. And the money agreed had always been paid without question. He had been on that basis between the islands. That was how his mind worked. To do something one must be paid. No use saying to him there was a glorious deed to perform. He performed glorious or inglorious deeds for cash. He agreed. It was a deal.

King Alexander, despite his dictatorship and the policy of coercion, always kept a warm corner in his heart for the Croats. He was very strongly drawn toward the Catholic parts of his dominion. He could not tolerate separatism and intellectual political leadership, but he had tried to keep Croats in his Cabinets. His friendship with Stephen Radich had not been insincere. In matters of church adherence he was impartial. That may perhaps explain how it was that a Serb king was still popular in Zagreb. Even the imprisonment of Machek had not deprived him of popularity. The Croats like a king, they like the attentions of royalty. So there was no obvious danger in the King's visit to the capital of the Savska province. The governor of the province, Perovich, was a Croat and the King stayed at the governor's palace. He was being received by the aged Catholic archbishop, Mgr. Bauer. With the Queen he would attend divine service at the cathedral of St. Stephen, a pleasing gesture. It was as if he chose to disappoint the Orthodox to gratify the Catholics. And he did not come with a parade of military force. He came with faith in his personal security. It was merely one more effort on the part of Alexander to show that he was a true Yugoslav and was as much at home among the Croats as among the Serbs.

The royal car with its Yugoslav pennant left the governor's palace at a quarter to nine on the morning of December 17. The people of Zagreb turned out *en masse* to shout for their King. Peasants by the thousands had rolled up in their carts from all the country round about. There were flags and bunting everywhere. Cannon boomed a royal salute. Peter Oreb was taken aback. Mobs were shouting "Long live the King!" There were no boos, no hisses, no sullen faces. Where were the fierce rebels Pavelich had promised? Oreb had taken up a position on one side of the Yelachich; Begovich and Pogorelats were across the way. He was to throw the first bomb but if it failed his confederates were to throw from the other side. The masses of the people delayed the progress of the royal car. It came forward slowly in a growing roar of cheers. Oreb became agitated. The gun fire shocked his nerves. Being tall, he had an excellent view of the King and Queen, who were smiling, smiling in the face of imminent death. He could not do it. He told his companions afterwards that he did not throw his bombs because so many innocent people might have been killed. But he did not think that at the time. He was bewildered. He caught the infection of king worship and followed the crowds to the cathedral.

The King and Queen stepped out of the car and the old archbishop blessed them in front of the cathedral. Oreb was a Catholic. He could not blow up the prelate with the King. He was moved by the blessing of the

Church descending upon the man he had been sent to kill. The organ of the cathedral of St. Stephen began to sound, and Alexander and Marie and all the court moved down the aisle. Oreb had proved recreant to Pavelich but perhaps true to some higher and hidden allegiance.

He rejoined his confederates, who reproached him bitterly for having failed in his duty. He was defiant and mocking. "I notice you didn't throw your bombs either," said he. "You had as good a chance as I had. You couldn't do it. You had a better chance outside the cathedral. But you couldn't kill the bishop. Same here. They deceived us. Didn't they say he was an enemy of the Church?"

"You were the principal," hissed Begovich. "If you are not a traitor you will have a chance tomorrow."

But the public street was no place for recrimination. They repaired hurriedly to the house where they had been put in hiding by a Zagreb agent. One can imagine they were not a happy party. But it appears that Oreb defended himself stoutly. Pavelich had been misinformed about the Croats. They were all for the King. What was the use of thinking there was going to be a rebellion?

That evening the police got belatedly on their trail. There were enough plain-clothes men in Zagreb to watch all suspected citizens. But they missed the three strangers. There were strangers in plenty arriving in the city for the occasion. But the police knew the Croat agents who had been in correspondence with terrorists abroad, men like Herentich, who received Oreb and probably indicated the lodging where the three men could stay. The police showed their usual lack of thoroughness in not arresting the conspirators before the

King's arrival. It was hardly thanks to them that Alexander and Marie escaped being blown to bits on this occasion.

But at seven o'clock the next morning two gendarmes were sent to arrest Oreb. They rang the doorbell and were admitted. The owner of the house held them talking for a moment and that gave the men time. They must have been prepared to resist arrest, because at the moment when the gendarmes opened the bedroom door the tall Oreb, pistol in hand, rushed to meet them and fired rapidly at them point blank. One gendarme was killed on the spot, the other seriously wounded. The three men then fled for their lives, the long-legged Oreb easily outdistancing the other two.

The wounded gendarme struggled out into the street and flung himself in the police car, which had brought him to the house, giving the driver orders to go in pursuit. The body of the dead gendarme lay in the doorway of the bedroom, and to escape, Oreb and the others had jumped over it. They had gone out at the front door, dashed past the waiting car, and bolted down the street.

Begovich and Pogorelats were speedily arrested but Oreb got onto a tramcar and was soon hurtling away to the outskirts of the city. He set off on foot into the open country. But he knew that a description of him would at once be telephoned to the rural police, so he stopped in a village and finding a house occupied by gipsies went in and made a deal with them, changing his clothes and offering money to the people if they would hide his bombs and pistol. It had been unnecessary to bring the bombs with him, but he must have had them in his pockets at the time the police had come to arrest him. Had he been more collected in his headlong flight he would have seen that it would have been safer to hide his weapons in some ditch. He lost his head when he took the gipsies into his confidence. They talked. The whole village soon knew of the strange visitor. Oreb thought that even if they got to know they would say nothing to the police. Again he was wrong. The police were soon told all about it and he was arrested.

Peter Oreb in custody showed another side of his character. He admitted his guilt freely and told no lies. Begovich and Pogorelats stoutly denied that they had been sent to kill the King, but Oreb made a clean breast of it. It might otherwise have been difficult to prove, except by circumstantial evidence. But Oreb had already killed a gendarme. For that he was certain to be executed. Even had he killed Alexander also, a man cannot be executed twice. There was nothing to deter him from confession unless he were a passionate devotee of Pavelich. That he was not. He had come to understand that Pavelich was a cheat. He had been told that the Croats wanted the King killed and that they would shelter him. He had found them all cheering for the King. He had been assured that there was going to be an armed rising, but that was wrong. All the men in uniform in the Italian camps were being cheated. He had been offered a large sum but he could never have got back to receive it. Oreb was simple minded, almost childish, and one should not judge him too hardly, although he did kill a policeman. He never had much of a chance to become an honest man and a law-abiding peasant. For he had the stigma of illegitimacy and was given into the hands of smugglers in his childhood.

He told the whole story to the Zagreb police. The Hungarian passport received much attention. In this document his name was given as Benedict Emil, a Hungarian subject. Oreb at once disclosed his true name and nationality. He declared he had never been in Hungary and he would not allow it to be assumed that he had entered Yugoslavia from the Hungarian frontier.

Had King Alexander been assassinated at Zagreb it was the intention of those Italians who were instructing Pavelich to allow the blame to attach to Hungary. Much the same situation might have arisen as arose after the murder at Marseilles when the rage of the Serbs was let loose upon the Magyars—somewhat unjustifiably, for the Italians were more compromised than the Hungarians. Hungary was incriminated in terrorism, but had in December, 1933, begun to check the activities of the Pavelich groups on her territory. The use of a Hungarian passport in Oreb's case tended to throw back the onus of international guilt upon Hungary.

Oreb gave explicit information about the camps in Italy, their location and the number of the men. He told all he knew about Pavelich. He enriched the archives of the sleepy Yugoslav police. The whole complicity of Italy was unveiled. It was a frightening and, indeed, dumbfounding story. Had Alexander been hotheaded it would have called for an ultimatum to Italy, possibly war. But the King, though agitated, was always on the side of peace. He would not kindle war just because of danger to his person. He did not even decide to bring the matter before the League of Nations. The most he would do was to sanction the free uncensored publication of Oreb's revelations and let his own people grasp that a foreign power wished to profit by disaffection to stir up civil war.

Although it was known that an attempt on his life had been contemplated, King Alexander went out on foot in the streets of Zagreb and mixed with the people as one of themselves, partly to show that he was not afraid. His agitation did not spring from knowledge of personal danger. He had faced death a hundred times with equanimity. What weighed on his mind was the thought of the blow intended to be struck at Yugoslavia through him, the calculation that the state would not hold together if he were killed.

Pavelich frequently referred to the King in his newspapers as "Alexander the Last." He predicted that there would be no more Karageorgevich kings. When Alexander went the dynasty would perish with him. The heir to the throne was only ten years old and such confusion must ensue before young Peter came of age that the dynasty might seem condemned. In December, 1933, after the arrest of Peter Oreb, Alexander gave this matter his serious thought. Only by God's grace had he escaped being killed on his birthday. No thanks were due to the police. Only the cheering Croats and an impulse in Oreb's heart had saved him. The men had been there in the Yelachich with their bombs and they had allowed him to pass. A great power had been helping these men. That power might not allow itself to be baffled or discouraged by one failure. The attempt might be repeated. And the danger could not be dealt with because it lurked beyond the frontier.

In the event of the King's sudden death the Prime Minister, Uzunovich, would be left in supreme power, but this old Serbian politician, a devotee of party politics, was hardly the man to lead a united people. All the irreconcilables would be clamoring for revolutionary legislation. Even if the Queen survived she had no experience of statecraft and was incapable of coping with Yugoslav politics. Some better provision must be made for the eventuality. The King stayed at Zagreb until

Christmas and then departed to his villa at Bled to make his will.

There was deep snow; the mountains were clad with dreaming pines. There was not one boat on the quiet, desolate lake, no tourists. Bled at Christmas time was a perfect place for meditation on life and death. He had sent his marshal, Dimitrievich, to spend the holiday with his family in Belgrade. He could not be bothered with him. He called Prince Paul for a long and serious talk.

Prince Paul was the only relative whom he could call to his assistance. His brother, Prince George, had been removed from the succession and though in middle age the unruly son whom King Peter had disinherited might prove to have outlived his early irresponsibility of character, Alexander could not appeal to him. The brothers were not on friendly terms. If Alexander nominated him Regent he might easily persuade the legislature to make him King. Alexander had abrogated the constitution which he had sworn to observe. Prince George would not find it difficult to get the act annulled which had excluded him from the throne. The only other male relative was his uncle, Prince Arsène, but Arsène preferred to live in Paris without responsibility. He was completely out of touch, and while the old man might consent to come and be the Sovereign he would hardly be ready to take the thankless task of being Regent. There remained only Prince Arsène's son, Paul.

Prince Paul was naturally in favor of the Queen being nominated Regent until her eldest son came of age. But there was always the possibility of the Queen being killed at the same time as the King. They went everywhere together. Had the bomb been thrown at

Zagreb there was as much likelihood of the death of Marie as of Alexander. And even should she survive him, Alexander did not like the idea of the responsibility of government resting on her shoulders. She would be a puppet in the hands of the politicians. Whatever went wrong would be blamed on her. And much was certain to go wrong. He did not wish any shadow to rest on his line. If Paul became Regent, and there should happen to be unfortunate developments, that would not matter so much. Young Peter would become more and more popular and the people would await his coming of age with impatience.

The King had not until that moment regarded his cousin as his right-hand man. The Prince had not been associated with affairs of state, never sat in conference with ministers, and had held no official post of any kind. His goings and comings were seldom remarked in the press and he was, in fact, a little-known personality. Likewise the Prince had no intimate knowledge of the personnel of Yugoslav politics. He was a private gentleman who followed the King's doings with sympathy. His position was that of family friend who shared the domestic confidence of Alexander and Marie. Some have greatness thrust upon them: that was Prince Paul's position. He demanded that the regency be shared, if not with the Queen at least with two others. The provisions of the constitution, in the case of the infancy of a sovereign, envisaged the appointment of three regents.

Two years previously the King had had a right-hand man whom he trusted more than anyone else in the realm, General Zhivkovich, to whom he had entrusted the domestic government of Yugoslavia under the dictatorship, but he no longer saw eye to eye with the general. He surmised that in Zhivkovich he had a passive critic

PRINCE PAUL, REGENT OF YUGOSLAVIA,
AND HIS SON, PRINCE ALEXANDER

of the regime and he could not tolerate critics. For that
reason the name of Zhivkovich was not mentioned in
the testament which he signed at Bled. It was a peculiar
disposition of power. To the name of Prince Paul he
added the names of Dr. Stankovich and Ivo Perovich,
the governor, at whose palace he had stayed at Zagreb.
General Tomich, commandant of the Belgrade garrison,
was named in reserve, in case one of the three Regents
should die before the heir came of age. It amounted
to giving the whole of the royal prerogative in trust to
his cousin. The other men had not sufficient weight to
outbalance him on any important question. Alexander
seems to have given but little thought to the question
of who were to be the other Regents assisting Prince
Paul. He had seen much of Perovich during his stay in
Zagreb and the name was uppermost in his mind. Dr.
Stankovich was a heart specialist and Minister of Education, otherwise only a friend. They were named as a
formality to spare his cousin the responsibility of having
to act alone. The testament was a secret document. It
came as a surprise to everyone but Prince Paul when it
became known after the King's death.

Nine months after these deliberations at Bled the
attempt on the King's life was repeated. And it was
organized by the same persons who sent Oreb to Zagreb
to kill him. December, 1933, Zagreb! October, 1934,
Marseilles! Much was said, after the event, of the
King's prescience, of his presentiment of the ultimate
tragedy. But if Alexander did have foreknowledge it
did not weigh upon his mind. He did not behave like
a doomed man. His life in 1934 was one of great energy
and freedom of action. He had made the provision for
the regency merely as a wise precaution.

In March, 1934, the trial of Oreb, Begovich, and

Pogorelats caused a sensation in Yugoslavia though not much attention was directed to it by the foreign press. The news agencies working through Vienna rendered Oreb's revelations as colorless as possible. It was hinted that the confession was obtained by torture and was not a free admission. Yugoslavia might have done more to seize the opportunity to impress European public opinion. No representations were made at Geneva regarding the Italian camps. Yugoslavia, with undue modesty, was unwilling to air her grievances against an influential fellow member of the League. Instead Yevtich sent a very full *aide mémoire* to the Yugoslav Ministers in London, Paris, Rome, and Geneva. There were official representations but the result was negligible. France at that time wanted to get to an understanding with Italy. Britain was also sympathetic to Italy. Italy was a lively guarantor of the independence of Austria which was a matter of first importance in London. In July the Nazis murdered Dollfuss and made an abortive attempt to seize the government of Vienna. Italy made a partial mobilization. She stood as a bulwark of Central European peace, and the powers were not willing to offend her. Mussolini was annoyed by Pavelich's failure but he would not break with him, would not expel him from the country, or dissolve his organization. Yet Borgotaro had come too much into the light. The men in that camp were ordered moved to other camps. Some of them were sent as far away as the Lipari Isles in the Mediterranean.

and condemned to life imprisonment. In prison he knew that there were those outside the prison walls who were working for him and he was not in the least surprised when in the following year he was set free.

One day he was a "lifer" wearing the striped prison garb, the next he was strolling in ordinary attire in the streets of Sofia as if nothing had happened. Though he never earned a penny by honest toil, there was always plenty of money for him. Mikhailov saw to that. He was in clover, dined at the best resorts, and had expensive mistresses. But he was watchful, because Nahum Tomalevsky had belonged to a faction only less powerful than Mikhailov's band. And the man he had murdered in the previous year had relatives. There is such a thing as the blood feud in Bulgaria, wherein it is laid upon the nearest of kin of a murdered man to take revenge. Blood must be paid for with blood.

Nahum Tomalevsky had a brother who belonged to the Danobist sect, a fraternity which abjured the taking of life. Vlada the Chauffeur traced him to the meeting place of the sect. To the surprise of the Danobist brotherhood the well-known murderer began to visit them. They were vegetarians and their pastor enjoined them not to destroy the life of man or of beast. It seemed a remarkable conversion, but though willing to receive Vlada the Chauffeur, the pastor considered that he ought to express public repentance for his life before joining them. The secretary said to him: "We know you to be a murderer. Are you sorry for the murders you have committed?" Vlada the Chauffeur said, "No." He had done as he was told for political reasons. He did not consider himself a criminal. The secretary said he must go away and not come back till he had repented of his murders, for the members of the cult were sworn never to take human life. Vlada the Chauffeur said he was glad of that. Tomalevsky's brother was a member, was he not? If he could be assured that there was no danger to him from that quarter that was all he wanted from them.

Pavelich and Perchets were interested in the man who had killed their old acquaintance, Tomalevsky. They shed no tears over the Bulgarian journalist. Perhaps they even rejoiced at his removal. Such a man having parted company with Mikhailov and entered upon more legitimate political activity might some time or other go to Belgrade and betray valuable secrets. Tomalevsky had paid the penalty of instability. But when a man had to be killed in Bulgaria the executioners made no mistake. Vlada the Chauffeur was the sort of man who could be of real service to Pavelich. He was more reliable than the Croats. There was some correspondence and the Macedonian Organization agreed to lend their assassin to Pavelich.

Vlada the Chauffeur disappeared from the streets of Sofia and was not seen again in the cafés. He had been married twice, once divorced: his wives never saw him again. Katia, his mistress at the time, never heard from him. The police lost track of him and yet he was not registered as having passed the frontier. It is probable that he departed with a false passport. In any case he turned up in Budapest in the summer of 1933, in the company of one of Mikhailov's henchmen, Cyril Drangov.

He was sent to Yanka Pusta and then to Italy. Little is known of his movements abroad and his activities until he was deputed to go to Marseilles. He must have lived rather idly. He was used to a free and profligate existence and could not be bullied or placed under severe discipline. At the trial at Aix-en-Provence he was described as Pavelich's bodyguard. Pospishil was certainly the bodyguard of Perchets, but Perchets was in danger because there had been disaffection in the Hungarian camp. Pavelich lived a much more secure existence than Perchets and it is not likely that he used Vlada the Chauffeur for his personal protection. The Serbs, especially after the Oreb revelations, might well have sent some men to kidnap or murder Pavelich. That would have been the Russian method of dealing with him; but, unlike the Russians, the Serbs will never venture on violence outside the limits of their territorial jurisdiction.

While Vlada the Chauffeur was in Italy the possibility of his returning to Bulgaria was destroyed. The Macedonian Revolutionary Organization was dissolved. The Mushanov ministry, which seemed to exist on the sufferance of the Macedonian Organization, fell as a result of the *coup d'état* of May 19, 1934. Georgiev, the new Premier, proclaimed the Macedonian Organization illegal and the army and police were given the task of rounding up the members and confiscating all arms in their possession. Many known to have been concerned in political murders were arrested and a warrant was issued for Vlada the Chauffeur. He was enrolled in the books of the organization as Vlada Georgiev Chernozemsky. He was not wanted for the murder of Nahum Tomalevsky, for which he had already been tried, sentenced, and amnestied. He was wanted for the murder of Christo Traikov, a Communist deputy whom Vlada the Chauffeur, with two others, had set upon in January, 1933, and also for an attack upon another man in March.

When the warrant was issued for his arrest, and the

society which paid him disbanded, Pavelich had a stronger hold upon him. He was a man without a country. His means of support had been cut off and he was absolutely dependent upon his new master. When he was chosen to kill the King he had but little choice of action.

Yugoslavia was pleased with the turn of events in Bulgaria. The Macedonian Revolutionary Organization had some time since ceased to send armed bands into Yugoslav territory, but it was a very strong organization influencing the policy of governments and it was hostile to the Serbs. It had stood in the way of *rapprochement*, perpetuating the national blood feud. The organization, founded in Salonika in 1893, antedated most disputes between Serbia and Bulgaria. Its original object had been to secure an independent Macedonian state and it had been as much directed against Bulgarian territorial ambitions as against those of Serbia. It developed on Bulgarian soil after the Great War to become a powerful terrorist organization, holding successive governments in thrall. It ceased to be possible for responsible ministers to dissociate themselves from the outrages committed in the name of Macedonia. Peace between Serbs and Bulgars was frequently jeopardized. The frontier was closed to raiding parties and Serb troops were massed there for war. Matters were made worse when the organization yielded to the intrigues of potential enemies of Yugoslavia—Italy and Hungary—and drew funds and direction from Fascist quarters.

But with Kimon Georgiev in power the whole situation changed. What is called "Macedonianism" was liquidated. The Bulgars became ready to waive their pretensions to "liberate" the Macedonians in Yugoslavia and elsewhere and the hatchet was buried. There was a mass meeting of Bulgars and Serbs in Belgrade, met to celebrate the prospects of friendship. Sofia newspapers began to explore the possibilities of alliance. King Alexander decided to make a state visit to the Bulgarian capital in September, 1933.

Bulgaria was excited. When, on July 12, Georgiev engaged the Royal Cinema Theatre in Sofia for a popular meeting to review Bulgaria's position there was scant room for the masses who wished to hear him. He gave orders that all citizens possessing radios must place them on the window sills of their houses and set them going at full blast so that all the people in the streets might hear his speech. The whole of Sofia barked with the voice of Kimon Georgiev. "Folk," said he, "I now turn one of the most somber and scandalous pages of our recent past. Recall how certain persons and groups of men have raised themselves above the law of the land! In extensive regions of Bulgaria the authority of the state was no more than a fiction. We have emerged from an era when foreign policy which ought to be conducted exclusively by the government was dependent upon frontier incidents. There were times when these incidents endangered the security of Bulgaria. . . . Recall the dead lying in the streets of Sofia and of provincial cities, the outrages with machine guns and infernal machines! Veritable battles took place in the very center of the capital, some few hundred yards from the Parliament House and in front of the gates of the royal palace. Bulgarian citizens were kidnapped from the capital and the government was powerless to obtain their release. . . . This lamentable state of affairs necessitated the decree contained in paragraph 14 of the manifesto of May 19, in applying which the government undertook the reëstablishment of the sovereignty of the state in the entire territory of this realm by dissolving the Macedonian Revolutionary Organization. The Ministry of the Interior seized the arms of this organization and the number of the weapons thus seized provoked general astonishment. The figures were: 637 revolvers; 15 automatic rifles; 3 grenades; 7,767 bombs; 10,938 rifles (now more than 11,000); 47 machine guns; 701,388 cartridges. . . . These figures of the armament of the Macedonian Revolutionary Organization, if we take into consideration the text adopted by the various Balkan States and others in the pacts which have been signed, wherein the London definition of an aggressor occupies an important place, demonstrate the dangers to which the Bulgarian state was exposed."

The resolute action of the new government entailed the complete failure of the Italian plans in Bulgaria. The amount of money wasted by such a great commercial nation as the Italians in an utterly unprofitable adventure is a paradox of history. Had Fascism been a limited-liability company it must long since have gone into liquidation. What did go into liquidation in 1934 was the Italian policy in the Balkans. Bulgaria was liberated from foreign intrigue and became ready to align herself with the Little Entente and the Left side in European politics. A fortnight after Georgiev's great speech in the Royal Cinema, Bulgaria recognized Soviet Russia. Yugoslavia had agreed to recognize Moscow. Russia, even Red Russia, must stand behind the Balkan Slavs as of yore.

The visit of Alexander and Marie to the Bulgarian capital in September, 1934, a month before he was murdered in Marseilles, was a brilliant success. The recep-

tion was not merely formal and official, but national.
A miracle seemed to have been accomplished. The Bulgars were won over. The Serbs shook hands with them
again. All Europe was impressed by the event. This
seemed the greatest achievement of Alexander, apart
from the exploits of war. He had made his name as a
man of peace.

But Fate lurked in the background. Warrants were
out for the arrest of all the more dangerous assassins of
the Macedonian Organization. The arch enemy, Ivan
Mikhailov, who fled to Asia Minor, was promptly arrested by the orders of Kemal, but a more dangerous
gangster was lodged in the security of Italy. The where-
abouts of Vlada the Chauffeur, lent to Pavelich, was
completely unknown to the police.

In the year 1934 murder as a political means was in
vogue. On June 30 Adolf Hitler took the short way in
dealing with Roehm and General Schleicher. On July
27 the Austrian Nazis murdered Chancellor Dollfuss.
In October Alexander was assassinated.

The Yugoslavs were not greatly shocked by the death
of Dollfuss. If they were sorry for the man they were
not particularly sorry for the state. No very friendly
relations ever prevailed between Vienna and Belgrade.
The more cultured capital had nothing to teach the
more uncouth Balkan city. The way Socialists and Lib-
erals were shot down and the workingmen's community
houses besieged did not hold up an example of enlightened democracy. Indeed Yugoslav politics were
far less bloody and brutal than Austrian politics. And
then Vienna was a center of intrigue, much of it directed against Yugoslavia. The government was venal,
supported by foreign loans and loans to pay back loans.
Added to that there were Italian money and subsidies to

politicians and groups. No one could tell what plot against the peace of the Balkans was being hatched in Vienna, what the adherents of the Hapsburgs were planning, what Perchevich and his confederates were conspiring. The ill will against Yugoslavia was manifest in the damaging news circulated from Vienna.

The Germans seemed more easy to understand and there was the admiration of one fighting people for another. The rise of Hitler did not alarm Alexander. He liked a man who was direct and knew his own mind. And the Germans did not approve the cowardly campaign of terrorism connived at by Vienna. They stopped the activities of Pavelich's agents in Germany. Serbs and Germans understood one another. In May, 1934, they signed a commercial treaty. Goering came to Belgrade shortly afterwards and visited Yevtich, expressing Germany's wish that Yugoslavia should become united and powerful.

King Alexander was asked whether it meant that Yugoslavia was thinking of deserting France. He said he would always remain loyal to his allies. His less strained relationship with Germany held nothing incompatible with friendship with France. That was true. France was considered to have done but little for Serbia after the war, but the King never wavered in his sentimental devotion to the country for which his father had fought in 1870, to the France he had been brought up to admire. In a way, Alexander, always reading the French classics, lived with the French. He had become almost French. It is characteristic of the French that they will take help where they can find it. They are logical. The Serbs also are logical, perhaps not so much so, but Alexander saw that there was some profit in having an understanding with Germany, the more so as at that time the Nazis did not see eye to eye with the Italians as regards the future of Austria. Hitler was laying claim to rule every German minority in the world and there was a minority under Italian rule.

The Nazi *coup d'état* in Austria in July, 1934, failed. It was not merely the murder of Chancellor Dollfuss that had been contemplated, but an armed rising and the seizure of the power of the state with a view to uniting with Germany. It got little further than the temporary conquest of the radio station of Vienna. The Nazi armed bands overestimated their strength and the support that might be forthcoming from Germany. Italy moved forces to the Brenner and was prepared to occupy Vienna. There ensued a speedy flight of the conspirators over the Yugoslav frontier, over the German frontier. The Yugoslavs interned the rebels on their territory but treated them hospitably. It would be a mistake to imagine that King Alexander was ready to coöperate with Mussolini on that occasion or that the Duce required his help. That was not a basis for reconciliation as some French writers assert. In 1934 it was not possible to come to terms with Italy unless the hired assassins were first expelled from Italian territory.

CHAPTER XIV

LOUIS BARTHOU

IF among his letters Alexander noticed an envelope that obviously contained a bookseller's catalogue he would generally open that at once. Pencil in hand he would scan the lists of old books. He collected rare French books and unique bindings and, in addition, bought books about his own country or the Balkan campaigns. The arrival of book packets at the palace was a joyous event. Queen Marie says the pleasure of acquisition was greater than the pleasure of reading. Her Majesty cleared out hundreds of books after his death and presented them to clubs. There was too great an accumulation of volumes at the palace. King Alexander did not employ a librarian and his collection was not catalogued during his reign. On a small stepladder, in dressing gown and pyjamas, he might sometimes be found by his Court Marshal, putting books in their right places or searching for some volume he wished to consult. He knew all his books but could not tolerate anyone else meddling with them. During the war the King's eyesight became weak and he made it worse by much reading of old texts.

The King said to the Queen: "You are happy, you can always find something to do with your hands in your spare time, whereas I can only read." That was true. He had few other recreations, never went to the theater or cinema, and although he had an ear for music he did not go to concerts.

One may judge of the King's taste and character by his library. There is nothing vulgar or indecent there, not a volume one needs to hide from children. There is little that is modern except books on Yugoslavia. Some interviewers from America were scandalized to find him reading Alfred de Musset and Racine instead of the latest successes of the Western world. He liked the formal and the classical, he did not care for humor, and he had no interest in scandal or in the difficulties of modern bourgeois marriage. But he liked modern books on natural science, read Henri Fabre aloud, and sometimes translated bits for his children and for Dimitrievich. He was a good reader and also a born *raconteur*. It seems he had a gift for military description and fascinated his entourage when he began telling of curious happenings in his campaigns or describing scenes in the Great War, such as those of the retreat through Albania. But like most Serbs he had no literary gift. He had a royal style of writing which was excellent but he had little flexibility of diction.

Visitors to the palace seemed to find the models of guns in the reception hall more significant than the books. But these models were merely presents from arms contractors desirous of obtaining orders. The books were bought from the private purse. The King had come to have more interest in books than in guns.

When the French government announced that the Foreign Minister, M. Louis Barthou, would visit Belgrade the King was delighted, not so much to be able to converse with him about policy as to exchange news about rare books. Louis Barthou, aged seventy-two, was a dear old grandfatherly person whom it was pleasant to receive. Alexander had met him before. They had corresponded, but mainly about books. Barthou had a very fine collection, better than that of the King, and was an enthusiastic bibliophile. In June, 1934, the plaudits of the populace faded into a rich bookish peace when Barthou entered the King's library at Dedinje. The conversation which took place had little to do with wars and pacts and understandings. It was of rare and curious volumes and, as a journalist put it, it was "heavily documented."

It is true that with his own hands, there in the library, the King decorated the old statesman with the Order of the White Eagle. But he also presented him with a very rare volume of Racine, and one can be quite sure which of these things the Frenchman valued most.

Barthou had not seen the royal collection before and must have been agreeably impressed by the serried ranks of French books, some in their original covers but many in luxurious and glittering bindings. The King was a connoisseur of bindings also and there were many fine specimens of French workmanship. No one who surveyed this library could doubt the King's devotion to France, and Barthou was impressed. Of all the countries he had visited on this summer mission of 1934, Yugoslavia seemed the most friendly to France.

He was concluding a tour of the capitals of the Eastern states whose destiny since the conclusion of peace had been linked with the support of France. Of these visits the one to Warsaw had been the least satisfactory. Poland had so far abandoned traditional policy as to conclude a pact of friendship with Germany. Poland also shared the Nazi hate of Bolshevism and would have nothing to do with a grouping of the powers of the Little Entente and the Balkan Pact with France if supported by Russia. The racial enmity of the Poles toward the Russians blinded them to the fact that the

Germans were the more dangerous enemies. The vanity of this nation never permits it to think that it is not a great power. It coöperates with the Germans as with equals and imagines the Teutons would value its military efforts against the Muscovites.

Prague, Bucharest, and Belgrade had no reserve in their welcome. There were great demonstrations. France could still feel the strength of her safeguarding alliances. But Czechs, Rumanians, and Yugoslavs also needed reassurance from France. Barthou's object was to give moral support and make it plain that France did not overlook the value of the little countries. That the visit did give moral support to the Little Entente is shown by the fact that his journey was resented in Hungary. There were violent demonstrations against Barthou at Budapest and when he passed through the city special police precautions had to be taken for his safety. Hungary was restively biding her time, awaiting the day when the Little Entente would be weakened and left unsupported by France, waiting to recover, with or without Italy's help, her lost territory.

Barthou was a quiet and benevolent old man. There was no fire left in him. He did not get excited by any welcome he received. There was a special session of the Yugoslav Parliament in his honor. Many members of parliament wore national costume. Barthou was invited to address the house from the benches of the ministry. He assumed that most members of foreign legislatures understood French, but there could not have been a great many who could follow him. In any case the speech was not electrifying. The impression that France was still supporting Yugoslavia was enough for Belgrade.

He was taken to view the impressive memorial to

KING ALEXANDER AND LOUIS BARTHOU

France done by Mestrovich, the only memorable monument in Belgrade and set in a place which dominates
the pleasure garden of Kalemegdan. And of course he
was taken to Avala to place a wreath upon the grave of
the Serbian Unknown Warrior. But there is no Arc de
Triomphe in Belgrade. The Serbs have placed their
unknown warrior on probably the highest point within
ten miles of the city, at the top of a steep and densely
forested hill. A visit to the shrine is an expedition into
the country. In choosing this eminence the Serbs seemed
to say: "We are a mountain people; do not seek to find
the meaning of Serbia in any city!"

It is difficult for the French to make contact in Yugoslavia. The country is not genteel. There are few shops
worth looking at. There is no fashion in the streets. In
the cities the women seem barely one stage removed
from peasants and are not adventurous in their behavior. There are no music halls. In the cafés there are
wildly painted gipsy girls who bellow forth oriental
songs too barbarous for a Frenchman's ears. In the few
bars there are Viennese and Hungarian girls, but they
have merely come to make a living out of tourists and
commercial travelers. They have little in common with
the Yugoslavs. In the houses of the people there is a
bare simplicity, no luxury. There are no millionaires,
no really rich people. There are few large country
houses and estates.

There are, in short, none of the trappings of a great
country and it is difficult for a Parisian to believe that
he has come to a place other than obscure. There has
recently been a decrease in the numbers of those who
speak French tolerably. Barthou stayed at a hotel in
the midst of Belgrade but he never heard anyone talking French in the streets of the city. He was not at

home. He was only at home with the King in the palace at Dedinje. It is the experience of most visiting Frenchmen. They may profess undying friendship, but they cannot grasp Yugoslavia. It means nothing more to them than a military force which might be at some time at their disposal.

On June 25 there was a grand luncheon for Barthou at the palace at Dedinje. Not only was the King present but his cousin, Prince Paul, and most members of the government and the Yugoslav Minister in Paris. In the course of that luncheon Barthou turned playfully to King Alexander and said: "Won't your Majesty come to Paris? Promise me you will!"

King Alexander replied good-humoredly: "I promise. I'll come to Paris to see you."

So lightly was the fatal meeting in France first mentioned and promised. Who could have guessed that in this pleasant interchange over lunch the two men were making a rendezvous with death? The King said: "I have long wished to visit a certain bookshop in Paris. I think the proprietor has something I want, but I cannot be sure from the description he sends me." He hoped to snatch a happy half hour rummaging in an old bookshop.

Thinking of old books, dim light, and faded print, King Alexander was reminded of another matter. His eyesight was degenerating rapidly and he was in a wretched state. Without spectacles he looked and felt like a blind man. He would use the opportunity of going abroad to visit his oculist at Lausanne. He did not trust his eyes to any oculist in Belgrade. He could stop at Lausanne on his way home from France.

Barthou was pleased with his achievement. To have obtained the King's promise was a diplomatic success.

He improved the occasion by divulging further plans for the future. At the beginning of the following month it was his intention to go to London. He undertook to explain to Sir John Simon the entirely pacific nature of King Alexander's policy. Great Britain seemed to look upon the new Balkan Pact with some suspicion and there were some who imagined that the Balkan States were again becoming aggressive. England was incurably suspicious of the Balkans, seeing that the Great War started out of Balkan intrigue and violence. Britain must come to understand both the Little Entente and the Balkan Pact as insurance against war. Barthou used a new phrase. He spoke of an Eastern Locarno. He thought the Little Entente and the Balkan Pact could be unified and that both Hitler and Mussolini could be persuaded to join in one comprehensive understanding for peace. If Hitler refused, Russia must be brought in despite Poland's obduracy. The old man had pactomania very badly. He wanted also a Mediterranean pact with France, Britain, Italy, and Yugoslavia.

One thing was very clear both to King Alexander and Yevtich. France was now concerned to come to terms with Italy. Why? The French could hardly fear a war with Italy. Italy still nursed the grievance that she had been cheated in the peace settlement after the Great War. But in 1934 she was not in a position to fight France. She was not on the best of terms with Nazi Germany and was watching jealously over the independence of Austria. She had no friends in Europe. But France perhaps foresaw the possibility of the two Fascist Powers coming together and wished to forestall it. Paris, equally with London, desired to see the appeasement of all conflicting interests in Europe.

After visiting London Barthou planned to visit Rome, but that would not be until the autumn; better after Alexander's visit to Paris. Alexander had promised to go to Sofia in September. October would be the best month for the King of Yugoslavia. Barthou noted November for Rome. He was going to Italy to try to obtain a complete settlement of all outstanding questions dividing the interests of Italy and France and then to propose an Eastern Locarno. He would go to Mussolini cap in hand. For the Duce flattered himself that he was going to be the arbiter of European destinies. "Let the nations come to me and arrange their future history!" The French in 1934 were approaching him rather too humbly, as if they had not the power to arrange terms as equals. When eventually Laval went to Rome in place of Barthou, who had been killed, he was received with deliberate coldness and the coldness endured until he had agreed to all the Duce required of him and France.

Incidentally, Barthou was desirous that the friction between Italy and Yugoslavia should be removed. France wanted peace with Italy and naturally did not wish to have to support her ally, Yugoslavia, should war break out between them. Alexander said he was far from desiring conflict with Italy, but if war broke out he was prepared. If Barthou could make peace between Yugoslavia and Italy the King would be pleased and grateful. But Barthou would have to persuade Italy to dissolve the armed camps and expel the terrorists from her territory. Barthou promised to raise the question of the relationship with Yugoslavia. They would discuss that again when the King arrived in France.

That the French had held a brief for Yugoslavia at Rome is clear. What Barthou would have done one

cannot say. He was a greater statesman than Laval
and more farsighted; he understood that in any ar-
rangement with Italy he must carry the interests of
those Eastern Powers who were at one with France in
a system of mutual support. In the upshot Laval did
nothing. When the Yugoslav Premier, Stoyadinovich,
asked him what he had been able to do for Yugoslav
interests, he replied, "We have done what we could.
We have come to an understanding with Italy." That
was all!

No word concerning the King's promised visit to Paris
was made public in the summer of 1934, though the
news must have been whispered because the promise
was made in the presence of a considerable number of
men. And little said to a Frenchman remains a secret
for long. But nothing had been definitely arranged.
There was some correspondence between Paris and Belgrade and it was not until September that an official
announcement was made.

The idea of the visit developed in the King's mind.
During the previous year he had unveiled a monument to the Greeks who had died on the Salonika front
in the war. His mind had been occupied with thoughts
of the soldiers of other nationalities. He would have
preferred to be honoring the French rather than the
Greeks whose share in the effort for victory had been
less great. He recalled a promise he had made to a
delegation of the *Poilus d'Orient* that he would one day
lay a wreath upon their monument at Marseilles.

It may seem evidence of an untidy mind that he
should not devote himself exclusively to his mission of
peace, but fit in a visit to his oculist, a visit to his bookseller, and a provincial function at Marseilles. But he
seldom had the opportunity of going abroad.

There was another consideration which weighed with him. He had found his warship, the *Dubrovnik*, very useful. It had enabled him to travel to Varna, Stambul, and Corfu during the previous year in comfort and with dignity. The most dignified way to arrive in France would be on a Yugoslav destroyer. It would indicate Yugoslavia as a sea power with pretensions to be included in a Mediterranean pact should Barthou prove successful. The Serbs are very proud of the fact that they are established on the Adriatic. At that time they had the words "Guard Our Sea" printed on most matchboxes. They had begun to talk of their fleet, though it amounted merely to the destroyer and a few small coastal vessels. By going on the *Dubrovnik* direct to Marseilles the King would not set foot on any intervening soil between France and Yugoslavia. The voyage would be a symbol of union.

But the French government was not very enthusiastic about the Marseilles plan. Paris ought to have the privilege of seeing the King first. To visit the commercial undistinguished port of Marseilles before the capital was undramatic and it would be a drawback having the Marseilles reception reported in the newspapers before the Paris reception. Moreover, Marseilles, swarming with the people of all nations, haunt of bandits and men wanted by the police, was not safe. The problem of guarding the King's person there was problematic. But when Alexander resolved on any course of action it was not easy to dissuade him. He was set on arriving in France at Marseilles. Barthou promised that he would be there on the quay to welcome him.

Shortly after M. Barthou's visit to Belgrade he was condemned to death by Pavelich. At least it was an-

nounced in one of Pavelich's newspapers that he and
the King were condemned. But that was long before it
was known that they would drive side by side in the
same car in Marseilles. Barthou was to be killed because
he was supporting the policy of King Alexander. Later,
at the murder trial at Aix-en-Provence, the president of
the court naturally called attention to this condemnation. Counsel for the defense was unable to make out
a strong case for his theory that the killing of Barthou
was unpremeditated. Nevertheless, it was probably an
accident. Vlada the Chauffeur had it in his power to
kill Barthou, but he only incapacitated him. He shot
him in the right arm. It was not a mortal wound and
had the Frenchman received prompt and efficient attention he would have walked out from the hospital a
few hours after the tragedy with his arm in a sling.
There is a theory that he was deliberately allowed to
bleed to death in Marseilles, but one can hardly credit
that.

However, Barthou's strengthening of the influence
of the Little Entente and support of Alexander had
made him powerful enemies. It was reported after his
visit to England in the previous July that revisionism
in London had lost ground. Following upon his visit
Sir John Simon publicly approved the Balkan Pact.
Alexander's enemies in Europe were Barthou's enemies.
There were no tears shed for him in Hungary and Italy.
His removal made it easier for Italy to bind France in
a dangerous agreement to passivity.

Three days after Barthou arrived back in Paris the
world was astonished by the Nazi murders. These were
so sensational that it was said the date, June 30, 1934,
would be forever remembered in history. Barthou's
peaceful mission to the Little Entente became a pale,

colorless event beside the fierce actuality of the new Europe that was coming into being, achieved by violence and founded on brute force.

There had been a conspiracy against Hitler. Its object has never been revealed, but one may surmise that it was the seizure of power in Germany. The leaders were accused of unnatural vice, but abhorrence of that could hardly have been enough to provoke the great leader to fly to Munich and shoot Roehm with his own hand. Roehm had been a right-hand man of Hitler. In the previous year he had been upon a mission to Yugoslavia feeling the way to an understanding between the two powers. Rumor has it that he was secretly received by Alexander. He was, in any case, a man of considerable significance, a potential leader. The murder of General Schleicher at breakfast with his wife was even more shocking, and unnatural vice could not be urged against him, nor against Von Papen who was held to be implicated in the conspiracy and was also in great danger.

Less than a month after this emerged another date which it was said would forever be remembered in history, July 25, 1934, when Dollfuss was murdered by the Nazis in Vienna. Previous to the murder there had been a terror in Austria partially hidden by press censorship, over a hundred acts of violence every month, most of them perpetrated by the Nazis.

The methods by which the Nazis intended to gain power and rule occupied men's minds for a space to the exclusion of other political interests. Within ten days of the murder of Dollfuss the ancient and ultrarespectable Field Marshal and President, Hindenburg, died and Adolf Hitler became the supreme dictator of the *Reich*.

The next date which was to be forever remembered in history was October 9, 1934, when King Alexander and M. Louis Barthou were assassinated at Marseilles; but from repeated bludgeonings Europe was becoming gradually insensitive and dazed. These great events soon became dim, half-forgotten tragedies. Other dreadful spectacles froze the imagination of civilized men, the destruction in succession of four members of the League of Nations, Abyssinia, Spain, China, Austria. The murder of nations followed the murder of men.

CHAPTER XV

HOW THE NEWS CAME TO BELGRADE

THE news was delayed. The evening newspaper in Belgrade on October 9 published an account of the King's disembarkation at Marseilles, the tremendous reception. It told how he had placed a wreath upon the memorial of the *Poilus d'Orient*, a reconstruction of an event which never took place. According to this paper, the only evening sheet in the Yugoslav capital, all had passed off happily in Marseilles and the King had left the city by train and joined the Queen at Dijon.

The people of Belgrade went about their ordinary occupations. There was the usual evening promenade on the Knez Mikhailova, a feature of the city, flocks of young folk chattering, laughing, flirting. The shops were open, café and restaurant life in full swing. There was one peculiar circumstance. Those who were sitting at home listening to their radios were surprised when the broadcasting program stopped in the middle of a song. They thought the wireless was out of order. They switched on to Zagreb and then to Ljubljana. Both were dead. But no announcement of the catastrophe was made on the radio. Foreign stations were bleating the news all over Europe but Yugoslavs do not care much for foreign programs and the majority do not understand foreign languages. It was late in the night before the baleful rumor spread.

People set off for the theater and found that it was closed, but there was no notice, no official explanation.

Among those on their way to the theater about a quarter to eight was General Zhivkovich. Someone overtook him with an urgent message. Would he repair at once to the Ministry of the Court? He was rather annoyed that he would be made late for the play. But at the office of the Minister of the Court he was put through by telephone to Prince Paul.

A low agitated voice said: "Peter, the King is dead. . . . Come at once to the palace!"

The news was withheld from the public and especially from the army lest it should prove the signal for disorder. Had it become known to everyone there would have been instant, uncontrollable agitation and possibly martial law and military dictatorship before the night was through. The Prime Minister, Uzunovich, had wireless reports but obtusely refused to give them credence. Paris was sensational and contradictory and he had little understanding of the French language. Rome blared information, which might be invented in order to cause a rising, and he did not know Italian. He told the Home Secretary that he believed it was a radio plot, and he ordered all stations to close down. About five o'clock he was told that Marseilles wanted him on the phone. "Now the plot thickens," said Uzunovich knowingly. He was entirely calm and unperturbed.

"This is Yevtich speaking from the Prefecture at Marseilles. I am sorry to inform you that his Majesty . . ."

Uzunovich chuckled and rang off.

The telephone bell buzzed insistently again but the Premier would not take up the receiver. The voice had been extremely clear but not quite the voice of Yevtich. It might very well be some charlatan speaking from Zagreb.

Half an hour later the telephone called him again. "This is Yevtich speaking from the Prefecture at Marseilles . . ."

"What, again? Well, what is your first name? Bogoljub . . . you've got that right. What was your wife's maiden name? Hm . . . what are the first names of your uncles? Yes. You seem to have made some study of Boshko Yevtich. But I don't believe you. You are an intriguer and you had better get off the line as you are obstructing other calls which may be important." He rang off, but Yevtich tried again and this time used Dimitrievich and other Serbs at Marseilles to convince the Prime Minister that it was indeed his Foreign Secretary who had been trying to give him a report, the most important imaginable.

Then Uzunovich allowed himself to be convinced and heard all that Yevtich had to say. It is difficult to credit the Premier with being as dense as he appeared. He was a longheaded but opinionated politician, always a schemer. It is just possible that he deliberately postponed hearing official confirmation of the news and that he required time for the maturing of certain plans. He did not inform either Prince Paul or Zhivkovich. But he closed all theaters and cinemas and he forbade the newspapers to issue special editions. The police were instructed to disperse any gatherings of people in the streets, but there were none.

Prince Paul was at his residence at Dedinje. As he had no official position, news telegrams were not forwarded to him. The Premier never asked his advice and the only official likely to get in touch with him, Antich, the Minister of the Court, had accompanied the Queen to France. His wireless was not working.

When he switched it on he had already missed the first reports. But then he was already agitated because he had had a telephone call from Dimitrievich who, unknown to Yevtich, had got in first with the news. The Court Marshal said there had been an attempt on the life of the sovereign. He was trying to break it gently and did not say that Alexander was already dead. He appeared to be too nervous to give more than a garbled account of what had happened. He must have bewildered the Prince with confused protestations of his grief.

"You say the King is now in the hands of the doctors? Very well, telephone me again directly a bulletin is issued."

There was a prolonged period of silence. Prince Paul sat watching the silent telephone which held the secret of destiny. At length Dimitrievich telephoned again. I give the Prince Regent's words describing his reception of the second message. "The general telephoned, 'The King is . . .' he waited '. . . dead.' I did not stop to hear any more. I hung up the receiver and took the necessary measures."

Prince Paul could see the empty royal palace from his windows; it was but a few minutes' walk. He strode out and went at once to the King's residence. The sentries saluted and let him pass. He hastened to the library, for the copies of Alexander's testament must be found at once, and acted upon. The regency must be proclaimed before midnight. His cousin had said that if he died the Prince would find the documents in the library. That was all. He had not said where. There was no safe. Cabinets, drawers, files, booksellers' catalogues, state correspondence, private letters, bills—the

distraught Prince rummaged a long while alone. At
length he found the two solid envelopes, sealed with the
arms of Yugoslavia, one addressed to the President of
the State Council, the other to the Queen. They had
been placed on a bookshelf between two volumes of
Molière.

Prince Paul then summoned three generals, two to
do his bidding and the third, General Zhivkovich, to
be a witness to the subsequent proceedings.

Paul knew that he was Regent. The whole weight
of responsibility of governing Yugoslavia had fallen
suddenly onto his shoulders. He had ceased to be a
civilian and an outsider and had become the central
personage in the realm. No politician had thought of
him as King's representative, as viceroy or successor. An
unknown quantity in Yugoslavia, not a soldier, never a
Cabinet Minister, not even a provincial governor, the
authority implicit in his person was but slight. He could
not face the government, the army, the people without
documents, with merely the verbal report of the King's
wishes.

The Prince was outwardly calm when General Zhivkovich arrived, more so than Zhivkovich. He had had
time to control his feelings. The presence of the general
was a moral support. But he had little to tell him beyond the bare fact that the King had been murdered.
He had given instructions for all messages from France
to be sent to the palace. Fuller information would arrive
later. "Meanwhile," said Paul, "we must produce the
King's testament," and he moved across to the library
shelves and took the two sealed envelopes from between
the two books. That was where Alexander had left
them. The one addressed to the Queen the Prince put

aside. The other, addressed to the President of the State
Council, the Prime Minister, he placed in the general's
hand. Zhivkovich had ceased to be premier two years
previously and he could not open the sealed envelope.
"This must be opened by Uzunovich . . ."

Prince Paul then sent an urgent message to Uzunovich, but the latter replied that he was busy and could
not come. He was making his own plans and had already summoned the boy King, Peter II, back from
school in England. He had given orders for the body
of Alexander to be conveyed at once to Yugoslavia,
unembalmed. He had become the most important person in the realm and was not taking orders from Prince
Paul. But the Premier was soon visited by an officer of
the royal guard and brought to the royal palace, practically by force. In the presence of Prince Paul and
General Zhivkovich he broke the seal of the envelope
addressed to him.

Uzunovich made no difficulty about recognizing the
authenticity of the signature of King Alexander and
at once signified his acceptance of the King's will. He
bowed to the authority of the Regent and gave instructions that all messages from abroad be conveyed
direct to the palace. Then the three men conferred as
to the form in which the declaration of the regency
should be made known to the public. Telegrams kept
coming in, punctuating their deliberations. "Marseilles
reports that Barthou has succumbed." "Marseilles reports that the King was wounded in two places, in the
stomach and near the heart. He was already dead when
he was examined at the Prefecture. The murderer's
name is given as Peter Kelemen, born in Zagreb in
1899, a shopkeeper. He passed the French frontier at

Vallorbes. . . . The murderer tried to commit suicide but the police prevented him. He was killed by the bullet of a gendarme."

This was followed by a long telephonic communication from Paris which added little except that President Lebrun was leaving for Marseilles. At nine o'clock Paris telephoned: "Her Majesty the Queen was informed by the prefect at Dijon of the tragic death of King Alexander. There are special editions of the newspapers dedicated to King Alexander, to his efforts for peace, and his friendship with France. There is consternation in Paris. The Cabinet has just met. General Georges is dead [incorrect]. The newspapers had been preparing an appeal that King Alexander, as peacemaker of the Balkans, be awarded the Nobel prize for peace. The President of the Republic, M. Lebrun, has sent to the Premier of Yugoslavia, M. Uzunovich, a declaration of his warmest sympathy. And also to the French Minister in Belgrade."

At half-past nine there was a telephonic message from the Yugoslav Minister in Vienna reporting the news being published in the Austrian papers, mostly fallacious. Yugoslavia had ordered the closing of the Austrian frontier. Orders were being given to mobilize troops on the frontiers of Hungary and Italy. The Queen had learned, while on the train journey across Italy, that an attempt would be made on the life of her husband in France. The heir to the throne, Prince Peter, had been recalled from England. News, true and untrue, poured through to the royal palace.

Meanwhile it was decided that all members of the Cabinet then present in Belgrade should at once take oath of allegiance to the new King Peter II, likewise all officers of the army and fleet. In the course of the

night many hundreds took the oath to the young sovereign. The proclamation of the accession of Peter II
was also issued with an official statement regarding the
death of King Alexander and black flags were ordered
to be hung on all public buildings.

All through the night there was a great discreet
activity as if conspirators were moving swiftly and
silently to achieve revolution while the masses slept.
But the object was not revolution but stability. The
assumption of enemies might be that the assassination
meant chaos, separatism, civil war. The resolution of
the government was that there should be disciplined
calm and a dignified acceptance of Fate.

Only in the early morning the newsvendors were
yelling the names of their papers in the streets and
waving their black-bordered sheets. Civilian Belgrade
awakened to its most tragic day. It stared at the proclamation confronting it on the front pages of *Politika*
and *Vreme:*

TO THE YUGOSLAV PEOPLE!

Our great King Alexander has fallen a victim to a treacherous
attempt on his life on October 9, at 4 P.M., at Marseilles.

With his blood the King-Martyr sealed that work of peace
on which he was engaged in allied France.

To the throne of Yugoslavia succeeds his first-born son, His
Majesty Peter II.

The ministry, the army, and the navy have taken the oath of
allegiance to His Majesty Peter II. . . .

GOD SAVE THE KING!

There followed the pent-up flood of news from
France which had been accumulating for more than
twelve hours, the terror-breathing sensational descrip-
tions from Marseilles. There were no comments, no

diatribes, no demands for vengeance, not even criticism of the French. All editorial space was taken by the biographical reviews of the King's reign.

And after reading the terrible news there was no shouting in the streets, no demonstrations of any kind. Only the shopkeepers added their black flags to the many that already hung in every street. The people were dazed and dumbfounded. There may have been some whispers against the Croats but they did not find audible voice. News came from Zagreb that the Croat city was hushed and apprehensive. It seemed that the murderer had been a Croat. All that was known of him was what was given on his forged passport. The assassination had no international aspect on October 10. It was a domestic tragedy, the pitiful culmination of the political differences separating Serb and Croat.

But late on the night of October 9 a Serb journalist had wrung from the prison authorities at Marseilles permission to visit the morgue and look at the corpse of the assassin. On a slab of concrete he stared at the naked body of the murderer, at the hideous face with open mouth and big gold-stopped teeth. It crossed his mind that it was not a Croat face and his opinion was confirmed by the inspection of one of the arms. The arm was tattooed with the sign of the skull and crossbones, under which were written the words "Liberty or Death," in Bulgarian. There were also the initials of the Macedonian Revolutionary Organization, I.M.R.O.

No comment was allowed on this discovery, as it was not thought desirable to throw any of the blame upon friendly Bulgaria. What King Alexander had wrought in reconciliating Serbs and Bulgars was considered too precious to be endangered by any rash accusation of complicity in the murder. It was characteristic of the new spirit in the Balkans that not one word was breathed against Bulgaria.

All day messages of sympathy arrived from the heads of states throughout the world. Among the first to express his grief was Adolf Hitler. The Germans were spontaneous in their sympathy and published in their papers many eulogies of their "ex-enemy." Their attitude made a strong appeal to the Serbs. The Germans were standing by them in their tragic hour. The Serbs are more drawn to the Germans than to any other nation and the way the Nazis did honor to the dead king made possible the closer political connection of later years. When, in 1938, Hitler overran Austria, the Yugoslavs did not even call a Cabinet meeting. A spokesman of the government publicly rejoiced that Yugoslavia had a nation of seventy-five million friends on its frontier.

Doubt of France was increased when, in response to clamor in Paris, the French Minister of the Interior resigned, an acknowledgment that the police had proved inefficient in safeguarding the person of the King in Marseilles. No messages of sympathy or promises of statues to Alexander could reduce the growing murmur against France in Yugoslavia. Official declarations of unchanged friendly relations have to be discounted. From the assassination of Alexander dates a coldness to France that was both governmental and national.

There were more conventional condolences from Austria and Hungary, but the Serbs did not think these states were very sorry. The death of the King might well be thought to help the cause of revisionism. What must have struck those powers who were hostile to the policy of Yugoslavia was the immensity of the sensation of the murder. It caused at least five times the stir that the murder of Dollfuss had caused. England, France, America, Belgium, remembered the heroic exploits of Serbia in the war and Alexander's great part in them. Yugoslavia, at least in the news, seemed a greater power than she had ever been. The whole postwar press campaign against the Serbs was ruined by the tragedy. No one dared to say that Alexander merely got what was coming to him. No one dared to breathe a word against the dictatorship. The big nations sensed the blow which the little nation had received and most of them gave their moral support. The ranks of the nations supporting the Yugoslavs were closed.

Mussolini saw how the land lay. There was no terror in Zagreb following the murder, no rising of the Croats. The French police were at first completely baffled by the problem of the crime. Mussolini could have given them much information, but he refrained. He sent a grandiloquent telegram to M. Uzunovich:

"The tragic decease of the exalted monarch of Yugoslavia as the victim of such a dastardly attempt has evoked the keen indignation of the Italian nation which shares the feeling of sorrow of the Yugoslav nation. Pray accept, Mr. Prime Minister, the expression of the most lively and profound sympathy of the Fascist power and of myself personally.—Mussolini."

He expressed his sympathy, but British warships moved up the Adriatic almost implying a hint to Italy: "Hands off Dalmatia!"

Mussolini had become more concerned to preserve good relations with France than to become embroiled with Yugoslavia. The Abyssinian invasion would require peace with France. The death of Alexander meant that he had nothing to fear from the other side of the Adriatic. The anti-Italian policy would probably fall to bits. It became important to avoid the blame of complicity in the murder. Fortunately the assassin was dead and could say nothing. No accomplice had been seen at Marseilles. The film pictures seemed to show that the crime was the work of one man, unaided, the deed of some isolated Croat fanatic, or of some mad Bulgarian. The only disconcerting item of news was that Vlada the Chauffeur was found to have been wearing new clothes which had obviously recently been bought at a shop in Paris. The conspirators had not had the sense to remove the tab of the shop *La Belle Jardinière*. That must put the detectives upon the trail of the assassin.

The French police, as if to make up for deficiency before the crime, had become exceedingly active. The frontiers were closed to foreigners trying to escape from France. On the 10th two suspects, Pospishil and Raich, were arrested near the Swiss border. They had come to France from Hungary and their activities did not cast a reflection upon Italy. Kvaternik and Pavelich reached Turin and their doings and correspondence were carefully watched by Fascist agents. Pavelich was not allowed to make any statement about the assassination. Otherwise he might have been tempted to boast that he had at last carried out the threat of execution.

There was no news explaining the murder in the Belgrade newspapers. Editors ought perhaps to have concentrated upon explanation. Instead they published day after day series of sensational photographs. The actual event at Marseilles had been photographed at every angle by the intrepid newsreel men. The public still stared uncomprehendingly at the assassin on the step of the car, at the snaps of confused gendarmes rushing forward and back, at the picture of Yevtich in

top hat running toward the royal car, at the picture of
the prostrate King lying in the car. Added to that,
they had distressing pictures of the little schoolboy,
King Peter II, on the steps of the Yugoslav legation in
London with swarms of people staring at him.

There was the intimation that the King's body had
gone back to the destroyer, the *Dubrovnik*, and was on
its way to Yugoslavia to be buried. More thought of
the coming funeral than of the crime! Whether due
to the complete success of measures to prevent agitation,
or due to national neurosis, the people gave way to
sentiment instead of anger; tears, prayers, and mourn-
ing instead of hotheadedness or fierce demands that the
government find an explanation of the catastrophe and
obtain satisfaction somewhere.

A change in the disposition of the Serbs was noticeable. After the conclusion of the Great War they had
had a tinge of megalomania, but in the course of sixteen
years of nervous peace they had become less sure of
themselves. King Alexander was the last man in Yugoslavia who was able to speak with a clear voice, seem-
ing to know the mind of himself and the nation. After
his death the Serbs were humble, rather confused in
mind and outlook, and inclined to wait upon events
rather than solve any problem by resolute action.

Belgrade was surprised, mollified, dumbfounded by
the honor to the dead, the great personalities of Europe
who followed with bare heads the bier of the hero King:
the President of the French Republic, the redoubtable
Goering, King Carol, the Duke of Kent, Prince Arsène
Karageorgevich, come out of his long exile in Paris,
Beneš, Titulescu, Ruzhdy Aras, Paul Boncour, Marshal
Pétain, Piétri, the Duke of Spoleto, Maximos, and
many other princes, statesmen, and generals accom-

FUNERAL CEREMONIES IN MARSEILLES

THE FUNERAL PROCESSION THROUGH BELGRADE

panied by French troops and marines, by detachments from the armies of the Little Entente, British naval officers and men of the Mediterranean fleet, kilted Greek soldiers and a hundred magnificent Turks from President Kemal's guards, aeroplanes of the nations roaring overhead. The funeral was an emotional experience stronger even than the news of the assassination. The cortege shut off fire like a safety curtain.

The police discipline of the crowds was perhaps a lesson as to how personalities could be guarded in rustic Belgrade. No chance for anyone to rush forward to use a revolver there. Not one doubtful person known to the police was allowed on the scene. Not a window was allowed to be open on the line of route.

But it was a demonstration of Europe in Belgrade rather than a funeral. For the coffin was not to remain in Belgrade. The dead King still traveled, as if the journey begun on October 4 to Kosovo, Cetinje, Zelenika, Marseilles, then back over the sea to Split, and by rail to Zagreb and Belgrade went on indefinitely. The body returned to Belgrade station and was put on another train for Mladenovats, in Shumadia, where peasants lifted the coffin and carried it to another hearse and again the journey was continued to Oplenats, the final resting place of the Karageorgeviches.

CHAPTER XVI

FERMENT

POSPISHIL and Raich had been arrested at Thonon, near the Lake of Geneva, which they wished clandestinely to cross; Kral at the crossroads beyond the outskirts of the forest of Fontainebleau. The stories they told upon arrest gave a sinister international significance to the crime.

Pospishil and Raich, as has been recounted, were left in the environs of Paris while Vlada the Chauffeur and Mio Kral were taken to Marseilles to make the first attempt on the King's life. Had the first attempt failed, Pospishil and Raich had to make a second attempt upon the occasion of King Alexander's visit to Versailles. Pospishil, who was nicknamed The Dragon, was a redoubtable assassin and had already killed several people in his time. His terrorist activities relate to Hungary, Bulgaria, and Italy. Achievement must have depended on Pospishil, because Raich, like Mio Kral, was not a tried man. But the pair were sufficiently dangerous and there is no reason to think that they would not have carried out the orders of Pavelich.

Their revolvers and bombs, an identical outfit to that which served Vlada the Chauffeur and Mio Kral, had been left in the checkroom of the Gare St. Lazare, in Paris. No need to risk these being discovered in their hotel bedroom. They could recover them when the moment came to act. No manner of suspicion was likely to attach to them. They were registered in their hotel as

Czechs. Their passports, forged in Hungary, showed them to be Czechoslovak subjects, curiously enough born on Italian territory—one at Zara, the other at Gorizia. Pospishil had the name of Novak. Raich had the audacity to take the name of the man who was until recently President of Czechoslovakia. He was Beneš. They had plenty of money and they amused themselves as men on holiday while waiting for news of the crime at Marseilles.

A telegram would arrive for Pospishil in the name of Novak at the post office at Fontainebleau. Failing that, the two men were to keep their eyes open for Kvaternik or Pavelich at the Café de la Paix, in Paris. The Place de l'Opéra was their rendezvous. So many thousands of various nationalities met there every day that no meeting of these conspirators was likely to be remarked.

October 9 must have been a day of tense expectation for Pospishil and Raich. They remained until afternoon in Fontainebleau. Nothing in the name of Novak had been received at the post office. That seemed to indicate that the journey to Marseilles had proceeded according to plan and that the organizers had had no difficulty with the assassins. Neither Vlada the Chauffeur nor Mio Kral had refused to go on with the perilous attempt. But, like Peter Oreb at Zagreb, they might get an attack of nerves at the last moment, or they might be arrested on the scene of action, or the street might be so heavily guarded by police and military that it would not be possible to get near enough to fire a shot. A bomb was a much less accurate weapon. Bombs might be thrown and yet the King escape. But if the attempt failed Pospishil would hardly get a telegram before evening. There was plenty of time to make further preparations because the King's visit to Versailles was not to take place until Wednesday. October 9 was a Monday.

In the afternoon they went into Paris by omnibus and visited the Place de l'Opéra. They thought they might see someone at the café. But there was no one there that they recognized or who recognized them, so they strolled along the Boulevard Haussmann and went into a cinema. Actually they were watching an American gangster film at the time when real gangsters of international politics were putting over a drama more fearsome than anything ever seen on the screen. Next day the cinema proposed showing in Pathé News the disembarkation of the King and the reception at Marseilles, but the cameramen at that moment were photographing a street scene that had never been equaled in news films. Pospishil and Raich were not men of imagination. They were only concerned with facts. Was the King killed or was he not? They had not long to wait. When they emerged from the theater onto the crowded boulevard the newsmen with *Paris-Soir* and *Intransigeant* were yelling their sensational titles. The papers, with the ink still damp and smudged, were being seized by all and sundry. People stood and read. Others having read shouted to one another. Pospishil, who knew some French, bought a paper. There was a bare telegram magnified by huge type: "An Attempt upon the Life of King Alexander in the Place de la Bourse, Marseilles. Twenty Revolver Shots Fired at the King of Yugoslavia. Several Soldiers Wounded. Consternation in Marseilles. The King Seriously Wounded. One of the Murderers Slain."

That was the sixth edition of *Intransigeant*. Pospishil and Raich hurried to the bus stop for Fontainebleau, but before the omnibus started the seventh edition was out announcing in big letters: "Le roi Alexandre de Yougoslavie et M. Barthou sont assassinés."

That was enough for the reserve assassins. They felt some relief. They would not have to do it. Vlada the Chauffeur and Mio Kral had done it. They must get out of France before there was a hue and cry, get to Italy. Curious that they wasted time by going back to Fontainebleau by bus instead of going to the Gare de Lyon. So soon after the event, that it was humanly impossible for anyone to have got from Marseilles to Paris in the time, they were relatively safe. Measures had not been taken by the police and they were not likely to have been asked any questions. But they went to Fontainebleau and there took return tickets to Évian, on the Lake of Geneva, slavishly following the route by which they had arrived. They explained afterwards that they took return tickets in order to divert suspicion. No one paid the least attention to them.

The midnight train for Geneva carried them away and in a second-class carriage Pospishil and Raich counted and watched the names of the stations. Raich had a notebook in which the names of the stations were scribbled in pencil. It was not their intention to go as far as the frontier station of Évian for which they had tickets, but to descend at a station before and get across the Lake of Geneva by boat. Pospishil got out his compass, which he had bought in Paris, and assured himself that it was working. The two men studied a map of Switzerland. They would cross Switzerland partly on foot, partly by car. The compass would be of most use when it came to dodging the frontier guards and slipping into Italy.

But luck was against them. There happened to be a certain M. Petit, chief of the special frontier police,

Annemasse-Geneva, who had made a hobby of studying terrorists, especially those of Pavelich's gangs. About 6 P.M. his wife telephoned him at Annemasse that she had heard on the wireless that King Alexander had been assassinated. He telephoned for confirmation to the French Consul at Geneva. Geneva said that both the King and M. Barthou had been killed. Then M. Petit, on his own responsibility, telephoned all the police posts in his department to be on the lookout for suspicious-looking foreigners. He said he was at once sure that the assassin at Marseilles had not acted alone. It was, nevertheless, remarkable that he took such rapid action, there being no possibility of accomplices getting from Marseilles to the Swiss frontier before the following day.

The only smartness Pospishil and Raich showed was in getting out of the train at Thonon. There was no inspection of passengers at Thonon. But then they went to a hotel to sleep off the effects of the train journey. They had no baggage and they were foreigners. The hotel proprietor asked for their passports and gave them rooms. The police of Thonon came to question them and, although they were quite polite, Pospishil and Raich realized that the game was up. They had no further chance of getting into Switzerland unobserved. Pospishil pretended to know no French; Raich prattled in Portuguese, which the police thought was Italian. M. Morel, of the Thonon police, telephoned M. Petit that there were two Italians with Czechoslovak passports at a hotel and that their behavior was suspicious. Petit did not think this communication important and did not hurry to Thonon. But at one in the morning the secret police from Paris telephoned the names Novak and Beneš, traveling from Fontainebleau, and requested M. Petit to be on the lookout for them.

M. Petit arrived at Thonon in the early hours of the morning, posted men to guard the entrances of the hotel, waked up the hotel porter, and had himself taken to the rooms occupied by the suspects. Two inspectors of police came up to stand by Pospishil and Raich while they dressed. Then having first searched them for arms, Petit had them taken under arrest to the police station.

The interrogation commenced. It is not the custom in France to caution prisoners or to inform them that any statement they may make is purely voluntary. The two terrorists were much more communicative then than they were afterwards, when interested parties warned them to give nothing away. They confessed their real names and gave abundance of detail in describing their activities since they had left Hungary. There were serious language difficulties, as Pospishil would not make use of the French he knew. He did not know enough to conduct an elaborate conversation. He preferred to speak broken German. Raich stuck to Portuguese, which nobody understood. The police had to wait for Serb interpreters before they could get a comprehensive statement.

Of the two men, Raich was by far the more communicative. But neither thought that they could be held for the murders at Marseilles. They must say they had been at Fontainebleau, because that was their alibi. They admitted they had been with Vlada the Chauffeur, whom they called Suk, that they were under the instructions of Pavelich, and that they had been told to wait for a poste-restante letter at Fontainebleau. They said they did not know what that letter might contain.

No one would know what he had to do until the last moment. They naturally said nothing about the arms which had been left at the Gare St. Lazare, but they gave much information about their life in the camp of Yanka Pusta in Hungary, their practice under the instruction of a Hungarian officer in the throwing of bombs and infernal machines. They said that if they had got through to Switzerland it had been their intention to go back to Hungary. They took no precaution whatever to shield the name of Hungary. They admitted that their passports had been forged in Hungary.

So the first international blame for the murders was thrown not upon Italy but upon Hungary. That may explain why the press went into full cry after Hungary, though the crime had not been organized from that country. The statements of Pospishil and Raich gave the first news of the conspiracy. They had made it appear that it originated from Budapest.

Four days later Mio Kral was arrested. To the first question as to his nationality he replied that he was a Hungarian. But he did not keep to that. He soon admitted that he was Mio Kral, a Croat, who had been in Hungary. In September he had been sent to Budapest to receive an automobile that was being delivered for use in one of the camps. He had met a man who had given him a forged passport and sent him to Zurich.

On the same day it was discovered in Sofia that the principal assassin was a Bulgarian subject going by the name of Vlada Georgiev Chernozemsky, commonly known as Vlada the Chauffeur. A warrant for his arrest had been issued long before the crime. It was stated in Bulgarian papers—and copied in Belgrade—that Vlada the Chauffeur had been afforded refuge in Budapest, that he had gone there with Cyril Drangov, a well-known member of the Macedonian Organization, and that he had been sent as an instructor to terrorists at the camp of Yanka Pusta. Even the movements of Vlada the Chauffeur pointed a finger of guilt at Hungary.

The representatives of the Little Entente, Beneš and Titulescu, who had come to the King's funeral, called a meeting at Belgrade and it was unanimously declared that the assassination had not been merely a blow directed against the King and Yugoslav unity, it had been a deliberate attempt to sabotage the existing order in Europe. Ruzhdy Aras and Maximos, on behalf of the Balkan Pact, associated themselves with that resolution and declared the solidarity of Turkey and Greece with Yugoslavia.

Yugoslavia was passive. The demonstration of European sympathy at the funeral had been flattering. The nation had many friends and did not stand alone. Both France and Britain had said that a strong Yugoslavia was necessary as a guarantee of stability in Central Europe. Yugoslavia had never felt so important during the King's life as she felt immediately after his death. That was enough; there was no disposition to pick a quarrel. Rumania and Czechoslovakia were much more indignant. They saw the stigma resting upon Hungary, Hungary which constantly menaced Rumania and Czechoslovakia because she wished to regain the territories lost in the war. It would be a fitting moment for Yugoslavia to square accounts with Hungary.

On the same day that the Little Entente made its declaration Italy, by way of showing coöperation and good will, placed Pavelich and Kvaternik under precautionary arrest. It is possible this action was taken upon representation from France and Britain. By October 19 the French were in possession of most of the important clues and all pointed to the crime having been organized from Italy with the connivance of Hungary. But France, on the eve of making a settlement of outstanding difficulties with her Latin neighbor, had to do all in her power to avert an open quarrel between Italy and Yugoslavia.

The chief concern of Great Britain was to prevent the outbreak of any war in which the Great Powers might become involved. The Great War of 1914 had sprung from a similar murder, and responsible British politicians were apprehensive in 1934. The first concern was to keep Italy immune. Italian pride must be shielded from a demand for satisfaction on the part of Yugoslavia. Hungary was in a secondary position, being a minor power, but Britain discouraged agitation against Hungary also. The quiet bearing of Yugoslavia during the weeks immediately following the assassination was due to various causes: first, the natural passivity of the Serbs; then British and French advice. The British Minister, Mr. Henderson, had several interviews and telephonic conversations with Prince Paul. The Regent inclined to the Minister's advice. He was proud of his personal connection with England and bore himself as an Englishman. He repressed his personal desire to avenge his cousin Alexander. The blood feud was in any case bad form. He was predisposed toward the Italians, having an admiration for their art and culture. Russian blood, which is not easily shocked, ran in his veins and he was not unbearably shocked by Italian Machiavellianism. He agreed that it would be better to overlook past differences and get into accord with the Fascists. He was ready to let bygones be bygones. For Hungary, he had some contempt: that was all. Hungary would be made the scapegoat at Geneva.

That might annoy the Magyars, but a little humiliation was a small price to pay for their guilt.

Yevtich had returned to Belgrade from Marseilles a national hero. No one, not even the Regent, had such popular backing. But he had no voice. The initiative was with Prince Paul who, though intending to install a more democratic regime, did inherit the power of King Alexander. What he said went. The Foreign Minister was still overawed by the throne. He was guided by Prince Paul's opinions and took no strong line of his own. He did not seize the occasion of his return to make a pronouncement on the international aspect of the crime, but tacitly accepted the plea that it was not a moment for presenting an ultimatum and threatening reprisals. The Serbs could show themselves more pacific and civilized in 1934 than the Austrians had done in 1914. They were members of the League of Nations, which had the right to settle grievances between states. They had signed the Briand-Kellog Pact and outlawed war.

Yevtich divulged to the Cabinet a very limited program. Complaint against Hungary had been made to the League during the previous summer. Hungary had agreed to disperse her armed camps and to cease sabotage of Yugoslavia but had not carried out her promises. The complaint would be renewed with additional accusation of complicity in the outrage of Marseilles. Uzunovich was for exposing and chastising Hungary. Yevtich's mind was not absolutely clear. In Belgrade he waived the case against Italy. Later, at Geneva, he wished satisfaction both from Italy and Hungary.

A mistake was made in not utilizing the opportunity provided by world-wide sympathy before that sympathy faded into the common light of indifference. It was a vital moment for a thorough testing of the authority of the League of Nations. The League should have been presented with the whole case and world opinion mobilized against international sabotage. France was shortsighted, for very soon her territory was secretly invaded by foreign agents storing bombs and arms for a Fascist rising, blowing up trains and houses. Britain was shortsighted and was soon, through the League, inviting an unwilling Yugoslavia to impose sanctions upon a power she had been persuaded to forgive.

But the Little Entente, which had more cause for animus against Hungary than against Italy, was pleased that Yugoslavia was taking up the cudgels against the Magyars. It approved. The direct attack upon Budapest began on October 16, when Yevtich informed the Hungarian government that the name of the assassin who had killed the King was Vlada Georgiev Chernozemsky, reported by the Sofia police to have been resident in Hungary and to have served as instructor at the terrorist schools. A photograph was enclosed and the Hungarians were asked to give further information.

After some delay and conventional promises to look into the matter the Hungarian government replied on October 26 that "in spite of the most minute and intensive research the royal Hungarian authorities have been unable, up to the present, to establish that the person named Vlada Georgiev Chernozemsky has ever been in Hungary. On the contrary, it appears almost absolutely certain that the above-named has never entered the territory of this country."

That closed the correspondence as far as Vlada the

Chauffeur was concerned. There is no definite proof
that he was even in Hungary. Yelka Pogorelets was in
Belgrade in October, 1934. Interviewed by the police
and afterwards by journalists, she did not admit that
she had ever seen Vlada the Chauffeur at Budapest or
at Yanka Pusta. She knew Pospishil very well, but she
did not know the Bulgarian even by sight. The Serbs
assumed, on too slender evidence, that Vlada the Chauffeur had been sent from Hungary to commit the crime.
It was shown afterwards that while Pospishil, Raich,
and Mio Kral did certainly come from Hungary, Vlada
the Chauffeur was brought into Switzerland by Kvaternik, who was living in Italy.

A French newspaper editor sent a journalist to make
investigations in Hungary. He was able to publish sensational revelations. He visited the farms which had
been used as schools for training terrorists and dished up
afresh the whole painful story of Yanka Pusta. According to him, the bomb throwers and train wreckers had
been still in camp after the assassination. They had
only been dispersed about the twentieth of the month,
when Hungary was becoming apprehensive of international action. French publicity was skilfully canalized
so that the blame should avoid Italy and go exclusively
to Hungary. Following the *Petit Journal*, the *Paris-
Soir* sent its special correspondent who, though nom-
inally under the protection of the Hungarians, reported much that was damaging. These articles were
freely quoted by Yugoslav papers and gave the impression of strong support in France for a campaign
against Hungary. Every day in the news the front
pages were given to Hungarian revelations with such
sensational headings as: THERE WAS A FACTORY
OF BOMBS AT YANKA PUSTA, say the French

authorities; SECRET STORE OF SIMILAR
BOMBS DISCOVERED AT BORDEAUX. Another
day it was: FORMER HUNGARIAN GENERAL
STAFF BEHIND MARSEILLES CONSPIRACY.

Colonel Perchevich had been arrested in Vienna and
the French had applied for extradition. There was a
movement to embroil the Austrians as Schuschnigg was
a strong supporter of the legitimists. A certain *agent
provocateur* allowed himself to be arrested in Marseilles, freely admitting that he was one of the terrorists. His task was to throw out as much confusing and
contradictory evidence as possible. This man pointed
to Colonel Perchevich as the master mind of the conspiracy, a crude attempt to shift the responsibility
from Pavelich and Italy to the Hapsburg supporters.

Italy kept Pavelich and Kvaternik strictly incom-
municado. It was Mussolini's intention to refuse extradition ultimately, but to keep France and Yugoslavia guessing until after the hearing of the case
against Hungary at Geneva. No journalists were allowed to interview them. No detectives had access to
them. The Fascist authorities did not subject them to
any examination. It would have been possible, while
refusing to surrender them to French justice, to make
an independent investigation of the part played by
these men and to publish the findings. Their evidence
was of cardinal importance and far outweighed the
question of punishment for crime. The French courts
were held up by the absence of Pavelich and Kvaternik
and but for the suspense of the extradition proceedings
they might have had the trial of Kral, Pospishil, and
Raich before the case of Hungary was judged by the
League of Nations.

Yevtich, in an interview to the *Petit Parisien*, declared that "our first duty is to await the investigation of the Marseilles crime," but it was important for him that the trial should take place before the session at Geneva. With Laval visiting Rome, however, to make a settlement with Italy, France had no interest in hastening the trial. She did not use much pressure in demanding Pavelich and Kvaternik. The tension in Europe was so great that had France mobilized opinion against the Fascists she could have forced Italy to cooperate in finding where the true blame for the crime lay.

The Hungarians were staunch. While hotly denying their complicity in the murder they never even hinted that Italy was involved. They had an understanding. The Hungarian Prime Minister was received by Mussolini in Rome on November 10. Hungary was to have the role of shock absorber, but in the long run she was assured that she had nothing to fear, as Italy stood behind her.

On November 28 the Yugoslav government presented its Memorandum to the League of Nations and on the same day Prince Paul set off for London and the wedding of his sister-in-law, the Princess Marina, to the Duke of Kent. It was thought that through his connection with the British Court he would obtain strong backing for the Yugoslav cause.

The Memorandum was moderately worded. It could have been edited to be a powerful indictment of Hungary, but it displayed no more literary skill than the average document emerging from state departments. It expressed the undue humility of the Yugoslavs, "We are a small people, but even a small nation has rights."

Nevertheless, it could have been made the basis of a strong denunciation of Hungary had it had a spokesman of the caliber, say, of Lloyd George.

Yevtich arrived at Geneva on December 3 and was warmly greeted by the representatives of the Little Entente. The session began on the 5th. There was a dramatic scene at the outset and Laval intervened to prevent a clash with Italy. The accusation must be pinned down to Hungary. Hungary obstructed and the case took on the usual Genevan dullness. Yevtich, with his slow speech, seemed in difficulties and the Serbs at home became displeased by the uncertain progress of the complaint. There was a whispering campaign against Yevtich in Belgrade. The Memorandum had proved to be an ineffective document, not sufficiently strongly worded, not comprehensive. Yevtich must be held responsible for the half-hearted way Yugoslavia went to Geneva. Why was Italy being spared? Italy was shielding Pavelich and Kvaternik from justice in order to avoid incrimination. Was there not even more against Italy than was being urged against Hungary? The Serbs were angry with Laval for eliminating Italy from the accusation. But if Italy could not be blamed at Geneva, Hungary at least should be denounced with vigor. Some politicians, especially of the faction of the Prime Minister, Uzunovich, grudged Yevtich the popularity he had won through being with the King at Marseilles. They saw their chance to bring him down. Either he must obtain satisfaction from the League of Nations or his career would be ruined. Uzunovich made it difficult for him.

The atmosphere of Geneva was oppressive to Yevtich. It must be so when a small country pleads its cause to the representatives of great states. There was no equality. A small country to succeed required the strong support of a great power. Thus in the following year Abyssinia was championed by Sir Samuel Hoare and the League applied sanctions against Italy, but Abyssinia by herself could not have got sanctions or anything else, which was clear enough when Britain changed her mind and withdrew her support of the Emperor of Ethiopia. Still later, the republic of Spain, for want of a champion, was unable to enforce her just claims.

At the inauguration of the League this dependence upon the leadership of great powers was not foreseen. The provision of "One nation one vote" implied an equality of voice. But it soon became apparent that a nation with great financial resources, or a powerful army, or world-wide influence had an ascendancy over all petty nations or groups of petty nations. Yugoslavia without backing made a poor show in the parliament of nations. Young in nationhood, that was to be expected. And youth was abashed at Geneva. "Now, how do you dare to try and make a disturbance?" asked the elder nations.

Yugoslavia comported herself with politeness and dignity in the person of Bogoljub Yevtich. But he was blindfolded by Laval and had to play blindman's-buff with some very slippery gentlemen. He tried repeatedly to pull off the bandage and grab Baron Aloisi and he was told that was not playing the game. It is easy but rather shameful to fool a child. It is not surprising that Yevtich became angry.

It was a game at Geneva; perhaps not a blindman's-buff, but none the less a game, and that offended the Serbs, who either take the League with deadly seriousness or are ready to resign membership. Still, the young

Serbs of today have learned to play games and shine internationally in football and tennis. If the skill, combination, and goal getting with which the postwar generation has learned to play football had entered into the composition of their politicians they would win victories. Do not Belgrade football teams win their matches at Rome and Budapest? But their politicians keep the ball to themselves and then fail to score.

Yevtich's strenuous and abortive efforts were gravely hampered by the doings of politicians in Belgrade. Uzunovich was not working with him but against him. While Yevtich was arguing the case, Uzunovich took the law into his own hands by starting a campaign of reprisals upon Hungarians. He did not consult his Foreign Minister beforehand and he made no public statement or explanation. Secret orders went to the Minister of the Interior that all Magyars living in Yugoslavia were to be harried and chased back over the frontier into Hungary. The Yugoslav public did not know the origin of these orders and had little part in the persecution, but the newspapers of the world at large knew about it soon enough. The victims of this unworthy act of revenge were mostly poor working folk who had no political activity or enmity. Some of them were old and feeble; some were very young, and the photographs of homeless children huddled at frontier railway stations made a painful impression. The privations of the evicted at once found voice in the European press, though not in the Yugoslav papers, and popular sympathy outside Yugoslavia was sidetracked at a critical moment.

The British government had never relished the prospect of a public chastisement of Hungary at Geneva, and Mr. Anthony Eden, on Friday, December 8, took advantage of the new sympathy for the Hungarians to diminish the prospects of a sharp decision. His speech that day made a painful impression on Serb public opinion and is not likely to be soon forgotten or forgiven. It put Yugoslavia in the false position of a state trying to exploit the murder of King Alexander to pursue her private ends. Eden evoked more animosity than the obstructionist, Laval. Unwittingly he diminished the prestige of Prince Paul, whose influence at the British Court was seen to have less weight than the Yugoslavs had imagined. Serbs never understand England and the paradoxes of her behavior; her generosity during the war, education of young Serbs at Oxford and Cambridge, nursing of the Serb wounded; and then after the war, coldness, indifference, misrepresentation.

Yevtich's anger and humiliation may not have been realized by Eden at the time, but that Friday brought war to the door. Yevtich told his secretaries to pack up: he would not stay after his country had been insulted. Some of those nations represented at Geneva had combined to murder the King and now England and France combined with the murderers to add insult to injury. Yevtich went to Titulescu's room that night and had a meeting with the representatives of the Little Entente and the Balkan Pact, telling them of his decision to quit Geneva and of the probable resignation of Yugoslavia from the League. They sympathized but did all in their power to smooth him down. Something still might be won. Instead of going away, which would cause a world sensation but might also enkindle European war, he might use the threat of going as a trump card.

But it proved very difficult to persuade him away from stubbornness to tactics. He kept to his decision.

The most he would promise was that he would see
Laval and make a complete explanation of his position
before he departed. So he went to Laval, who received
him with poker face. Laval was not backing him because he could not be sure that Yugoslavia was not going to insist on the complicity of Italy with Hungary. It
was not so much a question as to what would be the
verdict of the League. The question was, would Yugoslavia accept the verdict when obtained? But Yevtich
must not be allowed to leave. "France is with you," said
Laval. "France is devoted to Yugoslavia and our interests are united. What Eden has said does not matter,
because on Monday I will speak for Yugoslavia. I will
become a Yugoslav."

"But do you agree to our demands?" asked Yevtich.

That was the rub. Laval became sunk in thought.
"As I have said, if you eliminate Italy completely,
France is with you," said he.

"I am not asking for France's conditions. I merely
came to tell you that the Yugoslav delegation is leaving Geneva. We will settle our differences with our
neighbors on our own responsibility and the League can
take what action it thinks fit."

Laval's complexion went drab. "That amounts to an
ultimatum and I must have time to consider it," said
he. "Please make no public statement, but come to me
tomorrow morning."

"No," said the Serb. "You do not seem to understand yet that I am going."

That was annoying and might be true. These Slavs
were so impulsive. Laval grunted. He must keep Yevtich until he had made him compromise. "It is now all a
matter of the decision of the League Council," said he.
"If you can be guaranteed an acceptable verdict there

would be no reason for your going away and creating further international complications. If I agreed to support your legitimate demands, you would stay?"

"Well?"

"But we do not know, none of us know, what verdict would satisfy you. Come, Monsieur Yevtich, what are your minimum demands, your absolute minimum? Let me know that, and I will guarantee that they are accepted by a majority of the League."

It seemed that the Frenchman was being forced to compromise, though in reality the Serb was being forced. Yevtich talked again of his demands and that was all Laval required. If he could keep the Yugoslav case alive on any terms the situation might be saved.

Laval plied Yevtich with soft talk and with guttural assurances that came from the stomach and seemed to come from the heart. All the Serb said was very true, and every Frenchman sympathized. Let him reduce everything to a formula. The English loved formulas and would swallow almost anything if told it was a formula.

So Yevtich returned to his hotel and prepared a statement of his irreducible minimum. Next morning he presented it to Laval. The statement still harped on the responsibility of Italy and had to be reëdited. It must be strictly in accord with the Memorandum which made no mention of Italy. The Serbs must be logical and must not try to drag in extraneous considerations. If they won their case against the Hungarians they could lodge a further complaint against other powers subsequently, if they desired.

Yugoslavia decided to be satisfied with a signal victory over Hungary. The statement was rewritten. Laval seemed to be pleased and said that they must at once find Mr. Eden. But it was reported that Eden was out playing golf. Haste was necessary, if the powers were to be brought into agreement over the week end. Laval resolved upon a bold move. Without consulting the British delegate he would go direct to the Italians who, in his belief, held control of the situation. If Baron Aloisi could be made to agree the battle was more than half won. So he took Yevtich's irreducible minimum to Aloisi. He must have said, "We have reached an impasse. The Serbs threaten to go home and take their grievances back to Belgrade and publish a statement denouncing the League. The last state of this affair threatens to be much worse than the first. Now I have obtained an absolute guarantee that there will be no further accusations against Italy. It has not been easy but I have succeeded and France, with your approval and coöperation, will agree to a verdict on these lines. The necessary reassurances can be given to Hungary. It is not very much to ask this small country to take a certain measure of blame, thus making an insignificant sacrifice of prestige in order to save Europe from a conflagration."

Aloisi made no difficulties. He may have been flattered that Laval had come to him first instead of presenting him with a *fait accompli*. But the consent of Hungary must also be obtained in advance. They must have a united front in the League Council and then the voting of the necessary resolution would pass off without incident.

So Yevtich's minimum was taken to the Hungarian delegates, Eckhardt and Kanya, who both made wry faces. They were angry and uncompromising, but Laval dealt with them like a labor expert dealing with strike leaders. If they did not agree to the terms of the pro-

posed settlement let them state their objections and
he would see what could be done to meet their views.
So they set to work to whittle away the Yugoslav re-
quirements. Both Saturday and Sunday were very
wordy days. The only sort of blame Eckhardt and
Kanya would agree to accept was that of possible negligence on the part of obscure officials. It could not be
allowed that the Hungarian government had wittingly
connived at any part of the Marseilles conspiracy.

Yevtich, baffled and perhaps bamboozled, remained
on for the promulgation of the findings of the League.
With Italy completely eliminated Yugoslavia did not
have a good case for branding Hungary with the responsibility for the crime. The grievance against Hungary for harboring terrorists and issuing forged passports antedated the Marseilles murders by years, a
genuine but comparatively minor matter.

The Marseilles conspiracy had been followed by the
Genevan conspiracy. On December 11 the League
Council published its decision. It was held as established that the questions relative to the existence of
terrorist elements and their activity had not been regu-
lated to the satisfaction of the Yugoslav government.
It was established that certain Hungarian authorities,
at least through negligence, bore responsibility for
acts connected with the assassinations of Marseilles.
Convinced that the Hungarian government was willing
to fulfil its duty, the Council invited that government
to communicate to the League in due course the
measures it would take. A committee was set up to study
the subject of international collaboration in the sup-
pression of terrorism. Both Italy and Hungary were to
have representatives on that committee. For the rest,
the Council condemned the odious crime of the mur-

der of King Alexander and of M. Louis Barthou and demanded that all those responsible be punished, apparently a hint to Yugoslavia that the trial at Aix-en-Provence would make good any defects in the judgment of the League.

That was all the satisfaction that Yugoslavia obtained at the tribunal of the nations. Great Britain was pleased, because it seemed that the League had possibly saved Europe from war. France was pleased because the Yugoslavs seemed to have been pacified. Italy was pleased because no accusations had been tabulated against her. Hungary had been found guilty of negligence. It was rather like that type of English case where the plaintiff is awarded a farthing's damages. Even Hungary had cause for some satisfaction. Rumania, Czechoslovakia, Turkey congratulated Yugoslavia. It was the best they could do. But the Yugoslavs knew they had been fobbed off by the other nations. The best their papers could say was that there had been a "Victory of the Yugoslav thesis," as if what was involved was merely some abstraction of right and wrong.

Yevtich returned to Belgrade and had a hearty reception at the railway station, chiefly from youth, which still looked to him as its leader; but his reputation was not enhanced. He had not come back with glory and he was far from being the hero he had been when he returned from Marseilles. Most people knew better, though, than to hold him responsible for the colorless verdict. The main conclusion was that France and Great Britain had let Yugoslavia down. But as if by magic the grievances against Hungary and Italy faded away. The conviction grew that had Yugoslavia been allied with Germany instead of France she would have had stronger backing.

principal assassin to slip out of her hands she was going to commit a mortal affront to the Yugoslavs.

The friendship and international coöperation of Yugoslavia were important to France. The defection of Yugoslavia might mean the breakdown of her system of alliances. It would prove expensive to offend the strorgest country in the Little Entente; it might cause a pa_alysis of that combination of small powers.

But French policy, in 1935, was shortsighted and confused. There was no clear realization of the Yugoslav domestic situation. Prince Paul was an unknown quantity and the popularity of Yevtich was overestimated. With the strong backing of France, Yevtich's position would have been unassailable. And he was a loyal and honest statesman who would have stuck by France. The dilatory action of France had made Yevtich's foreign policy seem weak kneed. A week after he returned from Geneva Yevtich was made Prime Minister. A general election followed and had he brought real satisfaction to the wounded feelings of the nation he must have swept the country. There would have been no need to dragoon the voters. But there was no longer a semblance of unanimity. Uzunovich had been dismissed and the Serbs had become divided against themselves. Parliament, when it met, was turbulent and the Premier's position soon became untenable. He had to resign and his place was taken by Stoyadinovich, who did not follow the French tradition.

The new Premier represented a complete break with the past. He had no sentimental attachment to the memory of Alexander, as the late King had kept him out of office for nine years. Adroit, smart, tireless, bound by no sentiment or prejudices, a fresh mind faced the problems of international relationships. They thought he could not ride the storm of Yugoslav politics, but they were wrong.

Already when the first trial took place Stoyadinovich was in power. No one then knew which way he would go or whether he would last. Thoughts of the late King which had become dormant were reawakened and once more the Marseilles crime became front-page news in Belgrade. The Serbs were surprised that the trial should take place in little Aix-en-Provence and not in Paris, but they were expectant that at long last justice would be done. Yugoslavia sat up and stared over to France.

The president of the court, in opening the proceedings, invited those present to show homage to the memory of the great soldier of the World War and the passionate friend of France, King Alexander; and also to that of a great servant of France who never ceased to work for the cause of peace, "an apostle of the amity of peoples," M. Louis Barthou. The counsel for the defense, M. Desbons, agreed to that but added that he also bowed his head respectfully before the tombs of all the Croats and all the Macedonians who had died for liberty.

The president then proposed the names of certain interpreters and there commenced a quarrel over interpretation which lasted through this trial and was continued in the second. Desbons alleged that one of the Serb interpreters had almost driven the prisoners to suicide during the preliminary investigation. Apparently it had proved impossible to find a Frenchman with an adequate knowledge of the Serbian language, a curious comment on the Franco-Serb relationship. The only French interpreter relied on a knowledge of Russian, but a Russian can understand a Croat only by guesswork and haphazard, as a Dutchman can guess at the meaning of German. The Yugoslav interpreters were fairly effective, though none of them knew French perfectly, but the defense denounced them as being in the service of the Yugoslav government. Almost at once there was a great row about the translation of the expression *partie civile* as "lawyer." The accused refused to accept the interpreters and the president said, "We continue with the hearing whether they accept or not."

In the afternoon a supplementary French interpreter was provided, but the agitation against the Serb interpreter continued and Desbons accused the president of violating the law. The procurator general demanded that disciplinary action be taken against Desbons, it being the first time he had heard such words from a member of the French bar. The time of the court was taken up by a verbose defense of his behavior by M. Desbons. The three prisoners, Kral, Pospishil, and Raich, must have wondered what it was all about. This was not interpreted to them. Suddenly they were no longer on trial but their counsel, M. Desbons, was in the dock, talking tearfully of his soul, his honor, and all that he held dear. "You can punish me if you wish, but when you have punished me there will remain a joy which you will not be able to take from me, that, in receiving your sentence, I shall be conscious of having accomplished to the full my sacred mission which is that of defending counsel. The sentence you provoke, the sentence you will pronounce against me today, will have no other result than to make me adore this gown which up to now I have only loved."

The court was suspended and when, after an hour's private deliberation, it resumed, the president gave a summing up of the case against M. Desbons and taking into consideration the intercession of the *Bâtonnier de l'ordre des Avocats*, let him off with the formal penalty of an official reprimand.

Desbons remained silent for hours after that, and the case made some progress. Casteran, a journalist who had represented a French newspaper in Belgrade, was employed to interpret. As he was available only for the one afternoon his place was taken next day by a Yugoslav Moslem, whom Pospishil refused to accept. Desbons wanted to waste the time of the court by reading out all the evidence given at the session of the League of Nations in the previous December. The president refused. But the case proceeded more calmly because medical evidence on the point of Mio Kral's sanity was heard. It would be to the advantage of the defense to show that Kral was, if not mentally deranged, at least abnormal and not entirely responsible for his actions.

Kral had declared that while in prison an attempt had been made to hypnotize him. Instead of dismissing that as nonsense the doctors declared that he suffered from hallucinations. Those who followed the progress of the trial were astonished to encounter long disquisitions on the symptoms and proofs of hallucinatory neurosis devoid of any evidence derived from observation of the prisoner. The trial was not going well and Yugoslavs began to be indignant. For this also was obstruction; but even if it were not it must be designed to obtain an acquittal for the terrorist who had stood with Vlada the Chauffeur in the Marseilles crowd.

The doctor from the Toulouse Asylum indicated a "slight attenuation of responsibility." Dr. Digue was then called and gave the results of certain interviews with the prisoner in conference with other professors of practical psychology. They said that Kral had hallucinations which could be both created and cured by his emotions, that he was a nervous subject open to suggestion, implying that if it had been suggested to him in a certain state of mind that he should go to Marseilles and kill the King, he would take the suggestion as his own choice of action. Professor Digue therefore adduced a slight attenuation of responsibility, enough in the long run to save Mio Kral from the guillotine.

M. Desbons made further obstruction on technical grounds but was overruled. Then Dr. Euzière gave evidence that Kral bore no signs of being an epileptic, but that he had intermittent or delirious hallucination, that he had circulatory troubles, and a rapid pulse. Then came Professor Cornille, who was engaged by M. Desbons in an argument as to whether Kral commonly hesitated when asked a question, trying to have it proved that the reflexes of the prisoner were not normal. The president got tired of the word spinning that ensued and cut the argument short, asking the accused whether they had any comments to make. Pospishil said it was the first time he had ever heard tell of such matters.

Almost immediately after that the court usher handed a note to the president for transmission to the foreman of the jury. Desbons at once asked whether the note was in a foreign language and if so that it be translated and made public. The foreman read the note, which was obviously in French, and put it in his pocket. Had it been in Serbian it is hardly likely that he could have read it. The president said that whether the note be made public was a question that concerned the jury.

"But we do not know what is in it," murmured Desbons.

"Nor do I," said the president.

There was then an interval of a quarter of an hour. When the court resumed the president proposed to cross-examine Pospishil but Desbons returned to the subject of the contents of the note which the foreman had received. He had scented a first-class opportunity for causing a long delay, perhaps having the jury dismissed and a new jury called. The foreman of the jury said that the note referred to personal matters, but that the substance of it could be communicated if desired. In the interval the note had been destroyed, probably burned. Desbons seized upon the opportunity to try and get the whole of the trial up to that point quashed.

In doing so, of course, he would bring the court at Aix into disgrace. The whole world was watching its proceedings and the whole world was going to see it defeated and befooled by an obstructionist.

"A document has been received by the jury. The court does not know its contents, the defense does not know its contents, and the document has been destroyed." That certainly was an irregularity and the president of the court allowed the fact to be certified by the court, hoping that then they might be allowed to proceed with the cross-examination. But Desbons, having obtained the certification of the fact, said he desired to draw the necessary conclusions and he taunted the procurator with the words, "You will not have the heads of these three men, neither you nor your substitute the executioner."

He would draw the conclusion that the trial had become invalid and that the case must be dismissed, but he was provocative in his exclamations, shouting, "That's justice for you! That's republican justice!" The procurator was in a terrible rage and he and Desbons were shouting together and against one another.

At last the prosecution demanded the expulsion of Maître Desbons from the court.

In any case the trial was now destined to come to naught. If Desbons had his way, the court having been forced to admit an irregularity, any verdict the jury might find would be invalidated. If the counsel for the defense were expelled from the bar the case could not go on, the jury must be dismissed and a new trial called.

There is no doubt that the president of the court was angry, for some pressure had been exerted from Paris to insure that the case should be heard with a dignity befitting its international aspect. But from the beginning he had encountered an obstruction with which ultimately he could not cope. He was now determined to exact from Desbons the highest penalty the court could inflict. He would be excluded from the Paris bar and debarred from the further exercise of his profession.

Desbons defended himself first and the charges were made afterwards. He showed no repentance for his behavior and took nothing back that he had said. Instead, he made a hysterical appeal destined more for the press than for the ears of the president. He had been the subject of "abominable attacks in infamous journals." Because he was an honest man, devoted to the cult of justice like his father before him. He was the friend of the poor, yes, of the Croats and Macedonians, he admitted it. He risked his career for them, risked being broken. He had pleaded twenty-five years at the Paris bar and he had been decorated with the Legion of Honor. Now, because he was an independent man, they would take away from him the means of earning his daily bread. An ordinary delinquent might be brought up before them and sentenced to a few months' imprisonment, but for his offense they were going to punish him with hunger.

The president of the court, taking disciplinary action, dealt with him in a very matter-of-fact way, without heat, without epithets or abuse. He tabulated the charges against him: contempt of court; employment of maneuvers of obstruction; insinuations against the impartiality of magistrates; use of gross expressions in addressing the procurator general; and failure to accept the ruling of the court with regard to the conclusions drawn from the established fact of the transmission of a letter to the jury. He pointed out that in his defense the counsel had said nothing to extenuate his offense and taking into consideration that he had already received the censure of the court on the previous day, he gave the findings of the court. The court pronounced against M. Desbons the sentence of expulsion from the bar.

"Maître, you may leave the bar. You have nothing more to say," said the president.

"I will not leave the bar, unless expelled by military force," answered Desbons.

At a sign from the president a captain of gendarmes approached Desbons. He still protested that he wanted soldiers to remove him. Then he shook hands with the prisoners and was finally led away.

In an interview with journalists on the following day Desbons made a series of strange statements which can neither be contradicted nor confirmed. He said he had been offered, previous to the trial, a sum of 400,000 francs if he would pose a certain set of tendentious questions during the hearing of the case. The object of these questions was to inflame public opinion and hasten a European war. But he had refused. He said it had been known in advance that King Alexander would be killed at Marseilles. Alexander had been allowed to come to Marseilles because certain politicians, not Frenchmen, were interested in his death. "I have been expelled from the bar because it was not wished that I should demonstrate this fact." He said that only 5 per cent of the truth was contained in the dossier of the case. The other 95 per cent remained at the bottom of the well. Because he wished to get at the truth he had been represented as Public Enemy No. 1. Five months before the trial commenced he had been told he would be expelled. But he was sure that sooner or later the whole truth would be extracted from the well where it lay hidden.

But if Desbons had been so devoted to truth that he had sacrificed his career for it, he might have said who it was offered him 400,000 francs. If he knew that Alexander had been allowed to go to his death, he could at least have given sufficient detail to show who was inculpated. He hinted that certain Serbs had wished to have the King killed, but he avoided saying any names. If he had so many strong cards to play later in the trial, it is curious that he had retarded his effective entry into the proceedings by a whole series of obstructionary objections and questions, curious that he should have wrecked the trial instead of ensuing its steady progress toward the triumph of the defense; for the only real assistance the accused derived from the defense in this abortive trial was the evidence adduced to show that Mio Kral was slightly mad.

It is no secret that large funds were subscribed for the defense of the accused. But no one knows the exact amount of Desbons' remuneration, or exactly from what sources it was derived, or what precisely was required by those who put up the money. Was the amount he received commensurate with the risk he ran? He admits that he had been informed in advance that he would be disbarred.

He also admits that money from one source might gravely have imperiled the course of justice had he accepted it. And money from another source?

There was no need for this money at all. The best counsel obtainable would have been at the disposal of the accused. In such a *cause célèbre* there could be no trouble in finding able counsel. And the government had to defray the expense. It is quite legitimate to take money from a third party, but it may cause dangerous complications in such a trial as this. It is not unfair to assume that Desbons was paid to obstruct.

The impression made in Yugoslavia was appalling. The French had failed to protect the King at Marseilles. They had also let their Foreign Minister bleed to death. They had failed at Geneva. They had come to an understanding with Italy but had not exerted sufficient pressure to obtain the extradition of Pavelich and Kvaternik. They had postponed the trial of Kral, Pospishil, and Raich for over twelve months and then provided this spectacle of ineptitude at Aix-en-Provence.

The second trial took place in February, 1936, sixteen months after the crime had been committed. The president of the court was changed and the much more capable M. Loison took charge. The new counsel for the defense was the *bâtonnier* of the order of barristers, M. Saint-Auban, whose probity was undoubted. But this trial was conducted in a way that would cause astonishment to legal circles in England and America. Important witnesses were allowed to absent themselves for trivial reasons. M. Paul Boncour, who had been retained at a very high fee to represent the Queen of Yugoslavia, was not called.* The cross-examination was haphazard and important questions persistently sidetracked. The counsel for the prosecution did not know his brief, and the counsel for defense was allowed to make many statements, damaging to King Alexander, which could and ought to have been contradicted. It is said that the French government brought pressure to bear on everyone concerned, a pressure which M. Saint-Auban alone resisted. That may account for the fact that the report of the trial was not subject to severe criticism in French legal journals. The whole affair was governmentally managed and therefore hardly worth the attention of critics.

It has been explained that the Yugoslavs said to the French government, "Please, do not mention this!" and the Italians said, "Avoid that!" while the authorities in Paris also knew certain details of the crime which they did not want aired. The president was instructed to avoid the question of Italian and Hungarian responsibility and rule out all evidence bearing upon that. All

* It appears that the Yugoslav government in 1935 asked Queen Marie to withdraw her legal representative from the trial. M. Paul Boncour had been retained, on the advice of M. Yevtich, who fell from power in July, 1935. It is said that Boncour was in possession of highly important evidence and it had been the intention of M. Yevtich to obtain through him at the trial the satisfaction which had been denied him at Geneva.

On October 6, 1935, the Queen wrote to M. Paul Boncour that "having full and complete confidence in French justice I place my cause in the hands of its representatives, not desiring that any voice, however authoritative, be raised in my behalf, allowing it even to be supposed that I separate my cause from that of France herself."

This renunciation facilitated the task of the president of the court.

he had to do was to treat the accused as common murderers, obtain a verdict to that effect, and pronounce a
sentence which might be thought adequate to satisfy
Yugoslavia. It seems to have been important that the
life of Mio Kral should be spared. In Yugoslavia all
three men would have been executed. In London, supposing the prisoners to have been tried in England,
Pospishil and Raich could hardly have been held accessory as they were not in Marseilles at the time of the
crime. But Mio Kral, knowing the murder was intended,
being armed with bombs and pistols and being on the
spot, must have suffered the extreme penalty. It is possible that the international influence of Pavelich was
felt at Aix-en-Provence, shielding Kral from the guillotine. The same medical evidence as to his unhinged state
was adduced at the second trial, evidence which would
impress no reasonable man. For a short period during
his incarceration, waiting for trial, he was observed to
be suffering from hallucinations. And that saved him.

The accused resumed the tactics of obstruction in
which they had been primed by M. Desbons, but they
received short shrift from the president, who told them
that if they refused to answer questions the jury would
know what deductions to make and they must take the
consequences. At first they refused to be represented by
anyone except their chosen counsel, Desbons. But they
were won over by the tact of Saint-Auban, who defended
them with vigor, even with rancor. But they made the
same difficulties over interpretation and they went back
on the signed statements they had made after their arrest, saying that these statements had been mistranslated
and that they had never understood the contents of
them. Likewise they denied the evidence they had given
in the preliminary investigations. Kral said that shortly

after his arrest a Serb police agent had visited him and offered him his freedom if he would agree to go and kill Pavelich. The others said they had been threatened with reprisals upon their relatives.

Very little new evidence was elicited in the course of the trial. The defense might have shifted a great deal of the guilt onto Pavelich, the man who organized the assassination. The three men were only his tools, his instruments, and it is possible that they told the truth when they said they did not even know the purpose for which they had been brought to France. But the prisoners studiously guarded the name of Pavelich as if their future after the trial depended on his good will. And the defense had the audacity to depict him as a hero patriot. Saint-Auban stressed Serb brutality and invited the sympathy of the jury for him because, in 1929, he had been tried for treason and condemned to death at Belgrade merely on account of a harmless political speech at Sofia. The Serbs had no one to put up to refute this and give a full account of Pavelich's activities, showing that there was more reason for the condemnation of that man than of any other concerned.

According to Saint-Auban, the accused were patriots whose self-sacrifice and devotion to the cause of liberty ought to kindle emotion in the breast of every true son of republican France. According to the president of the court, who was never impartial, they were hirelings, men who were willing to do murder for reward. If they received so much money before the event and were lodged luxuriously in the best hotels, how much must one think was the amount promised them in case of success? But he would not explore the dangerous question of the source of the money. He interpolated a commentary of irony and sarcasm which delighted a French court but complicated the task of the interpreters. The interpreters were, in any case, inexperienced and when a witness spoke for five or ten minutes the translation was commonly given in a few seconds, a fact which rendered the prisoners extremely suspicious of the course the trial was taking.

The president, Loison, conducted the case, examining the prisoners on the lines he thought advisable. The prosecution scarcely asked more than a dozen questions during the whole of the hearing. The defense cross-examined most of the witnesses, or rather put questions to the president which he permitted the witnesses to answer or else ruled out of order. In conclusion, the procurator general summed up the case against the accused and then the counsel for the defense replied and made their various pleas. The jury then retired.

The last word had therefore been with M. Saint-Auban and he profited by it to make a strong appeal for acquittal. He began by applying the word "abnormal" to the proceedings. The abnormality was not due to the way the president had conducted the case but to the genesis of the case and its consequences, an abnormality rendered dangerous because of the obscurity which, despite all the efforts of the police, still enveloped it. Saint-Auban did nothing to disperse that obscurity. He touched on the internal aspect, quoting mendacious Hungarian evidence to the League without quoting the ultimate findings of the League. He quoted Pavelich to show that his program was one of legal action. He justified Italy in refusing extradition. Then he made a plea for the Croats fighting for their political freedom. Freedom cannot be attained, never has been attained, without acts of violence. The court must not forget that though the Serb was top dog in Yugoslavia at the moment, the position might be reversed some day later. It must not accept the Serb point of view with regard to the murder of Alexander. This was a purely political assassination.

He retailed the story of the murder of Stephen Radich, the Croat leader, though he was in the privileged position of having no one coming after him to contradict what he had said. He did not admit that the murderer of Radich was a Montenegrin, nor did he say that Radich was an intimate friend of the King, a court favorite on whose advice the dictatorship was inaugurated. He let it be implied that the murder of Alexander was a just revenge for the murder of Radich.

That provided the main line of the speech for the defense. If the accused were guilty of complicity, which he denied formally though unconvincingly, their actions could, nevertheless, be justified by the intolerable wrongs of the Croat people. Radich, the uncrowned King of Croatia, had been murdered. The murder of Alexander, though as indefensible, was, in a way, poetic justice. He told the story of the police murder of Professor Schufflai at Zagreb. Then, as if that was yet another wrong to Croatia, he reverted to the murder of the Archduke Ferdinand and his Slav wife at Sarajevo, in 1914. The people of Sarajevo had erected a magnificent monument to Princip. But in what respect did the assassins of Sarajevo differ from the assassins of Marseilles? The Serbs (and Croats) of Bosnia wanted freedom from the Austrian yoke. Pospishil, Kral, and Raich wanted freedom from the Serb yoke. The consequence of the murder of Sarajevo, which is glorified in the little cemetery with a splendid tomb erected to its memory, was a Europe drowned in blood. "Ah, gentlemen, when I recall this long series of murders I say to myself that the beautiful blue Danube is the beautiful red Danube."

Neither Sarajevo nor Marseilles is near the Danube. To show the Danube as red Saint-Auban might well have adduced Vienna, where political repression since the war had been far more bloody than anywhere in Yugoslavia. Had there been anyone to answer him in court it would have been easy to show that the number of Croats killed by Pavelich's gang far exceeded the number of Croats killed in the clashes with the police during the period of the dictatorship. There was never the ferocity of the Austrian repression of the Socialists, of the Nazi revolt at the time of the murder of Dollfuss, of Hitler against the Jews, or of Mussolini consolidating Fascist power. The cruel and haphazard explosions in trains and under trains in Yugoslavia, in churches, and barracks were not answered with a corresponding cruelty by the administration. Of all autocratic or almost autocratic rulers of his time Alexander was the mildest and most peace loving. As far as his political enemies were concerned he was never revengeful. He was fond of the Croats and after the Oreb affair he spent a fortnight moving about freely in the city of Zagreb. The terrorists sent by Pavelich to kill him were brought to book, but there was no hue and cry, there were no supplementary arrests. He did not seize the opportunity to have arrested hundreds of disaffected people and have them tried and shot for supposed complicity in the plot on his life. That would have been the course in Moscow or Berlin or Rome. It was not Alexander's way. He was a man of peace seeking, above all other things, the reconciliation of peoples.

But Saint-Auban made a strong appeal, the sort of

appeal that would have swayed the average jury in England and America, though the trial would never have been conducted in that fashion in those countries. It was highly necessary that after the prosecution and the defense had spoken the judge should have analyzed these two speeches *pro* and *contra*. But no; Saint-Auban was followed by his two assisting counsel who reinforced his pleas. Then the president asked the accused whether they had anything to say. They would not add a word. The case went to the jury. The president handed to the foreman of the jury thirty-two written questions to which they had to find the answer "Yes" or "No." Majority decisions would be accepted. Unanimity was not required.

The principal questions were: Was there a voluntary homicide of King Alexander and of M. Barthou? And, if it was voluntary, was it premeditated? Was there an attempt on the life of General Georges? Were the accused accessory? Did Mio Kral aid the author of the crime? Did Pospishil? Did Raich?

On almost all counts the jury brought in a majority verdict of guilty; the answer "Yes." But Pospishil and Raich were not considered to have helped Vlada the Chauffeur personally. And the police agent, Galy, was held to have been killed without premeditation. All three accused were held accessory to the murders. The verdict was qualified by a rider to the effect that in the case of each of the three men there were extenuating circumstances in their favor.

All three were condemned to penal servitude for life.

This trial had purported to be the trial of Pavelich, Kvaternik, and Perchevich also. Their names had appeared in the list of accused. But extradition having been refused they were judged in their absence. By decree and without assistance of jury the Court of Assize at Aix condemned Pavelich, Kvaternik, and Perchevich to death, and ordered their effects to be confiscated to the state.

CHAPTER XVIII

TO OPLENATS

A FEVERISH hand turns the pages of history, and those who look on have barely time to read, far less to understand them. The diary of the modern world is so sensational that each day successively obliterates, or partially obliterates, from the consciousness the memory of yesterday. October 9, 1934, is but yesterday, but how much has happened since then to change the minds of men! One needs but the spectacle of Britain in the fever of rearmament, heaping the Pelion of explosives on the Ossa of engines of war. But in 1934 she still nursed the happy dream of perpetual peace and had made no preparations for war.

On October 9, 1934, the League of Nations was still a vital organism. In a few years it became a shattered and helpless wreck.

Mussolini seized Abyssinia and then, unchecked by the League, made alliance with Hitler. He kindled civil war in Spain much in the same way as he had planned to kindle it in Yugoslavia, landing his legions to support one political faction against another. With the help of German big guns and aircraft he destroyed the greater part of Madrid and of many other cities, causing more suffering in a few years than Spain had, up to then, had in the course of her history.

At the same time there was revealed a foreign sabotage of France similar to that worked by Pavelich's agents in Yugoslavia, but on a much greater scale, so alarming that the French government was obliged to conceal its extent. Democratic France was being undermined and at any moment might be blown sky high.

In 1934 the independence of Austria was guaranteed by England, France, and Italy. In 1938 Austria was absorbed by force into the German *Reich* and ceased to exist. Germany then declared that she had at length won the World War. Just a striking statement on one of the fluttering pages of history!

Germany, Italy, and Japan bound themselves in a pact to resist Communism. Under cover of fighting Communism Japan invaded China. Another page—who runs may read!

The Moscow government—encountering sabotage worked by Germany and Japan through the agency of the Trotskyites—counterattacked with a reign of terror, bringing to trial and then shooting almost everyone who was implicated. The moral prestige of the Soviet, which stood high in 1934, entered a decline. The support of Russia became merely an added weakness to Czechoslovakia and a compromising entanglement for democratic France.

The word Disarmament disappeared and the word Rearmament took its place. The phrase "collective security" gave way to the phrase "safeguarding our national interests." There was no more progress along the road King Alexander was treading when he was removed from the European scene. The new states brought into being in 1918 and secured by the League Covenant began to tremble for their existence. Every state for itself, not each for all and all for each! They were too poor to compete in the armaments race. Yugoslavia would have had to toe the line with three hundred aeroplanes, about fifty modern tanks, one warship, a shortage of machine guns, and no heavy artillery worth the name.

King Alexander had been devoted to peace and believed that it could be maintained. His successor had to reckon with the fact that war was inevitable. Alliance with one's enemies afforded a greater sense of security than the sympathy of one's friends. Germany, Italy, and Japan were a stronger combination than the rest of the League put together; or so it seemed. Disillusioning England and astonishing France, the new Yugoslavia entered into close political relations with Germany and Italy. The wrongs which Italy had committed were overlooked by the Yugoslav government. In January, 1938, the Home Secretary, Koroshets, announced in Parliament that "the bandit camps in Italy are being dispersed. A considerable number of Yugoslav subjects not connected with the assassinations in Marseilles or with other acts of terror have already returned. They have become convinced that they were on the wrong road and that there was no place for them abroad. They have made declarations of loyalty and have been restored to their motherland. Others await the decision of the government for permission to return home. Thus, slowly and gradually, the camps in Italy are being definitely liquidated." *

* Among stories of fugitives from the Italian camps that of Ante Bilankov, printed in the *Khrvatski Glas*, of Winnipeg, Canada (April 5, 1938), gives some interesting detail. Bilankov, a Dalmatian, went to Italy in July, 1933, to serve Pavelich and was sent to Yanka Pusta and then returned to Italy.

"After six months at Yanka Pusta I was sent with six others to Italy and we were detailed to the camp of Olivieto in the province of Toscana. There I met some acquaintances to whom I recounted all that had happened to me in Hungary and they said that their position in Italy was as desperate as mine. We

Koroshets did not reveal what had happened to Pavelich, Kvaternik, and the blonde lady of Marseilles, or whether a friendly Italian government had made any proposals with regard to these terrorists. But the winter of Serb discontent seemed to have passed and the government basked in the sunshine of Mussolini's friendship. The blood feud stood away like a storm cloud on

---

put our heads together how to put an end to conditions of life which had become intolerable. We were all in danger that 'night would devour us,' as the phrase went. That was no exaggeration. One of us, a student named Vlado Kunich, wrote a letter to Mussolini airing our grievances and begging his intervention on our behalf. But when Mussolini received that letter he sent it at once to Pavelich. Kunich was arrested and subjected to the most frightful tortures and then made to dig his own grave before he was killed.

"Pavelich often came to the camp and he gave orders that we rebels be transferred from the camp of Olivieto to San Demetrio in the province of Abruzzi. There we were divided into two groups and some of us were sent to Fonteccio and others to San Lorenzo. Our opinions were denounced by spies set to watch us. Pavelich gathered us together and threatened us with these words: 'Serb blood is to me as water, but if any of you shows the slightest insubordination in camp or against officers his blood will be to me as the most stinking water in the canals.' Two men who joined us from Belgium protested against their treatment and were killed.

"As a result our indignation increased and Dr. Budak [one of Pavelich's henchmen] reported a number of us as anti-Fascists and enemies of Italy. We were arrested and subjected to dreadful torture. The torture went on for seventy-two days and I am incapable of describing our sufferings. . . . Every night we were visited by inhuman tormentors and put to the question. Some of us remained for days unconscious after these visits. Some had blood poisoning and died.

"Eleven of us were condemned to death and the rest were sent to Stromboli. There we heard that Perchets had been condemned to death for betrayal."

the horizon, sinking into night and oblivion, or awaiting the winds which, like the spirits of the dead, blow with restless violence round a pendant world.

The Yugoslav friendship with Germany was more natural because there was no outstanding account to clear. But it meant a departure from the long dependence upon France and it weakened the Little Entente, a success for Hitler in his effort to isolate Czechoslovakia. It made the Little Entente incapable of resisting *Anschluss*. That it could combine to resist Hungarian revisionism ceased to be clear. One result of the alliance of Mussolini and Hitler was the power to decree the destiny of the Danubian Powers. The Czechs, threatened by the Germans on the one hand and the Magyars on the other, were in a parlous plight. Yugoslavia seemed to have achieved a position of temporary security, but the system of mutual guarantee to which King Alexander had been devoted had crashed.

There was one clear relief. The specter of the Hapsburgs had been laid. Vienna ceased to be a center of intrigue against Belgrade. Budapest became quiescent. In the Nazi conquest of Vienna many documents relating to Colonel Perchevich fell into their hands, though they were not made public. And papers incriminating the monarchists were seized. Yugoslavia rejoiced when a Berlin newspaper referred to the Hapsburgs as a family of degenerates. So, after all, Princip at Sarajevo only murdered a degenerate!

But a tremor passed through the German-speaking populations of Croatia and Slovenia when the seventy-five million "friends" appeared on their boundaries. There was no longer any state capital of Vienna and their choice became Berlin or Belgrade. The domestic situation in Yugoslavia had not improved since Alexander died. The Croats still refused coöperation. The Regent had tried to revert to a democratic regime and found, like Alexander before him, that it would not work. And to make confusion worse confounded the Serbs were divided among themselves. Strong government, a virtual dictatorship, seemed the only practical means of holding the nation together and that accorded with the desires of Berlin and Rome. But it was a dictatorship of the Prime Minister, not of the throne. The Premier, Stoyadinovich, was a staunch supporter of Germany and Italy.

Prince Paul became in effect the only Regent. The other two did little more than sign their names to decrees. General Tomich, commander of the Belgrade garrison, who was reserve Regent, committed suicide. But there was no need for more than one man to represent the throne till the young King came of age. Paul Karageorgevich filled the bill.

Mr. Winston Churchill appealed to the Prince to throw in his lot with the Western democracies because Yugoslavia could never be more than a poor neighbor of the Fascist Powers. But action, not speech, is the best argument with the Serbs. Convincing action on the part of the Western democracies had for some time been lacking. France, slow to set her house in order, passed from crisis to crisis. Britain's prestige was weakened by her passivity. The function of nonintervention committees could not be understood, neither could the pretence that some mysterious unknown power was torpedoing ships. Germans punished: Britons protested. Serbs expected Britain to make war on Japan but again she kept peace under protest, almost any peace being considered better than the justest war. It was hard for the little states of Eastern and Central Europe to understand why the de-

mocracies of the West, though armed to the teeth, would
not resort to force. When great material interests were
at stake and yet they did not go to war it could be de-
duced that they would never take up arms in defense of
a small power unless the independence of that power
were a matter of life and death to themselves.

Anschluss only provoked more protests. Increases in
German man power derived from annexations such as
that of Austria would only cause France and Britain to
increase their efforts in rearmament equivalently and so
become more prepared for the ultimate world war. Let
the Sudeten Germans have their way! Let Czech Silesia
revert to the *Reich!* Let Hungary and Yugoslavia become servile states and Rumania with its oil and grain
serve the Central Powers alone!

Yugoslavia does not keep the memory of Armistice
Day. There is no great gathering to commemorate the
cessation of the "war to end war," or solemn honoring of
those who gave their lives that the world might be made
"safe for democracy." The anniversary passes without
even a mention in the newspapers.

But that the war stopped in November, 1918, is a
fallacy. There was merely an armistice, due to exhaustion, and then the strife was resumed. Many have died
in the Great War since it was supposed to have ended.
There were many other casualties and history may note
that *King Alexander also died.*

THE body of King Alexander was laid to rest in the
crypt of a cold marble church. The tomb which he prepared for himself has a timeless quality. It has the immense dignity and solidity of the sepulchers of ancient
kings. It makes one think of Egypt and Tutankhamen
or of the tombs of kings in the buried cities of lost At-

lantis. It is intended to last. For the Karageorgevich kings believed they were the first of a long dynasty. "And some I see which triple scepters bear." At Oplenats, in Shumadia, King Peter built the beautiful marble church. He had a Russian architect who copied a Byzantine model and he constructed a cathedral of which Justinian would have been proud.

The bare temple was even better in King Peter's time, for Alexander spent millions on beautifying it within and made it perhaps too rich. There is a disparity between wild and stony Serbia and the grandeur of the tomb of its sovereigns. Alexander embellished it all through his reign and it was only toward the end that it was open for worship. The Church approved his work. Bishop Nicholas Velimirovich says that this church alone might immortalize the memory of the great monarch. "From the era of Byzantium there has not been another church which in its interior so expressed the light and beauty of Orthodoxy," says Bishop Nicholas. "Not in the last six hundred years has there been a church in the Balkans so marvelously adorned and there is not its equal among newly constructed churches in all Europe. As if foreseeing his untimely death the King hastened the work and with the completion of the church came the completion of his time on earth. As the book of the King's life closed the temple was opened."

But the church should be full of worshipers to have beauty; otherwise the great glittering saints on the walls are lonely over the cold marble floor. There are fifteen hundred figures in relief, copied from twelfth-century frescoes and done in mosaic, covering all the walls with glittering facets mostly of purple and bright gold. The gigantic saints towering upward to the apse remind one of the interior of the cathedral of St. Vladimir at Kiev.

But the representation of the eternal must have the presence of the living to make one whole. The tourist, gazing at the mosaic, may be impressed or may be critical, but the worshiper in the midst of the congregation has more chance to find all in harmony.

The wide low crypt is not adorned. It is paved with glimmering polished marble, but one has entered the chill tomb. Someone has excavated to the basement under time and history. There is a sense of ancient Egypt: "My name is Ozimandias, look on my works, ye mighty, and despair!" Under gigantic separate slabs of stone lie the bodies of descendants of Karageorge. There are no pious inscriptions, just the bare names, and over the grave of Alexander an eternal lamp has been lighted.

It is a sixty miles' drive from Belgrade to Oplenats, over desolate hilly country where every turn of the road reveals a lay of the land which looks like a military position or an old battlefield. The land cowers as at the memory of the tramp of armed men, and nature herself seems to be in ambush. It is not like Belgrade. There is no futile hurry to change to the modes of peace. It is nothing modern; it is not even Yugoslavia. It is Serbian and Balkan. It does not possess much that any enemy would destroy except the superstructure of the church with its gorgeous mosaic. Even were the beautiful church shattered in another age, the crypt with its massive slabs of stone must endure.

So history rolls on but the sleep of Alexander, called the Unifier, remains undisturbed.

BIBLIOGRAPHY

"Procès de l'Assassinat du Roi Alexandre de Yougoslavie et de Monsieur Louis Barthou."
Verbatim report of the abortive trial at Aix-en-Provence on November 18–21, 1935. Unpublished.
Verbatim report of the second trial on February 5–12, 1936. Unpublished.
Communication du gouvernement Yougoslave au Conseil de la Société des Nations. Geneva. November, 1934.
Politika. 1920–38, files.
Alexander I, Creator of the State and Unifier. Stephen Vukojevich. Belgrade, 1937. In Serbian.
Our Heroic King. General Alexander Dimitrievich. Belgrade, 1936. In Serbian.
The Serbian Troops on the Albanian Golgotha. General Milan Nedich. Belgrade, 1937. In Serbian.
Alexandre I, le Roi Chevalier. J. Augarde et E. Sicard. Paris, 1935.
La Vie et la mort d'Alexandre I. Claude Eylan. Paris, 1935.
Speeches of Alexander I, the Unifier. Belgrade, 1934. In Serbian.
Administrations of Serbia and Yugoslavia: Years 1903–1935. Belgrade, 1935. In Serbian.
Brochures in English issued by the Yugoslav Government:
Vlada Georgiev Chernozemski (Vlada the Chauffeur).
Ante Pavelich.
Hungary and the Terrorists.
Les Secrets des organisations terroristes. Yelka Pogorelets.
La Restauration des Hapsbourg Menace pour La Paix Européenne.
The Heroic King Alexander. Vaso Glushats. Belgrade, 1934. In Serbian.
King Peter from Birth to Death. Milenko Vukichevich. Belgrade, 1924. In Serbian.

King Peter I, the Liberator. Zhivoyan Rankovich. Belgrade, 1932. In Serbian.

In the Times of Karageorge. Alexa Ivich. In Serbian.

The Balkan Pivot. Charles Beard and George Radin. New York, 1929.

Yugoslav Parliaments. Chedomil Mitrinovich and Milosh Brashich. Belgrade, 1937. In Serbian.

History of Yugoslavia. Vladimir Chorovich. Belgrade, 1933. In Serbian.

Life of Stephen Radich. Milan Marianovich. Belgrade, 1937. In Serbian.

Quatre mois chez les Comitadjis. A. Den Doolaard. Paris, 1932.

Bandits d'Orient. Jean Perrigault. Paris, 1931.

Nicholas Pashich. Sforza.

The Church of St. George at Oplenats. Z. Vukichevich. In Serbian.

The King Martyr. Bishop Nicholas Velimirovich. In Serbian.

INDEX